Codeswitching

Anthropological and Sociolinguistic Perspectives

edited by
Monica Heller

Mouton de Gruyter
Berlin · New York · Amsterdam   1988

P115. 96|0

Mouton de Gruyter (formerly Mouton, The Hague)
is a Division of Walter de Gruyter & Co., Berlin.

Library of Congress Cataloging in Publication Data

Codeswitching : anthropological and sociolinguistic
perspectives.
   (Contributions to the sociology of language ; 48)
   Bibliography: p.
   Includes index.
   1. Code switching (Linguistics) 2. Anthropological
linguistics. 3. Sociolinguistics. I. Heller, Monica.
II. Series.
P115.3.C6   1988   401'.9   88-7201
ISBN 0-899-25412-8 (Alk. paper)

CIP-Titelaufnahme der Deutschen Bibliothek

Codeswitching : anthropolog. and sociolinguist. perspectives /
ed. by Monica Heller. — Berlin ; New York ; Amsterdam :
Mouton de Gruyter, 1988
   (Contributions to the sociology of language ; 48)
   ISBN 3-11-011376-7
NE: Heller, Monica [Hrsg.] ; GT

Printed on acid free paper.

Typesetting and Printing: Mercedes-Druck, Berlin. — Binding: Lüderitz & Bauer,
Berlin.
Printed in Germany.

Codeswitching

Contributions to the Sociology of Language

48

Editor
Joshua A. Fishman

Mouton de Gruyter
Berlin · New York · Amsterdam

Table of Contents

Introduction

Monica Heller
The Ontario Institute for Studies in Education

Codeswitching, the use of more than one language in the course of a single communicative episode, has attracted a great deal of attention over the years, most likely because it violates a strong expectation that only one language will be used at any given time. It is seen as something to be explained, whereas the use of one language is considered normal. This notion can be so powerful that even those who codeswitch can be unaware of their behaviour and vigorously deny doing anything of the kind.

The perspective taken in this volume is that codeswitching constitutes one of many forms of language contact phenomena, and can best be understood by placing it in the double context of the speech economy of a multilingual community and of the verbal repertoires of individual members of that community. In order to understand the social significance of codeswitching, and in order to understand why it takes the particular linguistic and discourse forms that it does at specific historical moments in specific communities, it is necessary to place it in the context of other forms of language contact phenomena occurring in the community, including the absence of any such phenomena.

The approach taken here is essentially functionalist: codeswitching is seen as a boundary-levelling or boundary-maintaining strategy, which contributes, as a result, to the definition of roles and role relationships at a number of levels, to the extent that interlocutors bear multiple role relationships to each other. It is an important part of social mechanisms of negotiation and definition of social roles, networks and boundaries. At the same time, it is effective only where interlocutors share an understanding of the significance of the pool of communicative resources from which codeswitching is drawn. Conventions must be shared in order for their violation to have meaning.

Linguists have contributed greatly to the study of codeswitching, from two perspectives: 1) the study of codeswitching as a variable phenomenon, supporting arguments for the necessity of incorporating variability into any grammar; and 2) the study of codeswitching as a means to the discovery of universal linguistic categories. While these studies clearly contribute to the papers in this volume, the perspective taken here is more specifically sociological or anthropological in nature. The case studies, most of them ethnographic, attempt to address questions concerning codeswitching as social process.

The purpose of the papers in this volume, then, is to illustrate ways in which the study of codeswitching addresses fundamental anthropological and sociolinguistic issues concerning the relationship between linguistic and social processes in the interpretation of experience and the construction of social reality. By examining ways in which codeswitching is used to signal social, discourse and referential meaning, these studies work towards a model which unifies macro-level and micro-level approaches to the study of language change and social change.

It is argued that, while social and linguistic constraints on codeswitching (in the form of the existence and permeability of social and linguistic boundaries) obtain in any language contact situation, the form that codeswitching will take, when and by whom it is used, and the extent to which it can been seen to have social, discourse and referential significance, can only be understood by situating instances of codeswitching in the context of the community-wide distribution of linguistic resources (the community speech economy) and in the context of the relationship of code switching to other forms of communicative behaviour in individual speech repertoires. In other words, it is argued that codeswitching should be seen as a cover term for a wide variety of variable language contact phenomena, and that types of codeswitching and their relationship to other language contact phenomena are probably only interdistinguishable in community-specific ways in terms of their functions in social interaction. At the same time, in order to predict the forms and functions that language contact phenomena are likely to take in interpersonal interactions (whether in-group or intergroup) in the community, indeed, in order to predict whether codeswitching is likely to occur at all, the analyst must have an understanding of community speech economies (or how social boundaries constrain access to linguistic resources), of individual speech repertoires (or where individuals are located in the community speech economy), and of the linguistic relationship the grammars of the languages or language varieties involved bear to each other.

While codeswitching is not the only form of linguistic variability to carry social, discourse or referential meaning, it does provide a particularly clear avenue of approach to understanding the relationship between social processes and linguistic forms, because both the social and linguistic boundaries in question tend to be more evident than in other, monolingual, settings. It is also of interest in terms of the intellectual history of the disciplines within which codeswitching has been studied (the sociology and social psychology of language, anthropological linguistics and sociolinguistics, as well as theoretical and descriptive linguistics): these disciplines have tended to approach codeswitching as a structurally-unified phenomenon whose significance derives from a universal pattern of relationships between form, function and context (Genesee and Bourhis 1982; McClure 1981; Pfaff 1982). Increasingly, students of codeswitching have begun to approach it as a form of verbal strategy (Valdés 1981; Scotton 1976; Heller 1982; Gumperz 1982a), which represents the ways in which the linguistic resources available to individuals vary according to the nature of social boundaries in the community, and the ways in which individuals draw on those resources to communicative effect as part of their joint construction of interpretive frame in social interaction, based on the extent to which interlocutors share conventional associations between linguistic form and social relationships, or on the extent to which interlocutors can draw on their verbal resources to arrive at that shared understanding (Tannen 1979; Gumperz 1982b; Cicourel 1978).

The study of codeswitching has moved away from typological or deterministic models relating form and function to each other and to context, and towards a dynamic model in which codeswitching can be seen as a resource for indexing situationally-salient aspects of context in speakers' attempts to accomplish interactional goals. The study of codeswitching, then, becomes a means of understanding how such verbal resources, through use, acquire conventional social, discourse or referential meaning. Such a model further allows the relationship between these different kinds of meaning to be seen as a product of the history of the use of language contact forms, in much the same way as has been described for the social, stylistic and grammatical function of other types of linguistic variables (Labov 1972; Sankoff 1980; Thibault 1979). Codeswitching can be seen to pass from being an "exploratory" strategy (Scotton, this volume; Heller 1982), that is, one which permits interlocutors to discover to what degree they share understandings about the situation and their roles in it, from among the alternative frameworks available. This exploration permits them to establish a shared framework, and codeswitching can then become an index of that framework. It then becomes available as a discourse strategy (for signalling thematic ties, old vs. new information, and so on, as well as for signalling participants' perspectives on the discourse; cf. Valdés 1981; Gumperz 1982a; McClure 1981; Calsamiglia and Tuson 1980). Finally, language contact phenomena may not bear any indexical relationship to interpretive frames at all, as the alternative frames collapse, and so the linguistic forms come to carry referential meaning only.

In this volume, Scotton and Poplack argue that it is the difference between social and discourse meaning, on the one hand, and referential meaning, on the other, that distinguishes codeswitching from other forms of language contact phenomena. Along with Auer, Poplack also argues that the degree to which language contact phenomena are similarly used by community members distinguishes codeswitching and borrowing from individual language learning phenomena such as transfer. By situating the interactional social, discourse or referential meaning of language contact phenomena in the context of the community distribution of strategies for negotiating, defining and indexing shared frames of reference, this model provides a means of understanding the processes linking social and linguistic change.

Two related sets of concepts underlie this model: the first concerns the existence of multiple frames of reference, and the second concerns multiple roles and role relationships, or multiple identities, which are associated with those frames.

Multiple frames of reference, or the social separation of domains of social activity associated with different language varieties, underlies the availability of codeswitching for social and discourse effect. This notion was perhaps most influentially expressed by Blom and Gumperz (1972). They proposed a basic type of code-switching, *situational codeswitching*, which is rooted in a social separation of activities (and associated role relationships), each of which is conventionally linked to the use of one of the languages or varieties in the community linguistic repertoire. Through this association linguistic varieties come to symbolize the social situations, roles and statuses and their attendant rights and obligations, expectations and assumptions. Use of each variety in unconventional contexts has the effect of calling into play all the meanings associated with the variety in situations where normally other frames of reference are operative: this is what Blom and Gumperz refer to as *metaphorical codeswitching*, because the unexpected variety is a metaphor for the social meanings the variety has come to symbolize. As an example, consider the case of French-English bilingual students and teachers in a French-language school in a predominantly English-speaking city. Everyone knows everyone else is bilingual (or how would they survive in that city?) but teachers are careful to insist that students speak French at school; teachers themselves never speak English while on school grounds. However, students have heard one teacher speak English at softball practice, because her English-speaking father-in-law joins her in coaching the team. During the school day one student comes up to her to plead for a favour in English. She refuses to speak to him in English, and won't even consider granting the favour unless he speaks French. He gives up and walks away, even though he *could have* asked her in French. The point here is that the boy felt he only had a chance at getting what he wanted if he appealed to the teacher in her non-French guise, that is, outside her role as teacher. When she insisted on French, which he associates with her teacher status, he no longer saw the point of even attempting to plead his case. Use of the unexpected variety can also merely suspend the meanings (rights and obligations, expectations and assumptions) normally operative and indexed through conventional associations between language and situation. These associations are the basis of what Scotton (this volume) refers to as *unmarked* (conventional) and *marked* (unexpected) uses of language, and are linked to the multiple role relations individuals may bear to each other. McConvell and Heller (this volume) describe social processes which can lead to the development of multiple role relationships associated with different languages, and so to codeswitching as a strategy for defining or managing those relationships.

While Blom and Gumperz only discuss situational and metaphorical switching with respect to homogeneous groups who share the same experiences of the two languages or linguistic varieties, the concept is equally applicable to inter-group interaction. In the case of inter-group interaction there are usually conventions of language choice which govern both in-group and inter-group interaction and which constitute the set of situations on the basis of which language associations are set up. Any violation of those conventions constitutes a reference to other situations or distancing from the currently operative one; here, the interpretation is ingroup vs. outgroup role relations, as opposed to two different kinds of ingroup role relations. For example, if an English-speaking Quebecer is used to speaking French with French-speaking colleagues at work, he or she might feel put at a distance — put out of the group — if one of those French-speaking colleagues suddenly started speaking English with him or her.

Thus at the heart of codeswitching is the separation of languages in different domains, a separation that is undoubtedly behind the fact that many people who codeswitch are not aware of their behaviour until it is brought to their attention — and even when it is they often resist the notion that they really speak that way. An example: I was talking to a group of French-English bilingual seventh- and eighth-grade students in Toronto about codeswitching. I was trying to get a grasp of the syntactic limits on acceptable codeswitching for this group, many of whom codeswitched. I used the standard linguistic methods of trying out variations of codeswitched utterances, asking the students if any of the example utterances sounded like things they would say. They all denied that they ever talked like that, but they did allow that they knew people who said things that resembled some of the sample sentences (cf. Blom and Gumperz 1972: 428–430 for another example from Norway). At most, some codeswitchers might admit that that is how they talk amongst themselves when no one else (no outsider) is listening, but often this type of talk is presented as not being "real" language.

However, the sparse amount of ethnographic evidence that we have regarding this subject indicates that in some communities codeswitching is not only widespread but also accepted as the normal way of speaking. Poplack, for example, states that code-switching is the norm for *ingroup* talk among Puerto Ricans in Spanish Harlem (1980). On the other hand, I have argued else-where (Heller 1982) that codeswitching may become the norm for *intergroup* talk between francophones and anglophones in Quebec. However, even in those communities there is a basic separation of domains: for Puerto Ricans in New York this probably corre-sponds to the homeland on the one hand and English-speaking mainstream society on the other, while for Quebecers this corre-sponds to separate francophone and anglophone in-group domains. It is possible that it doesn't really matter whether within each separate domain the "sanctity" of the language is maintained, but that it is the dominance of one language over the other that matters, or to be more precise, the dominance or conventionality of sets of rights and obligations conventionally associated with the languages. Moreover, codeswitching itself becomes conventional when it indexes a shared frame of reference which represents the neutralization of tension at the boundary between separate domains.

In examining the separation of domains two questions stand out: the first has to do with the actual distribution of codeswitch-ing in the community, and the other has to do with speakers' awareness of codeswitching as a way of speaking and their accept-ance of it as a normal way to talk. The answers to these questions can then be used as evidence to explain the social uses of code-switching and the linguistic consequences of it. The notion of separate domains, whatever it corresponds to in linguistic struc-ture, is, I believe, fundamental to codeswitching, while code-switching itself, seemingly paradoxically, is the direct contradic-tion of separation. This has implications both for our ideas about how languages work and for our ideas about the organization of social life.

While the social separation of domains implies the existence of social boundaries regulating or constraining access to linguistic resources which form part of the social life of those domains, the existence of codeswitching necessitates that at least some individuals have access to all the domains in question, and therefore have access to those linguistic resources. More importantly, perhaps, for understanding the nature of codeswitching, those individuals have access to certain kinds of roles and role relationships within each of those domains: that is, they have access to *multiple* roles and role relationships. However, as several papers in this volume point out (Woolard; McClure and McClure), even where multiple domains exist in a community, codeswitching may be totally or relatively unavailable, because the social boundaries separating the domains are relatively impermeable. Put differently, the social consequences of crossing the barrier may be too costly for individual members of the community (see Heller, this volume). Finally, even where codeswitching exists, it may not be universally available: only those who are so socially situated with respect to the social boundaries that they have access to multiple roles will be likely to be able to use codeswitching to communicative effect, for they are the only ones for whom the significance of the multiple frames of reference is at all pertinent. Lieberson (1970) describes, for example, the social separation of domains between French and English in Montreal in the 1960's, in which most francophones and anglophones never came in contact with each other, and so never became bilingual. A notable exception, indeed one which was crucial for the economy of the community, concerned francophone working class males of an age to be in the labour market, most of whom provided the labour in anglophone-owned and -managed private enterprise. The degree of bilingualism, as might be expected, was much higher for these members of the community than for any others (francophone or anglophone). Further, not only did they have access to the linguistic resources of both anglophone and francophone domains (at least to some of them), they carried out different roles in each of these domains, and shared with each other a multiple set of roles and role relationships (neighbours or kin, for example, whose role relationship would conventionally be associated with French, could also work together in a domain where the conventional language was English). They would therefore be plausible as candidates for codeswitchers. Many other such examples have been cited in the literature (cf. Blom and Gumperz 1972; Gal 1979; Scotton 1976; Gumperz and Hernandes-Chavez 1971).

There are other ways in which individuals may bear multiple role relationships to each other. The above examples all focus on codeswitching among members of one group, but intergroup inter-action is another area where participants of necessity bear multiple role relationships to each other, as members of different groups, and as participants in a particular kind of social interaction (e.g. a service encounter, as in Heller 1982 or Scotton, this volume; or a gate-keeping encounter, as in Scotton, this volume; etc.). Here, on the boundary, is another area where codeswitching is at least potentially available.

❜It is evident that codeswitching does not occur in all multi-lingual communities, and even in communities where it does exist not everyone codeswitches; further, even among those who do codeswitch, codeswitching does not necessarily occur in all social situations. Unfortunately, not enough attention has been paid to negative cases, that is, cases where there is no codeswitching; nevertheless, several papers in this volume (McClure and McClure, Woolard, Heller, Poplack) have addressed the question of the conditions under which one finds or does not find codeswitching and it is possible to derive some generalizations from these case study analyses. Specifically, it seems that when groups occupy separate economic niches the multiplicity of role relationships across groups is unlikely to occur; boundary-levelling has severe economic consequences.

An analysis of the sources of codeswitching may, then, begin with the separation of domains upon which codeswitching rests. I believe that intra-utterance codeswitching will not occur in situa-tions where, for social reasons, it is important to maintain that separation, whereas it will occur when it is important to overcome the barriers. On the other hand, situational switching (or language choice conventions) may occur in boundary-maintenance condi-tions: the individuals may speak different languages depending on the situation, but the language spoken in that situation does not vary. This analysis also accounts for interactions in which speakers each use their own preferred language (while communication is not blocked because of the at least passive bilingualism of the speakers), since we can infer that while cross-cultural interaction may be necessary, speakers find it important to maintain the social boundary between them.

However, the question remains of when it is going to be important to maintain or overcome boundaries. Here I believe the analysis must rest on the short-term and long-term social goals of individuals, goals which will necessarily be informed by their social status and the various social, economic and political processes which may affect that status. In analytic terms, codeswitching, as mentioned earlier, can be approached as a function of what it accomplishes; the consequences of codeswitching link long-term social consequences (e.g., acceptance of an individual into a group, access to certain activities, etc.) to short-term discourse or conversational consequences (e.g., making a point, getting the floor). It is at the level of social interaction, then, that analysis can link the form that codeswitching takes to its discourse and conversational functions or effects and eventually to longer-term social consequences in the light of ethnographic information which permits the interaction to be situated in the first place. This ethnographic information must situate codeswitching within the linguistic repertoire not only of codeswitchers, but of the community of which they may form only one sub-group; similarly, such an ethnography must situate codeswitching encounters in the context of community encounters in many of which codeswitching may be absent, including the context of the appearance, evolution or disappearance of the use of codeswitching over time.

Codeswitching, then, provides a clear illustration of the ways in which sociohistorical context is tied to the use of language in social interaction. These papers detail the ways in which the socio-ecological framework constrains possibilities for individuals to have access to multiple roles and role relationships (multiple identities) and therefore to a variety of linguistic resources, which are then used in the negotiation and articulation of social identity and social action. Put somewhat differently, codeswitching provides a clear example of the ways in which individuals draw on their linguistic resources to signal changes in the different aspects of context which they wish to foreground, to make salient, thereby opening opportunities for the redefinition of social reality, exploiting or creating ambiguity in the relationships between form and context to do so. The approaches adopted here tie together historical, community-level and interactional/inter-pretive approaches to the study of language change and social change, and of language use and the construction of social reality.

The social, discourse and referential function of linguistic resources cannot be inferred solely from a study of the form these resources take, in isolated texts or utterances; they must be situated in the community speech economy and in historical context. In other words, since individuals in a community have differential access to multiple roles and linguistic resources, and experience differential consequences of the use of those resources, they are, according to their own socioecological position and the distribution of resources in the community (i.e. the nature of social boundaries in the community), more or less likely to be able to use certain resources to social, discourse or referential effect, given also the nature of the social interactions in which they are participating.

Consequently, specific forms may be ambiguous, and the nature of codeswitching is not amenable to purely structural analysis, although within a speech economy structural factors will convey the communicative effect of codeswitching. It is therefore unlikely that a universal linguistic grammar of codeswitching exists, or that codeswitching can be distinguished from borrowing or other lan-guage contact phenomena on purely formal grounds; rather, cer-tain structural strategies (some of which are widely available) will be used in each speech community to set off socially-, discourse- and referentially-significant forms from each other. However, even within an individual's speech repertoire, or in a community speech economy, ambiguity may still exist due to the changing nature of social boundaries. Indeed, this ambiguity may itself be successfully exploited in the negotiation of interpretive frames of social action.

Different disciplinary perspectives have in the past been brought to bear on various aspects of the role of codeswitching in linking the interpretive processes of interpersonal interaction to processes of maintenance and change of social boundaries between groups.

The sociology of language (cf., e.g., Fishman 1972; Fishman et al. 1971; see also Ferguson 1964) has addressed the nature of the conventional association of languages or language varieties to activity in identifiable social domains, pointing to the importance of studying the nature of social boundaries in a community, and the ability of individuals or groups to cross them (cf. also Barth 1969).

Work in this area has established that it is often the case that language choice is but one of many conventional aspects of the enactment of roles and role relationships, and is therefore tied to a complex of other behaviours and contextual factors. The major issue raised by such an approach is how best to account for cases where a more or less one-to-one correspondence of language to domain does not exist. The question arises of the extent to which codeswitching can itself be conventionalized, or whether the language-domain model requires that codeswitching be seen as evidence of change (of language shift on the community level or of change at the level of re-definition of individuals' roles or role relationships). This book attempts to address that question by situating conventional language choice and codeswitching in the framework of community speech economies and individual speech repertoires. In other words, both conventional codeswitching and codeswitching-as-change are theoretically possible; identification depends on understanding the relationship between codeswitching and boundary-maintenance or boundary-levelling processes, on situating codeswitching in the context of other language practices of individual codeswitchers and across the community.

However, it is also necessary to address the relationship between changes in language use practices and social changes: to what extent does one influence the other, or to what extent are they dialectically related? This question is difficult, if not impossible, to address within the confines of the sociology of language; it is argued here that micro-level approaches (as exemplified by studies in the social psychology of language, the ethnography of communication and ethnomethodology) must be explored within the speech economy/speech repertoire framework. The linking of micro-level and macro-level approaches enables the analyst to go beyond description of social and language use changes as they co-occur to address the mechanism of such changes.

The social psychology of language (cf. Genesee and Bourhis 1982; Lambert et al. 1960; Lambert 1967; Ryan and Giles 1982; Clément and Beauregard 1986) has examined codeswitching from the point of view of the kinds of evaluative inferences interlocutors might make about each other on the basis of their verbal behaviour, both in terms of speakers' social and personality characteristics and in terms of the extent of their willingness to accommodate their own conventions of behaviour to those of their interlocutor (and what that signals about the interlocutors' role relationship).

In the first case, social psychologists drew on the insights of the sociology of language: if language choices (or even codeswitching) were conventionally associated with certain roles or role relationships, then those language use patterns should be evaluated themselves in ways similar to the ways in which speakers and the situations they regularly participate in, or the roles they regularly assume, are evaluated. The second approach grew out of the realization that the first approach is likely to be most valid only for the most stable of language contact situations and for univalent role relationships. Judgements about others can vary from stereotypes based on interlocutors' experience of interaction with each other, and indeed individual's language practices can vary depending on the processes and events of conversation (i.e. within communicative situations). The issue for the social psychology of language has thus become, in part, to identify speaker intent at the levels of conveying information both about relationships as representatives of ethnolinguistic groups as well as about relationships as representatives of other kinds of social categories or about individual characteristics (R. Clément, personal communication).

The approach that is favoured is essentially experimental: speech samples are simulated and controlled, and judges provide evaluative reactions. The difficulty, of course, lies in the assumption that judges react the way they would were they themselves party to the interaction. Second, issues about the consequences of evaluative reactions have to be made by inference: we cannot observe what happens to people's relationships as a result of conversational events. Yet it is this question, the question of *social outcome*, which is most central to the problem posed here: what do people gain or lose by using language in certain ways in certain interactions?

The ethnography of communication has addressed this question by examining the relationship between language varieties and the definition and articulation of social roles in social situations (Blom and Gumperz 1972; Irvine 1974; Zentella 1981). By examining how speakers use language in specific social interactions to accomplish conversational goals, this approach has been able to make the link between local conversational tasks and the significance of their accomplishment for the development of relationships between speakers. It has, moreover, drawn attention to the interpretive process relating linguistic form to the indexed salient aspects of context, a process in which interlocutors must participate in order to arrive at shared ways of understanding the social or stylistic significance of codeswitching (Gumperz 1982a; Gal 1979). In other words, speakers who are part of the same social network, or more broadly, of the same speech community, share both general background knowledge and conventions concerning communication within and about that context. They know how to exploit the communicative resources available to them due to their position in the speech economy of the community (and to the position of the interaction at hand) to call into play the relevant aspects of context which render their action meaningful. The ethnography of communication approaches this analysis by explicitly situating recurring patterns of language use in their social context.

Ethnomethodological approaches (e.g. Auer and di Luzio 1983) have focussed on the ways in which recurring patterns of language themselves provide a contextual framework in which to situate the significance of variable verbal behaviour. These approaches have as their goal precisely the understanding of the significance of behaviour from "the members' point of view", and take the position that patterns of language use are strategies for the social construction of reality. Conversational inferences are based on conversational events and are reflected in the evolution of the pattern of conversational events or processes. Again, the central question remains of the way in which codeswitching enables speakers to define both conversational reality (organize information, highlight new or important information, etc.) and social reality (to define one's social role through the definition of one's conversational role, and through situating oneself with respect to the conversational resources currently available, that is, by accepting or rejecting the sets of language choice conventions that are available).

In this volume, the attempt is made to unify these approaches within a single framework which accounts for patterns of code-switching, interpretive processes and conversational inferences, and the social distribution of multilingualism, by focussing on the social consequences of patterns of verbal behaviour in social interaction, in terms of the location of situations and interlocutors with respect to social boundaries, in terms of short- or long-term changes in the rights and obligations which individuals bear to each other as part of their social relationship, and in terms of the ability of interlocutors to establish and maintain shared frames of reference within which their communicative behaviour makes sense.

Moreover, as indicated earlier, this perspective attempts to account for the relationship between different forms of language contact phenomena, an issue to which much of the literature on codeswitching has devoted a great deal of attention (e.g. Gumperz 1982a; Haugen 1953; Mougeon et al. 1982; Beniak et al. 1985; Muysken et al. 1985; Lance 1975; Pfaff 1982; Poplack 1980; Timm 1975; Woolford 1983). Much effort has been devoted to establishing typological characteristics which universally distinguish one type of language contact phenomenon from another (transfer, interference, borrowing, codeswitching, codemixing, calquing, etc.), i.e., which are equally valid no matter which language pair is involved. The difficulty of establishing such criteria has led some authors to conclude that it is necessary to apply multiple criteria, which range from internal structural criteria (such as the extent to which morphological or phonological constraints of either language are violated), to criteria pertaining to the extent to which forms are part of a community-wide pattern of speech as opposed to individual, and possibly ephemeral, phenomena. Several papers in this volume (Scotton, Poplack, Auer) argue that, while the structural problem posed by codeswitching is the same across languages (i.e. that of reconciling potentially mismatched or conflicting grammars), the strategies adopted for so doing may be quite different across language pairs; further, several different strategies may be adopted within one language contact situation. (Some of these, of course, such as framing through the use of hesitations, pauses, or framing phrases, may be widely available). What is significant is not the exact linguistic nature of the strategies used, it is the contribution they make to the verbal repertoire of individuals and to the speech economy of the community, and to interlocutors' ability to successfully negotiate and infer social, stylistic or referential meaning. The analytical problem posed, then, is to pass from a description of the variability of forms and their patterns of occurrence to an analysis of how they come to acquire social, stylistic or referential meaning, and how they come to be restricted to developmental phases in an individual's verbal repertoire or distributed widely across a speech community. In attempting to find a solution to this problem, the papers in this volume address themselves to different aspects of the relationship between social boundaries, speech economies and verbal repertoires, conversational inference, and variability in linguistic form.

Papers by McClure and McClure, Woolard and Heller focus on the ways in which social boundaries restrict access to multiple roles and role relationships, and on the ways in which codeswitching may be unavailable (as part of boundary maintenance processes) or, conversely, adopted as a strategy (as part of boundary levelling processes).

McClure and McClure discuss the sociohistorical processes which contribute to the social organization of language in a multilingual Romanian village. They point out that it is not enough that language contact occurs for codeswitching to be present in a multilingual situation: it is necessary that community members have access to social roles in social situations where languages other than their mother tongue are conventionally used. In other words, where social barriers between groups are strong, conversational codeswitching is not very likely to occur, although individuals may speak more than one language in clearly separated domains of social life. The important point here is the cultural ecology of the community and its relationship to the village speech economy, which allows for the identification of likely arenas for codeswitching and of the framework which allows Saxons a shared set of conventions for codeswitching and for understanding the significance of codeswitching. It is crucial that only Saxons codeswitch, and that the nature of their codeswitching differs as between Saxon-Romanian and Saxon-German, just as the nature of their participation in Romanian and German domains is qualitatively different.

Woolard makes a similar point regarding the relative absence of codeswitching between Catalan and Castilian in Barcelona, examining closely a negative case, where codeswitching at least appears to be rampant. The case, similar to that of the bawdy Saxon-Romanian songs described by McClure and McClure, is that of the monologues of a stand-up comedian, and Woolard argues that the monologues are funny precisely because they violate the separation of languages in the community. Moreover, since that separation also reflects a certain degree of interethnic tension, the boundary-levelling produced by the comedian's monologues serves to release that tension. Finally, Woolard shows that the effect of "rampant" codeswitching in this case is produced by manipulation of a very limited set of features along a continuum (phonology, prosody, lexis, etc.); since the two languages involved are very similar, it is possible to create the impression of speaking two languages at once at a more finely-grained level of linguistic organization than is possible when the two languages are less similar. In other words, the degree to which grammars overlap constrains the kinds of linguistic strategies speakers may adopt; see also the paper by Poplack in this regard.

Heller develops the points made regarding the importance of codeswitching in levelling social boundaries, focussing on specific types of social situations in French-English contact in Canada. In these social situations, despite social separation of languages in the wider community, certain individuals (for reasons having to do with their role, and the role of different ethnolinguistic groups, in the evolution of Quebec's economy) find themselves in a position where either they must take on roles in domains which are otherwise mutually exclusive, or they must act as brokers in situations which form the interface between mutually exclusive domains. Codeswitching is used as a strategy for levelling boundaries for the purposes of the interaction, while behaviour in other situations simultaneously maintains barriers.

Papers by McConvell and Scotton focus on the multiple role relationships individuals bear to each other, whether in ingroup or in intergroup interaction. McConvell discusses a specific type of situation where otherwise mutually exclusive social arenas can be called into play during the course of a single social interaction, in this case the butchering of meat by multilingual, multidialectal Australian Aborigines. Using as an analogy the variable use of kin-terms, McConvell shows how the rights and obligations obtaining between people bearing certain role relations to each other are defined in terms of the roles conventionally associated with specific social domains, which in turn are conventionally associated with specific dialects or languages. However, as individuals participate in increasing numbers of social arenas, they may bear multiple role relations to each other, each of which can be invoked through codeswitching in the course of single encounters, in order to invoke certain rights or obligations which are tied to the accomplishment of participants' particular conversational goals of the moment. He further shows how social change affecting the economy of Western Australia, and the position of Aborigines in it, affects the access of members of diffrent generations to different social arenas and so affects their role relationships and patterns of language use.

Scotton further develops the idea of multiple role relations, and focusses on the idea of markedness as a basis for understanding the effectiveness of codeswitching in defining social rights and obligations in specific interactions in East Africa. She shows how certain sets of rights and obligations are conventionally associated with certain social situations, and how language use in those situations is unmarked. She goes on to discuss two ways in which situation and language use co-vary: externally-motivated changes signal changes in situation and so change in unmarked language choice, while within single encounters participants can deviate from conventional verbal behaviour, and through such marked switches re-define role relations and consequently situations.

Auer uses a conversation analysis approach to account for the ways speakers (in this case children of Italian migrant workers in Germany) use codeswitching either to manage social relations or to accomplish discourse objectives. In his view, codeswitching and language transfer can be distinguished operationally, and shown to function differentially in face-to-face conversations to establish various kinds of *footing* (in Goffman's terms) on the basis of which conversation can be interpreted by participants. Finally, operational distinctions between codeswitching and language transfer can be shown to be related to the degree of shared membership of participants in social networks.

These six papers, then, link codeswitching in social interaction to the social organization of language use in the community, by demonstrating the effectiveness of codeswitching as a
boundary-levelling strategy, either in situations where participants
bear multiple role relationships to each other, or where they are
involved in situations at the boundary of intergroup relations.
They also demonstrate the ways in which codeswitching can
become available in in-group talk (that is, where frameworks are
shared) for the accomplishment of discourse objectives: since the
management of social relations occurs through conversation,
conversation must be structured through the use of linguistic
resources to accomplish the discourse objectives which in turn
serve to accomplish larger-scale interactional goals.

Poplack describes the different forms that codeswitching can
take in different communities, even if the languages concerned
resemble each other. She contrasts the embedded codeswitching
used by Spanish-English bilinguals in New York with the "flagged" codeswitches of French-English bilinguals in Ottawa/Hull
(Canada), showing how two very different strategies are used to
avoid grammatical conflict in the two communities. She goes on to
discuss the place of codeswitching in the set of language contact
phenomena (borrowing, transfer) in the verbal repertoires of the
communities, arguing that distinctions cannot be drawn on purely
formal, structural, linguistic grounds, but must be analyzed in
terms of their distribution in the community and with respect
to the use members make of different forms to signal social,
discourse or referential meaning. While Poplack asserts the superficial similarity of the two language contact situations, it also
seems possible to hypothesize that underlying differences in the
situations (hence different patterns of access to multiple identities,
different sets of values and linguistic ideologies) have led to
different patterns of language use in the two communities, due to
differences in the social consequences of codeswitching.

Gal's paper provides a theoretical and methodological framework
for the analysis and interpretation of codeswitching. She argues
that the meaning of codeswitching, both at an interpersonal and at
a collective level, as well as explanations for the pattern of distribution of codeswitching across speech communities, lie in an

examination of ethnolinguistic groups' roles in international economic and political relations. She shows that local issues of boundary maintenance and levelling are the products of long histories of struggles for political and economic resources and other forms of power, symbolic and material. She shows further that the value of resources (in whatever form) is itself conditioned by a region's position in worldwide processes. She argues that often the differences in patterns of language use, across both space and time, can be as revealing as the similarities, and that we cannot fully understand the significance of either if we do not examine the historical configurations and processes which inform the value of the linguistic resources which speakers possess, as based in the value of other resources to which the deployment of linguistic resources facilitates access.

As a whole, then, this volume attempts to provide a synthetic approach to the study of the relationship between social and linguistic processes, and to provide a model in which individuals, while constrained by social processes, can also, by drawing on the linguistic resources available to them, contribute to processes of social change.

While the emphasis here is on language use in social interaction as the preferred focus for examining exactly how those processes work, it is clear that future research must increasingly take into account the situation of that interaction in the speech economy of the community (and across communities) and in individual socio-linguistic repertoires. The study of codeswitching will thereby be increasingly able to contribute to an understanding of the nature of speech communities and the creation and distribution of linguistic resources within them. Finally, closer examination of relationship between the use and distribution of those resources themselves will contribute to an understanding of the functioning of linguistic structural processes and of the ways in which linguistic, cognitive and social constraints on the communicative process can be said to influence each other. The papers collected here represent an attempt to begin to lay the groundwork of careful, comparative ethnographic research on which rests the accomplishment of such an ambitious research agenda.

References

Auer, J. C. P. and A. di Luzio
1983 "Structure and meaning of linguistic variation in Italian migrant children in Germany", in: R. Bauerle, C. Schwarze and A. von Stechow (eds.), *Meaning, Use and Interpretation of Language*, Berlin, N.Y.: Walter de Gruyter, pp. 1–21.

Barth, F.
1969 "Introduction". In: F. Barth (ed.), *Ethnic Groups and Boundaries*, Boston: Little, Brown, pp. 9–38.

Beniak, E., R. Mougeon and D. Valois
1985 *Contact des langues et changement linguistique: étude socio-linguistique du français parlé à Welland (Ontario)*. Québec: Centre international de recherche sur le bilinguisme.

Blom, J.-P. and J. Gumperz
1972 "Social meaning in linguistic structures: code-switching in Norway", in: J. Gumperz and D. Hymes (eds.), *Directions in Sociolinguistics: The Ethnography of Communication*, N.Y.: Holt, Rinehart and Winston, pp. 407–434.

Calsamiglia, H. and E. Tuson
1980 "Us i alternança de llengües en grups de joves d'un barri de Barcelona: Sant Andreu de Palomar", *Treballs de sociolingüistica catalana*, Valencia, pp. 11–82.

Cicourel, A.
1978 "Language and society: cultural, cognitive and linguistic aspects of language use", *Sozialwissenschaftliche Annalen*, Band 2, Seite B25–B58, Wien: Physica-Verlag.

Clément, R. and Y. Beauregard
1986 "Peur d'assimilation et confiance en soi: leur relation à l'alternance des codes at à la compétence communicative en langue seconde". *Canadian Journal of Behavioural Science* 18 (2): 189–198.

Ferguson, C.
1964 "Diglossia", in: D. Hymes (ed.), *Language in Culture and Society*, N.Y.: Harper and Row, pp. 429–439.

Fishman, J. (ed.).
1972 *Readings in the Sociology of Language*, The Hague: Mouton.

Fishman, J., R. Cooper, R. Ma et al.
1971 *Bilingualism in the Barrio*, Bloomington, Ind.: Indiana University.

Gal, S.
1979 *Language Shift: Social Determinants of Linguistic Change in Bilingual Austria*, N.Y.: Academic Press.

Genesee, F. and R. Bourhis
  1982 "The social psychological significance of code-switching in cross-cultural communication", *Journal of Language and Social Psychology* 1 : 1–28.

Gumperz, J.
  1982a "Conversational codeswitching", in: J. Gumperz, *Discourse Strategies*, Cambridge: Cambridge University Press, pp. 59–99.

Gumperz, J.
  1982b *Discourse Strategies*. Cambridge: Cambridge University Press.

Gumperz, J. and E. Hernandez-Chavez
  1971 "Bilingualism, bidialectalism and classroom interaction" in: J. Gumperz, *Language in Social Groups*, Stanford: Stanford University Press, pp. 311–339.

Haugen, E.
  1953 *The Norwegian Language in America: A Study in Bilingual Behaviour*, 2 vols., Philadelphia: University of Pennsylvania Press.

Heller, M.
  1982 " 'Bonjour, hello?': negotiations of language choice in Montreal", in: J. Gumperz (ed.), *Language and Social Identity*, Cambridge: Cambridge University Press, pp. 108–118.

Irvine, J.
  1974 "Strategies of status manipulation in the Wolof greeting", in: R. Bauman and J. Sherzer (eds.), *Explorations in the Ethnography of Speaking*, Cambridge: Cambridge University Press, pp. 167–191.

Labov, W.
  1972 *Sociolinguistic Patterns*, Philadelphia: University of Pennsylvania Press.

Lambert, W.
  1967 "A social psychology of bilingualism", *Journal of Social Issues* 23 (2): 91–109.

Lambert, W., R. Hodgson, R. Gardner and S. Fillenbaum
  1960 "Evaluative reactions to spoken language". *Journal of Abnormal and Social Psychology* 60: 44–51.

Lance, D.
  1975 "Spanish-English codeswitching". In: E. Hernandez-Chavez, A. Cohen and A. Beltramo (eds.), *El lenguaje de los chicanos*, Arlington, Va.: Center for Applied Linguistics, pp. 138–154.

Lieberson, S.
  1970 *Language and Ethnic Relations in Canada*. N.Y.: Wiley.

McClure, E.
  1981 "Formal and functional aspects of the codeswitched discourse of bilingual children", in: R. Durán (ed.), *Latino Language and Communicative Behavior*, Norwood, N.J.: Ablex, pp. 69–94.

Mougeon, R., C. Brent-Palmer, M. Bélanger and W. Cichocki
  1982 *Le français parlé en situation minoritaire* (vol. 1), Québec: CIRB.

Muysken, P., A. di Sciullo and R. Singh
  1985 "Code switching and government", *Journal of Linguistics* 23.

Pfaff, C.
  1982 "Constraints on language mixing: intrasentential codeswitching and borrowing in Spanish/English", in: J. Amastae and L. Elias-Olivares (eds.), *Spanish in the United States: Sociolinguistic Aspects*, Cambridge: Cambridge University Press, pp. 164–197. Also in: *Language* 55 (2): 291–518 (1979).

Poplack, S.
  1980 "Sometimes I'll start a sentence in English Y TERMINO EN ESPAÑOL; towards a typology of code-switching", *Linguistics* 18: 581–618.

Ryan, E. B. and H. Giles (eds.).
  1982 *Attitudes Towards Language Variation: Social and Applied Contexts*, London: Arnold.

Sankoff, G.
  1980 *The Social Life of Language*, Philadelphia: University of Pennsylvania Press.

Scotton, C. M.
  1976 "Strategies of neutrality: language choice in uncertain situations" *Language* 52 (4): 919–941.

Tannen, D.
  1979 "What's in a frame: surface evidence for underlying expectations". In: R. Freedle (ed.), *New Directions in Discourse Processing*, Norwood, N.J.: Ablex, pp. 137–181.

Thibault, J.
  1979 "L'expressivité comme source de changement linguistique". In: P. Thibault (ed.), *Le français parlé: études sociolinguistiques*, Edmonton: Linguisitic Research, pp. 95–110.

Timm, L. A.
  1975 "Spanish-English code-switching: el porqué y how-not-to", *Romance Philology* 28 (4): 473–482.

Valdés, G.
    1981   "Code-switching as a deliberate verbal strategy: a microanalysis of
           direct and indirect requests among bilingual Chicano speakers" in
           R. Durán (ed.), *Latino Language and Communicative Behaviour*,
           Norwood, N.J.: Ablex, pp. 95–107.
Woolford, E.
    1983   "Bilingual codeswitching and syntactic theory", *Linguistic Inquiry*
           14 (3): 520–536.
Zentella, A. C.
    1981   "Tá bien, you could answer me en cualquier idioma: Puerto Rican
           codeswitching in bilingual classrooms", in: R. Durán (ed.), *Latino
           Language and Communicative Behavior*, Norwood, N.J.: Ablex,
           pp. 109–131.

Macro- and micro-sociolinguistic dimensions of code-switching in Vingard

Erica McClure
University of Illinois-Urbana

Malcolm McClure
Illinois State University

Introduction

In 1972 at the Third International Congress of Applied Linguistics, Jean Ure indicated the potential value of a sociolinguistic survey of the incidence of code-switching on both macro- and micro-dimensions: "a macro-sociolinguistic study of the relevant features of the types of community in which such mixing occurs and a micro-sociolinguistic study of the occasions on which it is used (Ure 1974)." The subsequent decade witnessed the publication of a multitude of studies addressing the latter functional issue and also the issue of the formal linguistic characteristics of code-switching (see for example Kachru 1978; Gumperz 1982; and for a review of analyses of code-switching in Hispanic communities, Baker 1980). However, there continued to be a paucity of analyses directed at the macro-sociolinguistic level although the need for such analysis continued to be acknowledged as is attested by Jonas Nartey's suggestion that "a universal theory of code-switching would need to look beyond mere linguistic behaviour and examine the socio/political environments of the code-switchers" (Nartey 1982). This paper is in answer to Ure and Nartey's call. In it we will first discuss the relationship between the macro-sociolinguistic context of code-switching and the formal linguistic and functional (or micro-sociolinguistic) parameters of code-switching in a multilingual Saxon community in Romania and then compare this situation with that existing in some of the other communities across the world whose formal and functional patterns of code-switching have been described.

The social situation in Transylvania

Diachronic view: a synopsis of Transylvanian history

Romania, as a result of its strategic location between Asia and Europe, has known the influx of multiple ethnic groups. The earliest existing records show it to have been the home of the Dacians. However, in A.D. 101 to 107 the Romans, annoyed by Dacian interference with trade, seized the area. When, in response to internal disruption and external attack, the Romans withdrew in A.D. 271, they left behind a population which in a period of only 170 years had been so Romanized as to have adopted the Latin language to the complete exclusion of Dacian.

After the Romans' departure, a series of migratory populations took possession of the area. Archaelogical sites attest to a Slavic presence in Transylvania by the beginning of the seventh century. At the time of the Hungarians' arrival in the tenth to eleventh centuries, Transylvania was occupied by a mixed Slavo-Romanian peasant population ruled by Slavic voivodas. In the course of the twelfth century, the Hungarians conquered the southern part of Transylvania, and by the thirteenth century Transylvania was under the rule of Hungarian kings and the subject Romanian population had completely assimilated the Slavic element.[1]

The period between A.D. 1150 and 1322 witnessed the immigration to Transylvania of a Rhine Franconian population from the area of Germany near Cologne. This population, known in Romania today as the Siebenbuergen Saxons, arrived at the invitation of the Hungarian kings. The invitation was prompted both by the need for a frontier guard to repulse invading barbarians and the desirability of a middle class to counterbalance the power of the nobles. In return for their services, the Saxons were granted privileged status. Under the charter of A.D. 1224, they held their lands directly from the king and had the exclusive right to ownership of land within their territory, the Fundus Regius. Furthermore, they were granted: (1) complete self-government under an elected count, including the right to elect their own judges and clergy; (2) exemption from taxation and freedom from all tolls and dues throughout the country for their merchants; and (3) exemption from direct military conscription. These provisions held, however, only within the Fundus Regius, not in villages established outside its perimeter (such as the village focused upon in this study, Vingard – Weingartskirchen in German, Van^yərškirx^y in Saxon). In these villages the Saxons were legally serfs, as were their Romanian neighbors, however, in practice they were initially accorded much the same rights as their compatriots within the Fundus Regius.

By the fifteenth century, the multitude of ethnic groups in Transylvania were organized into "received" or privileged nations – Magyars, Szekels, and Saxons – and "tolerated" nations without rights of citizenship – Vlachs, Greeks, Jews, Moravians, Poles, Russians, Serbs, Sclavi, Zingari, and Romanians – the latter group probably constituting the majority of the total Transylvanian population. From 1526, when central Hungary was taken by the Turks and Transylvania became independent, through the periods of native rule (1540–1690), Hapsburg rule (1691–1867), and Austro-Hungarian rule (1868–1918) until Transylvania was united with the Regat (Romania south of the Carpathians), the situation of the Romanians and that of the other tolerated peoples progressively worsened. The Hungarians first sought to subordinate them, then to assimilate them completely. Legislation enacted in the 1800's made Magyar the sole language of government, public notices, and the schools. Romanian societies, songs, and national colors were prohibited, and there was constant pressure to Magyarize family names.

Since the Saxons were one of the "received" nations, they were not subjected to the same harassment as the "tolerated" nations. However, following the inauguration of Hapsburg rule in Transylvania, relations between the Magyars and the Saxons slowly deteriorated, and "there were constant efforts to undermine Saxon holdings in land, and especially to reduce the standing of those who had settled outside the Fundus Regius" (Seton-Watson 1934: 172). Nevertheless, the Saxons retained a separate corporate existence and accompanying privileged legal status until the union of Transylvania and Hungary under the dual monarchies in 1868. This union dealt a strong blow to the Saxons for they lost their traditional privileges in exchange for a bill of rights whose provisions were never honored. Thus they became subject to the same Magyarization pressures that confronted the Romanians, although in general they retained a superior economic position.

A synchronic view: the modern period in Transylvania

Sovereignty over Transylvania passed to Romania at the end of World War I, occasioning an alteration in the balance of power among the coresident ethnic groups. The relative positions of the Hungarian and Romanian populations were reversed and so therefore to some extent were the positions of the Saxons and Romanians. The Romanians, who had been a completely subordinated population, now found themselves the dominant population. The Saxons, who had been subordinated to the dominant Hungarians, were now subordinated to the Romanians. However as the Romanians saw the Saxons as co-victims of Magyarization, rather then as oppressors, their accession to power saw an improvement in the Saxons' status, including the guarantee of their autonomous church and of their schools. Life in the villages, however, changed little until the advent of World War II.

Romania entered World War II allied with the Axis powers. Therefore, since the Germans considered her Saxon citizens to be Volksdeutsch, many were recruited directly into German regiments. At the end of the war, some of these soldiers who found themselves in Germany remained there, making new lives for themselves.

Other Saxon soldiers, prisoners of war, remained in forced labor camps in the USSR. In 1945 they were joined by an influx of Saxons from Romania. Although Romania had ended the war on the side of the Allies, the USSR demanded laborers as part of the reparations to be paid by Romania for the destruction she had wrought during her participation in the Axis. Romania sent the Saxons. Beginning on January 8, 1945, all healthy Saxon men seventeen to forty-five years of age, and all women eighteen to thirty-five years of age, were sent to Russian forced labor camps. Only pregnant women and women with children under one year of age were exempt (Hartl 1958: 128–130). Many died in the USSR from privation, many others did not return to Romania until 1951. When they returned, they found their homes and land occupied by others, since decree number 187 of March 23, 1945, expropriated without compensation all lands and equipment of those who had aided Nazi Germany in any way. Ninety-eight percent of the population of German ancestry in Romania were included (Hartl 1958: 128–130).[2]

The Saxons were just the first to experience the radical changes World War II was to introduce. The end of the war brought with it the gradual Communization of the country, resulting in an almost complete removal of the means of production from private hands by 1961. The proletarianization of the peasant, now a paid worker in a collective farm or on a state farm, had begun. The process has been accelerated by the linking of village and town through improved transportation and communication networks.

Vingard

The social setting

Saxon residence in Vingard is of long duration. Records indicate that the Saxon graf Daniel established a Saxon community there between 1271 and 1309, and, according to the ministry of architectural landmarks, the Saxon church in current use dates from 1461. It is not known whether the Saxons are the original inhabitants of the village or whether there were previously resident Romanians or Hungarians (Thomas Nagler, personal communication). In the period 1968–1970 in which the research reported here was carried out, Vingard was a multiethnic village of over 1200 individuals, about 650 of whom were Romanian, 450 Saxons, and 100 Gypsies.[3] This ethnic division is reflected in residence patterns, social interaction networks, schooling, religious affiliation, and linguistic repertoires.

Vingard is essentially a line village, the line running along the bottom of a shallow valley. With a few exceptions, the Saxons live in the broader, flatter part of the valley, the Romanians in the narrower top of the valley, and the Gypsies on the hillside. As a result of this arrangement, the Saxons have better gardens and flooded basements. The civic center — school, post office, state farm office, collective farm office, library, barber shop, dyer, weekly market, shoe repair, bar, one cooperative store, and the Romanian church — is in the Romanian area of residence. The Saxon church, the abandoned Hungarian church, the cultural center, the village clinic/maternity ward, and the other cooperative store which also serves as an alternative bar are at the border between the Romanian and Saxon neighborhoods. The Gypsies are also located there.

The ethnic neighborhood separation does not imply hostility. However interaction in work brigades tends to follow ethnic divisions, as does socializing, which generally involves neighbors (a number of Romanians live in the Saxon area, and both they and those at the border have normal, although slightly reserved, neighborly relations with the Saxons). Neighborhoods are formally organized into vecinătăţi. There are six Romanian vecinătăţi and four Saxon vecinătăţi. Their principal function is to provide necessary help at funerals and weddings. Funerals and weddings are occasions at which both Romanians and Saxons will extend invitations to members of the other ethnic group, but only to those few with whom they have a history of greater social interaction. In the memory of our informants, only one case of Saxon-Romanian intermarriage occurred within the village. Cross ethnic feuding was equally rare. In the past, when one went at night and set fire to ones' enemies' barns and poisoned their wells, Saxons attacked Saxons and Romanians attacked Romanians, probably because no means of interethnic conflict resolution existed. Thus should an interethnic dispute have occurred, there was always the risk that it would escalate into a villagewide fight, whereas intraethnic disputes were subject to arbitration based on pressure applied by common relatives and by the priest.

Religion was historically also a divisive factor in interethnic relations. Romanians and Gypsies were Orthodox, while Saxons were Lutheran. Although in general this pattern still held true at the time this study was conducted, there existed then a mixed Romanian and Saxon Baptist congregation. The government had refused to sanction two Baptist congregations within the village, so unified meetings were held, the sermon given by a lay preacher being translated into German or Romanian from its original language. However, toward the end of our stay in the village, the Romanians began to meet separately saying the original place "is too far to walk."

Language also separated the ethnic groups of Vingard. Everyone spoke at least some Romanian, but some older Saxons spoke it only minimally. Saxon, the first language of the Saxons, was known by only a few of the Romanians and Gypsies. Likewise, all Saxons had some knowledge of German, but only a few Romanians spoke it. However, many of the Gypsies (but no one else) spoke Romany. A few older people of all ethnic groups spoke Hungarian, a result of the Magyarization period in Transylvania. The linguistic separation of the Saxon population was also augmented by the fact that the first four grades in the village school had double classes, a class theoretically conducted in German (but actually in Saxon) for the Saxons, and one conducted in Romanian for the Romanians and Gypsies. Upon completion of the village school (grades 1–8 in 1970, subsequently increased to 1–10), Saxon children could attend a German high school in a nearby town.

Despite the cohesiveness of the Saxon community of Vingard, exterior ties did exist: (1) Almost everyone had relatives in one of the Romanian industrial centers and some individuals had relatives in Germany; visits were exchanged in both cases. (2) Most houses had radios, and in 1970 twenty-eight had television sets, two movies were also shown a week. Only a few hours of radio broadcasting per day were conducted in German. Television broadcasting and motion pictures were entirely in Romanian with the exception of films of foreign origin which had Romanian subtitles. (3) Daily newspapers, magazines, and books were available in German, but the selection was not nearly as broad as that which existed in Romanian. While a number of villagers subscribed to German-language newspapers, some preferred Romanian newspapers and some alternated. (4) All males spend two years in the army. (5) Some young adults commuted to nearby towns to work in factories. (6) Almost all older people had spent five years in the USSR at forced labor.

Code-switching in the Vingard Saxon community

The verbal repertoire

The verbal repertoire of the Saxon community in Vingard at the time the data for this study were collected included Vingard Saxon, Sibiu Saxon, German, Romanian, and Hungarian. Vingard Saxon was the first language of the entire Saxon community and everyone spoke it fluently. Sibiu Saxon, the dialect spoken in a nearby city (Hermannstadt in German) with a large Saxon population, could be understood by all as Vingard Saxon and Sibiu Saxon are quite similar, coming from the same dialect area. However the Vingard Saxons differed in their ability to speak Sibiu Saxon. The people who spoke it more fluently were those who had worked as servants in town and those who had been educated during Romania's participation in the Axis when the Germans encouraged the use of Sibiu Saxon as the standard language of the Siebenbuergen Saxons. Vingard Saxons considered Sibiu Saxon to be more cultured than their Vingard Saxon; nevertheless they felt a loyalty to their own dialect. One widely-travelled informant, after saying how much nicer and more civilized the Sibiu dialect was, cocked his head to one side and said "but you know, of all the Saxons we're the only ones that speak clearly." Another informant who had spent several years in town, returning to Vingard only in the summers, related how in town she was laughed at for saying bɔks (⟨Rom. box) instead of šagəkrem for shoe polish while in Vingard she was laughed at for saying šagəkrem instead of bɔks. She herself ridiculed for having used šteyədəš ("city talk") one of our other informants who in a recording had used gəgyəŋən instead of gyəŋən 'gone'.

The Saxons' fluency in German also varied and was influenced by some of the same factors affecting their fluency in Sibiu Saxon (urban residence and degree of formal schooling) and also by having relatives in Germany. Fluency in Romanian depended upon school attendance during Romanian rule of Transylvania and upon the degree of social interaction with Romanians, just as fluency in Hungarian depended upon school attendance during Hungarian rule of Transylvania and the degree of social interaction with Hungarians.

Situational code-switching

John Gumperz (1982: 60–61), in describing code alternation of
the situational type, notes that "Distinct varieties are employed
in certain settings (such as home, school, work) that are associated
with separated bounded kinds of activities (public speaking,
formal negotiations, special ceremonials, verbal games, etc.)
or spoken with different categories of speakers (friends, family
members, strangers, social inferiors, government officials, etc.)
. . . only one code is employed at any one time . . . There is a
simple almost one to one relationship between language usage and
social context so that each variety can be seen as having a distinct
place or function within the local speech repertoire." Among
Vingard Saxons, it was the category of participants that was most
salient in determining situational code-switching, although setting
and kind of activity ('genre' in Hymes' 1972 framework) also had
a effect.

Vingard Saxon was considered to be the appropriate code when
all participants in a speech situation were Vingard Saxons except
in two settings, the church and the school. Church sermons were
conducted entirely in German, although church announcements
were made in Saxon. German was also the de jure language of
instruction for the first four years of education for Saxon children
in Vingard schools. However, de facto, much more Saxon than
German was used in the school not only because the children
came to school with little knowledge of German, but also because
the instructors were more comfortable in Saxon. When Vingard
Saxons conversed with Saxons from other communities, code
choice depended on the degree of similarity of the participants'
dialects. If the dialects were from the same dialect area, each
person spoke his own, attempting not to use any lexical items
which were not shared. If the dialect was quite different, German
was used.

Romanian was the choice when one's addressee was Romanian
or Gypsy.[4] According to convention, Romanian was also the
choice when there was a Romanian audience even if the addressee
was Saxon, "because we don't want them to think we are talking
about them." Saxons felt that this rule was usually observed,
while Romanians felt that it was usually broken. Perhaps the

discrepancy results from different definitions of audience. It appears that Romanians define any person within hearing as part of the audience while Saxons so define only those they consider to be part of the conversational grouping.

The use of Hungarian was very restricted. Only a few Saxons had conversational fluency in Hungarian, and they used it only when conversing with Hungarians. Since only three Hungarians remained in Vingard, Saxon use of Hungarian occurred only in the infrequent occasion of interaction with one of these co-villagers or in interaction with a Hungarian in an urban marketplace or store.[5]

Conversational code-switching

Gumperz (1982: 59) defines conversational code-switching "as the juxtaposition within the same speech exchange of passages of speech belonging to two different grammatical systems or subsystems." He further notes that "the items in question form part of the same minimal speech act, and message elements are tied by syntactic and semantic relations equivalent to those that join passages in a single language (1982: 61)." Stating that the relationship of language usage to social context is much more complex than in situational code-switching, he suggests that "Rather than claiming that speakers use language in response to a fixed, predetermined set of prescriptions it seems more reasonable to assume that they build on their own and their audience's abstract understanding of situational norms to communicate metaphoric information about how they intend their words to be understood." In discussing the functions of conversational code-switching, Gumperz (1982) introduces a preliminary typology which included the following six categories: quotations, addressee specification, interjections, reiteration, message qualification, and personalization versus objectivization. Additional factors which have been cited include: parenthesis, emphasis, contrast, narration, and preformulation (Valdés-Fallis 1976). Qualitatively quite different motivations for specific switches are gaps in the codes of the bilingual. These may be of three types (Baker 1980): gaps in denotation (Elías-Olivares

1976; Huerta 1978; McClure 1981) gaps in connotation (Huerta 1978; McClure 1981), and gaps in register (Baker 1980; Elías-Olivares 1976). Finally, the code-switched register itself, rather than any specific switch, may be used to convey social information about the speaker, serving to mark him for example as knowledgeable about a specific topic, generally well educated, urbane, sophisticated, etc. This function of code-switching has been called 'role identification' by Kachru (1978) and Sridhar (1978).

Among the Vingard Saxons, conversational code-switching occurred relatively infrequently. Since Vingard Saxon was defined as the appropriate language for intragroup communication, and generally only other Vingard Saxons shared the multilingual verbal repertoire, much such code-switching involved the use of Vingard Saxon as the base language, with limited switches to Romanian, Sibiu Saxon, or German. Furthermore, only a small subset of the factors mentioned in the literature were involved. These included quotation, parenthesis, reiteration, gaps, and the use of a code-switched register to indicate education. Examples of each are given below:

Quotation

Marking direct quotation was by far the most frequent motivation for conversational code-switching, the narrator switching from Saxon, the language of the narrative frame, to Romanian or German in accordance with the language of the original speaker. However, such switching was not consistent. In example 1, FT, a Saxon woman, narrates her experiences in trying to obtain the appropriate documents to travel to Germany, quoting her conversation with a Romanian policeman and a Romanian travel agent in Romanian and her conversation with a German-speaking border official in German. The narrative frame is Saxon. However, in example 2, the same informant narrates the story of a search to find a cure for an epileptic villager, quoting several Romanians in Saxon. The only marker of the fact that the original conversation took place in Romanian is a parenthetic remark, an example of the type of code-switching discussed next.

EXAMPLE 1

FT was supposed to go on a visit to West Germany, and was unsure whether the information which she received from the Romanian passport office and travel bureau was correct. At the Austrian border she was in fact turned back because she lacked an entry visa for Germany.

frame	ən do vor əzi ə gaŋ məlitsyán ən zot ke mix^y:
P	"Aici e paşaporta, acumă poţi să pleci în Germania."
FT	"Dar primă data mă duc − trebuie să mă duc la Bucureşti."
P	"Ce aia? Nu trebuie să te duci!"
.	
.	
.	
frame	ən sprax^{y}t day haran:
TA	"Numai la ora unşpe puţeti veni după acte."
.	
.	
.	
frame	Zæt an də pɔs ən zæt ba mix^y:
BO	"Wohin reisen Sie?"
FT	"Nach Westdeutschland."
BO	"Nirgends reisen Sie," sprax^{y}t ə "Nirgends reisen Sie, Sie haben keine Einreise."

TRANSLATION

frame	[Saxon] And there was a young policeman and he said to me:
P	[Romanian] "Here is your passport, now you can leave for Germany."
FT	[Romanian] "But first I go − I need to go to Bucharest."
P	[Romanian] "What's that? You don't need to go!"
.	
.	
.	
frame	[Saxon] and the woman says:
TA	[Romanian] "Only at 11:00 can you come for your documents."
frame	[Saxon] Looks at the passport and says to me:
BO	[German] "Where are you travelling?"
FT	[German] "To West Germany."
BO	[German] "You are not going anywhere," [Saxon] he says, [German] "You are not going anywhere, you have no entry visa."

EXAMPLE 2

FT is reporting what FC told her about a conversation between FC and some other Romanian women in a market place regarding an herbalistic cure for epilepsy.

Rom   "ət az ən dwəktər an Krayóvə ən dey hwət mæn^y mon gəhəyəlt."

frame   Naw zay hwət zix^y ux geyə ken deyə fraan:

FC   "Zot mər vət hwəd ir, vət reyət ir hay əzi?"

frame   Zay hwəd ər fen un tsə zon:

Rom   "Zax^y mæ mon hwət ux də amfola kriŋkət"

frame   (epilepsie vaa zə ət həysən)

Rom   "ən mər hu gəheyrt fun dyəzəm dwəktər"

frame   (zay hwət gəzot tver ən dwəktər)

Rom   "fun dyəzəm dwəktər ən mər zyə gyəŋən ux mæ mon as gəhəyəlt vwərdən, tazəm nast mey "

frame   Dyəs hwət gəzot:

FC   "Bast əzi gawt ən gist mər dadrés fun dyəm dwəktər har.
Yəx^y kænən ux — cunosc şi eu un cetăţean,"

frame   vaa zay zon,

FC   "Yəx^y kænən ux yənə faar har vo mæn^y kant^y vorən an deyər gəməyn ugix^y væd gaarən halfə vun ət zix^y væt kænən."

TRANSLATION

Rom   [Saxon] "There is a doctor in Craiova and he healed my husband."

frame   [Saxon] Now she went up to those women:

FC   [Saxon] "Tell me what you have, what you are talking about here thus?"

frame   [Saxon] She began to tell her:

Rom   [Saxon] "You see, my husband had the falling sickness"

frame   [Romanian] (epilepsy, [Saxon] as they call it)

Rom   [Saxon] "and we heard of this doctor,"

frame   [Saxon] (she said it was a doctor)

Rom   [Saxon] "of this doctor and we went and my husband was healed, he has nothing more."

frame   [Saxon] This one said:

FC   [Saxon] "Be so good and give me the address of the doctor. I know also — [Romanian] I also know a citizen,"

frame   [Saxon] as they say,

FC   [Saxon] "I also know someone far away where my children were in a village and I would like to help him if it can be."

Parenthesis

In this type of code-switch, the speaker stepped out of the role of impersonal narrator to make comments about the code usage itself as in Example 3 below, which is also taken from FT's description of her abortive trip to Germany.

EXAMPLE 3
FT is quoting her dialogue with a Romanian policeman at the passport office in Romanian:

FT⟩P   "Dar primă data mă duc — trebuie să mă duc la Bucureşti."
P⟩FT   "Ce aia? Nu trebuie să te duci!"
FT⟩P   "Ba da, eu ştiu aşa de la noi s-o dus puţin, dar care s-o dus o trebuit să meargă la Bucureşti la ambasadă ca să-îşi scoată . . . də Einreise."
FT⟩aud   Ixᵛ bəštanyət væys va zə zon əf dot.
aud1   Ieşirea
aud2   Întrarea
Aud1   Întrarea în Germania

TRANSLATION
FT⟩P   [Romanian] "But first I go — I have to go to Bucharest."
P⟩FT   [Romanian] "What's that? You don't have to go!"
FT⟩P   [Romanian] "Yes I do, I know that from our village few have gone, but each who has gone has had to go to Bucharest to the embassy to get . . . [Saxon] the [German] entry visa."
FT⟩aud   [Saxon] I don't remember how they say that.
aud1   [Romanian] Exit visa.
aud2   [Romanian] Entry visa.
aud1   [Romanian] Entry visa for Germany.

Reiteration

Reiterative code switches seem to fulfill two functions in Saxon speech: clarification and emphasis. Examples 4, 5, 6, and 7 are of the former type while 8, 9, and 10 are of the latter type. In 4 and 5 the switch is from Saxon to German, in 6 from Saxon to Romanian, in 7 from Sibiu Saxon to Vingard Saxon, in 8 and 9 from Romanian to Saxon, and in 10 from Vingard Saxon to Sibiu Saxon.

EXAMPLES
4   Hæf gəzot xᵛa hey hæf a Vaanən študeyrt, an Wien.
T   [Saxon] He said, yes he had studied in Vienna, [German] in Vienna.

5   Tsa minútə vorən amtsvášə mad ast az əm dər odəm əwsgyəŋən,
        əwz yənəm əzi layxᵛt <u>ausgehaucht</u> vaa dər dæč zot.
T   [Saxon] Then there were ten minutes and a little, then the breath
        went out of him, suddenly he lightly [German] exhaled/expired
        [Saxon] as German says.

6   Zay hwəd ər fen un tsə zon, "zaxᵛ mæ mon hwət ux də amfola
        kriŋkət" <u>epilepsie</u> vaa zə ət həysən.
T   [Saxon] She began to tell her, "See, my husband had also the
        falling sickness" [Romanian] epilepsy [Saxon] as they say.

7   Ux nast zyəld ər geyən əws dər harbrixᵛ − əws dər <u>stuf</u> har.
T   [Vingard Saxon] And you should give nothing out of the
        household − out of the [Sibiu Saxon] household.

8   ən dey manč hæt gəzot "da, prietini" hæf ə gəzot "să şti că
        sanătate e foarte scumpă. Dar eu m-am vindicat. Am fost bolnav
        în ultimul grad," <u>am ləytst graat ver ə gəveyəst − hərt hərt ux</u>
        <u>ivərneyn mat dyəzər kriŋkət.</u>
T   [Saxon] and the man said "[Romanian] yes, friends" [Saxon] he
        said "[Romanian] know that health is very precious. But I got well.
        I was sick to the ultimate degree," [Saxon] to the last degree he
        was sick − strongly, strongly taken over by this disease.

9   "Dar m-am vindicat. Dar eu nu-ţi spun cu ce numai ătît îţi spui de
        nişte băi reci" <u>əws ništᵛ æy kold bɨwədər.</u>
T   [Romanian] "But I got well. But I won't tell you with what, I'll
        only tell you about some cold bath" [Saxon] about some cold
        baths.

10   Dyət vor lwənst Krayóvə, yəxᵛ kon ən əvər nyət zon də gəməyn −
        <u>an ə gəməyn, an ən dwərf.</u>

T   [Saxon] That was near Craiova, I can't tell the village − in a village,
        [Sibiu Saxon] in a village.

Gaps

While no code-switches in our data appeared to be occasioned by
gaps in register, gaps in denotation and gaps in connotation or
specificity appear to motivate minimal code-switches. We have

considered the following examples to be code-switches rather than borrowings because they were unmodified phonologically and had not been assimilated into the grammatical system of the matrix sentence, criteria commonly employed in the code-switching literature (Gumperz 1982; McClure 1981; Poplack 1979).[6] Examples 11, 12, and 13 are instances of denotative gaps while 14 and 15 are instances of connotative or specificity gaps. While Saxon has a word durx^v grívəlt 'bad, naughty', it does not capture the same image as the Romanian mişel 'a naughty mischievous rascal'. Nor does Saxon giptərtsəgunən 'gypsies' capture the three-way distinction according to residence and economic patterns that Romanian makes among the Romany with the words ţigani, lăieţi, and corturari.[7] In 11 a Saxon noun phrase with a German borrowing is switched into a Romanian sentence while in 12–15 Romanian nouns are switched into Saxon sentences. In 11 and 13 the nouns are plural and their pluralization is Romanian.

11   O trebuit să meargă la Bucureşti la ambasadă ca să-îşi scoaţă də Einreise.
T   [Romanian] They had to go to Bucharest to the embassy to get [Saxon] the [German] entry visa.

12   ən gon an Hermannstət mat də aaktə fun də agencie de voiaj fun day ix^v də kortx^vər hu gəvanən . . .
T   [Saxon] and I go to Sibiu with the documents from the [Romanian] travel agency [Saxon] from which I got the tickets . . .

13   əzi ken dox hevə zə gəzaan dər old ver ɔfgəštondən ən hæf am bax an^v gəleyəzən ən hevəm iwəfgəšrivə mat tsve indigouri.
T   [Saxon] So in the morning they saw how the old man had gotten up and had read extensively in a book and had written it down for him with two [Romanian] carbon copies.

14   ə vor əzi mişel.
T   [Saxon] He was such a [Romanian] naughty one.
15   Ux hay əzi baa aws vorən dyəzər lăieţi.
T   [Saxon] And here near us were these [Romanian] gypsies.

Role identification

In Vingard Saxon the use of a few lexical items from German or Sibiu Saxon marks the speaker as more educated, urbane, or sophisticated, although if one's claim to this status is not accepted by the audience, such use may lead to ridicule. The speakers in the examples below receive community acceptance for their usage. In 16 the speaker is the individual who acts as master of ceremonies at Saxon weddings and other ceremonial occasions while in 17 the speaker is a middle-aged woman with better than average educa· tion who in addition is quoting the Saxon minister. In 16 the switches involve insertion of German lexical items in a Saxon sentence while in 17 a Sibiu Saxon lexical item has been inserted.

16 Dru moecht' ixᵛo vančən dər laaf hargot zol dyəzər gaŋər Jugend halfən dət zə zər xᵛo trɨwa zyən.
T [Saxon] Then [German] would [Saxon] I wish that the dear God should help these young [German] youths [Saxon] that they should be true to each other.

17 ən hwət dər har for ɨwəfšəyt gəneyn ən hwət gəzot, "Yəxᵛ fɨwərən an urləf."
T [Saxon] And the minister took his leave and said, "I'm going on [Sibiu Saxon] vacation."

Language play

A final category of within speech act code-switching found in our data but not commonly discussed in the literature, is that of language play. Two songs, one in Saxon and Romanian and the other in German and Romanian are illustrative:

18 Hai naw go mir an gəyskən ɔfən,
    tra la la lalala
    repeat
    Mat dəm kradᵛə lčə no vosər
    tra la la lalala
    repeat
    Hai naw go mir tsər lele Floare
    tra la la lalala
    Cu cupiţa după moare
    tra la la lalala

Şi mi-o dat şi o căpăţene
tra la la lalala
Să mai am o săptămînă
tra la la lalala
Hu yu yu gəfodər Træn^V
tra la la lalala
Gaf mər mat dəm kwənčə væn^V
Tra la la lalala

T   [Saxon] Now we go up the alley,
[Saxon] With the pot for water,
[Saxon] Now we go to [Romanian] Ms. Floare
[Romanian] with a cup for sauerkraut water.
[Romanian] And she gave me also a head of cabbage
[Romanian] So I would have enough for a week.
[Saxon] Hu yu yu cogodmother Katherine
[Saxon] Give me wine with a cup.

19   Tu draga iubita, was hast du gemacht?
Eu nu pot s-adorm die ganze Nacht.
Şi dacă adorm, so traeum' ich von dir,
Şi mă gîndesc du waerst bei mir.
Hai gib mit dein guriţa, gib mir dein Mund
Să te sărut eine halbe Stund'.
(repeat)
Şi dacă mă duc wohl in der Wald,
Nu plînge tu draga, 'ch kom' wieder bald.
Şi dacă mă duc wohl ueber die Brueck',
Nu plînge tu drage, 'ch kom' wieder zurueck.
Şi dacă mă duc, bei dir kehr' ich ein.
Şi mă învîrtesc auf einem Bein.

T   [Romanian] you dear loved one, [German] what have you done?
[Romanian] I can't sleep [German] the whole night.
[Romanian] and if I go to sleep, [German] then I dream of you,
[Romanian] and I think [German] you were with me.
[German] Hai give me your [Romanian] mouth, [German] give me your mouth
[Romanian] To kiss you [German] a half an hour.
[Romanian] And if I go [German] in the woods,
[Romanian] Don't cry dear one, [German] I'll come back soon.
[Romanian] And if I go [German] over the bridge,
[Romanian] Don't cry dear one, [German] I'll come back again.
[Romanian] And if I go [German] I'll stop in with you
[Romanian] And I'll turn around [German] on one leg.

Formal linguistic constraints on Saxon code-switching

The range of syntactic patterns in our data on Saxon code-switching is quite limited. Since by far the greatest use of code-switching is for direct quotation, the vast majority of code-switches in our corpus is at the level of the sentence. However code-switches at the level of the clause, prepositional phrase, and lexical level also occur. Lexical switches to Romanian almost always involve substantives, but lexical switches to German include adjectives and even modal auxiliaries and pronouns as in example 20:

20   ən moecht' ix^v bidən treyət ər un yənər hand^vərəm ondərən ən jeder
      græyft an də toš ən zol geyən vodəm moeglich as.

T   [Saxon] And I [German] would like [Saxon] to ask that you step up
      one after another and [German] everyone [Saxon] reaches in his pocket
      and should give what is [German] possible [Saxon] to him.

In this example, three previously proposed constraints on code-switching are violated. The use of moechte 'would like' is in violation of the constraint on switching between auxiliaries and main verbs (Timm 1975; Lipski 1978), the use of jeder 'everyone' is in violation of the constraint on switching between pronominal subject or object and verbs (Timm 1975; Lipski 1978; Gumperz 1982), and the use of moeglich violates the constraint on switching the simple adjective (Lipski 1978; Gumperz 1982). Perhaps the explanation for these violations is the extreme structural similarity between the two languages involved. It is normally possible to translate any German sentence into Saxon morpheme by morpheme (the reverse does not always hold as Saxon only optionally places the verb in sentence final position in cases where that is obligatory in standard German). Moreover, in most cases it would be possible to carry out such a translation employing only cognates.

While our data violate some of the more specific proposed constraints on code-switching, they are in conformity with the following more general constraints:

21   An immediate constituent or phrase structure boundary constraint
      (Hasselmo 1970; Poplack 1977; Schaffer 1978) which states that
      code-switches occur at phrase structure boundaries and that higher level

constituents have a greater probability of being switched than lower ones (Gumperz and Hernandez-Chavez 1972; Poplack 1977).

22   A homology or equivalency of structure constraint (Poplack 1977; Lipski 1978) stated by Lipski as "Whereas, the portion of a code-switched utterance that falls before the code-switch may indeed contain syntactically divergent elements, those portions falling after the switch must be essentially identical syntactically (1978: 258).

23   A frequency constraint which limits the number of code shifts that may be accommodated in a given stretch of discourse (Lipski 1978).

24   A free morpheme constraint (Poplack 1977) which rules out code-switching where the switch is between a free and bound morpheme.

The relationship between macro- and micro-sociolinguistic and formal linguistic parameters

In generalizing about the macro-sociolinguistic context of code-switching Gumperz states:

"Code-switching is perhaps most frequently found in the informal speech of those members of cohesive minority groups in modern urbanizing regions who speak the native tongue at home, while using the majority language at work and when dealing with members of groups other than their own. The individuals concerned live in situations of rapid transition where traditional intergroup barriers are breaking down and norms of interaction are changing (1982: 64)."

This description quite neatly characterizes the situation of Spanish-English code-switching in the United States. It does not fit the situation of Vingard. In the United States, English, the majority group language, is the primary language of education and of the workplace while Spanish is primarily the language of the home. As a result, observers of Spanish-English code-switching have repeatedly noted that topic or domain shift often occasions code-switching (Huerta 1978; Baker 1980; McClure 1981). Topic shift as a motivation for code-switching is also mentioned by those describing code-switching in former British colonies where English became the language of domains such as economics, education, politics, and modern technology (Kachru 1978; Sridhar 1978; Nartey 1982). Topic shift was not, however, a factor in Vingard Saxon code-switching. The explanation we believe is threefold. First, Saxon borrows quite freely. Second, no single language was associated with education. While traditionally Siebenbuergen Saxons travelled to Germany for higher education, according to our informants no Vingard Saxons had ever had that opportunity. Instead, whatever grade school education they received was through the combined media of Saxon, German, and Romanian or Hungarian. Third, there were no activities of daily life which were carried out in only one language. Life in Vingard, an agricultural village, was much less fragmented than life in the urban communities whose code-switching patterns have been described. The language used depended upon the participants.

That code selection frequently depends on characteristics of the participants has also been quite widely noted in the literature (McClure 1981; Gumperz 1982).[8] Much has been written about the use of code-switching to mark social identity (e.g. Kachru 1978; Sridhar 1978), role relationships (e.g. Blom and Gumperz 1972; McClure 1981), and social solidarity (e.g. Elías-Olivares 1976; Gumperz 1982). In Vingard Saxon code-switching, it was primarily the language competence of the participants which determined switching. Sibiu Saxon and German could be used to indicate erudition but their primary use was for communication when speakers did not share a local Saxon dialect. Romanian and Hungarian were only used for the latter purpose. Furthermore, although one can identify Romanian and Hungarian as "they codes", Vingard Saxon as the "we code" and Sibiu Saxon and German as intermediate forms ("we codes" in contrast to Romanian and Hungarian and "they codes" in contrast to Vingard Saxon), this wealth of resources was apparently not manipulated to convey metaphorical meaning. Perhaps the absence of such usage is related to a firm, positive sense of identity as Saxons, based on their history of privileged status in Transylvania and the respect they are still accorded by all ethnic groups as excellent, conscientious workmen.

Our data on Vingard Saxon code-switching also contained a much narrower range of stylistic use of code-switching than has been described for Hispanic communities in the United States. This relative poverty of usage may be related both to differences in the degree of integration of the bilingual communities in their respective dominant monolingual communities and to differences in the prestige of the respective "they codes". In the United States, the Hispanic community finds itself in a situation in which "intergroup barriers are breaking down." Thus the bilingual has the opportunity to develop the sophisticated command of English which appears to be necessary before one can exploit the full range of syntactic codeswitching patterns (e.g. Poplack 1979; McClure 1981) without which it is difficult to exploit the full range of stylistic motivations for code-switching.

In Vingard, at the time of our study, the Saxon and Romanian communities were still quite separate. This fact, together with the fact that as peasants the Saxons had little need to develop a sophisticated command of Romanian, meant that most had only a basic conversational grasp of Romanian. They also had little need or opportunity to develop a greater command of German as there is no local group of native German speakers. Finally, as neither Romanian nor German had the status of being the language of a local group of acknowledged superior social status, larding one's speech with conversational switches would not function as a means of increasing one's social status through demonstration of a native-like grasp of a prestige language.

Conclusion

In response to the suggestions of Ure and Nartey in this paper we have tried to situate the formal linguistic and micro-socio-linguistic dimensions of Vingard Saxon code-switching in their macro-sociolinguistic context. We have seen that the history of Saxon residence in Transylvania has involved a very different pattern of social interaction between the small multilingual community of Saxons and their neighbours than that of either the multilingual communities in former British colonies or the immigrant or minority bilingual communities so widely described in the code-switching literature. In the latter cases, structural inequality clearly existed or had existed, in which the bilingual and multilingual communities had clearly occupied subordinate positions. In the Saxon case, no such structural inequality existed. Indeed, for many centuries the Saxons had an advantaged position. The Saxon situation also differed in that at the time of our study the Saxon community for the most part interacted in closed social interaction networks while the bilinguals described in the studies of immigrant and minority groups seemed to participate in open networks (Gumperz 1982). These macro-sociolinguistic differences were associated with formal linguistic and micro-sociolinguistic differences. In the Saxon data, code-switching has more limited functions and there is much less diversity in the linguistic form of the code-switching than is characteristic of the two other types of community.

Situational code-switching of all three types mentioned by Gumperz (governed by setting, activity and participants) occurred, but it was the latter that was dominant. Conversational code-switching, while present especially for purposes of quotation but also for parenthetical remarks, reiteration, gaps, role identification, and language play, was clearly subordinate to situational code-switching. These facts suggest two possibilities: (1) situational code-switching may be historically prior to conversational code-switching; and (2) social identity may be the first trigger not only of situational but also of conversational code-switching; switching to mark quotation seems to be the most commonly mentioned form of conversational code-switching (see McClure 1981 for further support of this thesis). Further functional development of code-switching may require more intimate contact between bilingual and monolingual communities.

Nartey suggests that linguistic constraints on code-switching may differ in immigrant and former colonial settings. Our data and that of Dozier (1956), Bright (1960), and Diebold (1962, 1964) with respect to borrowings suggest that a finer typology may be necessary. Our data also suggest that for code-switching, as for borrowings (e.g. Sapir 1927; Haugen 1956), the structure of the two languages involved is important. In the last decade, major advances have been made in describing the formal and functional properties of code-switching in a wide variety of communities. We would like to join Ure and Nartey in urging that researchers now also consider the relationships of macro-sociolinguistic variables to these well-studied variables.

Notes

1. The outline of Transylvanian history presented here is in accordance with the Romanian view. In general, Hungarians and Germans claim that Aurelian's withdrawal from Dacia was complete, that the Roman colonists were not Romans, that Romanization could not have been complete in 170 years, and moreover, that whatever was left of the population of Dacia after Roman withdrawal was subsequently pushed out of the Northern Region and restricted to the Southern Region until the thirteenth century, when it was invited back by the Hungarian kings. The Slavic viewpoint coincides with the Romanian – namely, that Transylvania has been continuously inhabited by Romanians, the descendants of a Romanized Dacian population, Roman colonials, and an admixture of Slavs.
2. Vingard Saxon informants (unlike Hartl's informants) state that they were able to buy back their houses in installments and that after the first year they were granted title free. Furthermore, recently Saxon collective members have been granted pension rights as if they had donated their land directly to the collective, rather than having had it expropriated.
3. The three elderly people who are the remnants of a pre-World War II Hungarian population of about forty families may be ignored for the purpose of this discussion.
4. An exception was the situation in which one of the Gypsies who spoke Saxon was addressed. For conversational purposes these Gypsies were treated as Saxons.
5. Speaking Romanian to a Hungarian in a commercial interchange is often the way to ensure poor service.
6. Saxon does have numerous loans from German and Romanian (see E. McClure 1976; M. McClure 1973). These loans have however undergone characteristic sound changes and many Saxons are unaware of the fact that they are indeed borrowings.
7. The term *ţigani* is used in Romanian at two levels of specificity – as a cover term for all Romany and as the term for Romany who are settled out living in a fixed location and earning their livelihood there. In the latter use *ţigani* contrasts with *lăieţi*, Romany who live in a fixed location but whose trading activities take them on a circuit of communities, and

corturari, Romany with no fixed abode who live in wagons and follow traditional Gypsy occupations such as tinsmithing, horsetrading, and fortune telling.

8. Indeed, if one Guttman-scaled factors affecting code-switching, participants would probably rank as number one.

References

Baker, Opal Ruth
  1980 Categories of code switching in Hispanic communities; untangling the terminology. Working Paper No. 76. Austin, Texas: Southwest Educational Development Laboratory.
Blom, Jan-Petter and John J. Gumperz
  1972 Social meaning in linguistic structures: code-switching in Norway. In John J. Gumperz and Dell Hymes (eds.) *Directions in Sociolinguistics.* Chicago: Holt, Rinehart and Winston, Inc., pp. 407–434.
Bright, William
  1960 Animals of acculturation in the California Indian languages. *University of California Publications in Linguistics*, Vol. 4 pp. 215–246. Berkeley: University of California Press.
Diebold, A. Richard, Jr.
  1962 A laboratory for language contact. *Anthropological Linguistics* 4 (1): 41–51.
  1964 Incipient Bilingualism. In Dell Hymes (ed.) *Language in Culture and Society.* New York: Harper and Row, pp. 495–510.
Dozier, Edward P.
  1956 Two examples of linguistic acculturation: the Yaqui of Sonora and Arizona and the Tewa of New Mexico. *Language* 32: 146–157.
Elías-Olivares, Lucía
  1976 *Ways of Speaking in a Chicano Community: A Sociolinguistic Approach.* Ph.D. Dissertation. The University of Texas at Austin.
Gumperz, John J.
  1982 *Discourse Strategies.* New York: Cambridge University Press.
Gumperz, John J. and Eduárdo Hernández-Chávez
  1972 Bilingualism, bidialectialism and classroom interaction. In Courtney Cazden, Vera John, and Dell Hymes (eds.) *Functions of Language in the Classroom.* New York: Teachers College Press, pp. 311–339.
Hartl, Hans
  1958 *Das Schicksal des Deutschtums in Rumänien (1938–1945–1953).* Würzburg: Holzner-Verlag.

Hasselmo, N.

1970 Code-switching and modes of speaking. In G. G. Gilbert (ed.) *Texas Studies in Bilingualism.* Berlin: De Gruyter, pp. 179–210.

Haugen, Einar

1956 *Bilingualism in the Americas: A Bibliography and Research Guide.* Publication of the American Dialect Society, No. 26. Tuscaloosa: University of Alabama Press.

Huerta, Ana Graciela

1978 *Code Switching Among Spanish-English Bilinguals: A Socio-linguistic Perspective.* Ph.D. Dissertation. The University of Texas at Austin.

Hymes, Dell.

1972 Models of the interaction of language and social life. In John J. Gumperz and Dell Hymes (eds.) *Directions in Sociolinguistics.* Chicago: Holt, Rinehart and Winston, Inc., pp. 35–71.

Kachru, Braj B.

1978 Toward structuring code-mixing: an Indian perspective. *International Journal of the Sociology of Language* 16: 27–46.

Lipski, J. M.

1978 Code-switching and the problem of bilingual competence. In M. Paradis (ed.) *Aspects of Bilingualism.* Columbia, S.C.: Hornbeam Press, pp. 250–264.

McClure, Erica

1976 Ethnoanatomy in a multilingual community: an analysis of semantic change. *American Ethnologist* 3 (3): 525–542.

1981 Formal and functional aspects of the code-switched discourse of bilingual children. In Richard P. Duran (ed.) *Latino Language and Communicative Behaviour.* Norwood, New Jersey: ABLEX Publishing Company, pp. 69–94.

McClure, Malcolm

1973 *A Grammar of the Weingartskirchen Dialect of Transylvanian German.* Ph.D. Dissertation. University of California at Berkeley. University Microfilms.

Nartey, Jonas N. A.

1982 Code-switching, interference or faddism? Language use among educated Ghanians. *Anthropological Linguistics* 24 (2): 183–192.

Poplack, Shana

1977 Quantitative analysis of constraints on code-switching. Centro de Estudios Puertoriqueños Working Paper. New York: CUNY.

1979 Sometimes I'll start a sentence in Spanish y termino en español: toward a typology of code-switching. Centro de Estudios Puertoriqueños Working Paper. New York: CUNY.

Sapir, Edward
  1927 *Language.* New York: Harcourt and Brace.
Schaffer, D.
  1978 The place of code-switching in linguistic contacts. In M. Paradis
        (ed.) *Aspects of Bilingualism.* Columbia, S.C.: Hornbeam Press,
        pp. 265–274.
Seton-Watson, R. W.
  1934 *A History of the Romanians from Roman Times to the Completion
        of Unity.* Cambridge: Cambridge University Press.
Sridhar, S. N.
  1978 On the function of code-mixing in Kannada. *International Journal
        of the Sociology of Language* 16: 109–118.
Timm, L. A.
  1975 Spanish-English code-switching: el porque y how-not-to. *Romance
        Philology* 28: 473– 482.
Ure, Jean
  1974 Code-switching and mixed speech in the register systems of devel-
        oping languages. In A. Verdoodt (ed.) *Association Internationale de
        Linguistique Appliquée Third Congress Copenhagen 1972 Proceed-
        ings, Volume II: Applied Sociolinguistics.* Heidelberg, Germany:
        Julius Groos Verlag, pp. 222–239.
Valdés-Fallis, Guadalupe
  1976 Social interaction and code-switching patterns: a case study of
        Spanish/English alternation. In G. D. Keller, R. V. Tichner,
        and S. Viera (eds.) *Bilingualism in the Bicentennial and Beyond.*
        New York: Bilingual Press.

Codeswitching and comedy in Catalonia

Kathryn A. Woolard
University of Wisconsin, Madison

Introduction

Many case studies have contributed to the understanding of the extent to which conversational language mixing or codeswitching in bilingual communities is orderly, systematic, and meaningful. A large number of those studies that attempt to move beyond the descriptive and taxonomic draw on two important approaches, one more narrowly linguistic, the other more social in its explanatory assumptions. The first approach is that which identifies syntactic constraints on codeswitching, and takes the sentence as the level of analysis; an important example is Poplack's (1980) "equivalence constraint", which states that the order of sentence constituents at a switch point must not violate the grammar of either language involved. While the emphasis in this perspective has been on constraining rather than facilitating conditions, some attention has nonetheless been given to identifying sentence-level syntactic points that might be particularly vulnerable to codeswitching (ibid., Gumperz 1982).

From the more social orientation, the emphasis is less on constraints against and more on motivations for or functions of codeswitching; the interaction event rather than the sentence is usually the unit of analysis. One of the most influential explanatory notions in this second perspective has been that of "metaphorical codeswitching" developed by Gumperz (Blom and Gumperz 1972). Metaphorical codeswitches are seen to acquire their meaning through reference to a basic "we/they" social dichotomy that is reflected in the associated languages. The social meaning of a particular instance of language switching will vary, depending on context, but in each case meaning is captured by filtering it through this "we/they" contrast and through the typical association of each code with particular domains of use.

Both of these approaches have yielded significant insights into the organization of multilingual speech repertoires, but neither alone nor together can they account for all the codeswitching phenomena encountered in various bilingual communities. In the following pages, rather than either the sentence or the interaction, the unit of analysis emphasized is the discourse structure of narrative in an extended case of Catalan-Castilian codeswitching. The aim is to contribute to an intermediate approach to identifying the orderliness and meaning of codeswitching that combines linguistic and social concerns, and that stresses the discourse functions of language variation as a necessary preliminary step to understanding the ultimate social force of such switching (cf. Gumperz 1982, Auer and Di Luzio 1983).

While my interest ultimately lies in understanding the social effect of language mixing, an interpretive approach to code-switching can productively address not just psychological facts and (transitory) personal, interactional goals of participants, but the larger social and political context in which communicative exchanges occur (cf. Gal 1986). Social effects achieved can depend not only on the personal attitude or emotional stance that might be said to be encoded by a particular switched chunk of speech (cf. Gumperz and Hernandez-Chavez 1978), but on the structural slotting and informational load of such switches in the development of a narrative. I will suggest (as have others, including Sankoff 1980, Scotton 1983, Auer and Di Luzio 1983) that while metaphors of "we/they" are crucial in understanding the over-arching meaning of the use of two languages in a speech event, any *particular* switched phrase is best understood not by direct reference to different social worlds associated with the two languages, but to other structural demands or possibilities in the development of a discourse.

The Socio-Political Context

The winter and spring of 1980 was a tense time politically and linguistically for the people of Barcelona, Spain. The Statute of

Autonomy for Catalonia had been approved by public referendum the preceding fall, and now the people would go to the polls in March for the first Catalan parliamentary elections in nearly forty years. The numerous political parties were jockeying to define and attract their own constituencies, and some were playing upon divisions between Catalan-speaking natives (all bilingually competent in the state language, Castilian) and the large population of Castilian-speaking immigrants (predominantly monolingual or at best passively bilingual). Partly at issue in the elections was the role of the two ethnolinguistic groups in creating the new Catalonia.

At the same time, language choice in and of itself was stirring considerable feeling in segments of the city. Public debate centered on a polemical publication forecasting a dismal fate for the Catalan language if it was not aggressively protected (Argente et al. 1979). Moreover, refusals on the part of public figures to speak Catalan in some cases and Castilian in others created occasional uproars. Traditional norms for language choice in this bilingual community were challenged, and the population was unclear where change would or should take them. What language to speak and how to speak it were very live issues in Barcelona (Woolard 1986).

Much talk about talk could be heard, as well as varying choices of code for conversation. But one style that did not occur with any frequency was that of extended conversational codeswitching. There are very few naturalistic studies of code selection and switching in Barcelona in that period (or any other), but those that exist indicate that the interlocutor's linguistic affiliation was the primary determinant of code choice and of conversational switching (Calsamiglia and Tuson 1980, Woolard forthcoming). While in their study of teenage groups Calsamiglia and Tuson did find instances of conversational codeswitching not attributable to interlocutor's linguistic identity, which they identified as "metaphorical", almost all the examples in their data are of single nouns, many of which may well be legitimized borrowings, or frozen formulaic expressions such as curses.

The metaphorical and rhetorical possibilities of a bilingual repertoire were rarely exploited in Barcelona in the ways that have been documented for, e.g., Spanish-speaking communities in the

U.S. (Poplack 1980, Woolford 1983, Zentella 1981). Two reasons can be given for this absence: first, what might be thought of as the in-group code among active bilinguals, Catalan, had considerable prestige of its own, thus reducing the usefulness of switches to Castilian to invoke power, authority, formality, etc. (Woolard 1984, 1985). Equally important, the predominant interlocutor cue for code choice interacted with generalized anxiety about ethnic boundaries to inhibit codeswitching strategies. Most Catalan speakers (all bilingual) habitually and automatically switched to Castilian upon detecting the presence of a native Castilian-speaking interlocutor. Thus, to introduce Castilian extensively into a conversation might too easily be taken as indicating doubt about the Catalan identity and/or Catalan loyalty of an interlocutor, an identity and loyalty much prized by most natives (Woolard 1985, forthcoming).

During this same period, a professional comedian was building toward what came to be massive popular success in Barcelona. Eugenio, a nightclub entertainer, was in demand in both live performances and on commercial tape. It was hard to be unaware of Eugenio. He first came to my attention when the waiters at my neighborhood restaurant began recounting his jokes and insisted on lending me a copy of his tape. Within the next month, Eugenio was a smash hit. In the center of the city, one of the large department stores piped the recorded jokes onto the street, and passers-by stood on the sidewalk to listen and laugh. Long lines formed outside the Club Sausalito every night that Eugenio performed. The newspapers reviewed or mentioned him frequently. By late spring, Eugenio's jokes were being recounted to me spontaneously by teenagers I interviewed in the working class suburbs of the city.

There are undoubtedly many factors that account for Eugenio's remarkable popularity: good public relations and a good media response, quick distribution of the commercial cassettes, simple faddism. There was nothing particularly new about Eugenio's jokes; most were standard set pieces of the "did you hear the one about . . ." variety. (Several were already known to me in an English version.) Clearly Eugenio's dry delivery and almost unfailing comic 'timing' were important factors in his success. But one feature of his performance stood out in most people's minds, and they pointed to it repeatedly to account for Eugenio's comic appeal. As one newspaper put it, the most distinctive feature of Eugenio's joketelling was his "promiscuous" mixing of Catalan and Castilian.

A variety of informants told me that what was appealing –"la gracia"[1] – about his style was that "you can't tell what language he's speaking." This judgment was heard from native Catalan speakers as well as Castilian speakers. Even when questioned immediately after listening to a comercial tape, some listeners said that Eugenio speaks basically **la barreja** – 'a mixture' – when telling his jokes.

There has been considerable discussion in the literature on how to identify particular stretches of speech as codeswitching, borrowing, interference, etc. This problem is greatly exacerbated in the case of Catalan and Castilian, which are closely related languages that share much syntax and vocabulary, and differ primarily in phonetics and phonology; moreover, due to political constraints on language learning, many Catalan speakers use non-standard forms greatly influenced by contact with Castilian. However, even allowing for such difficulties, on examination one can identify a basic language for Eugenio's humorous narratives, and this language is Castilian. By an admittedly rough count, approximately 80 % of the overall performance analyzed here is in Castilian, and only 20 % in Catalan.[2]

This situation provides a new twist on the phenomenon of categorical perception described by Labov (1966), in which deviation from a norm is perceived as far more salient than its actual frequency would warrant; variable performance is perceived as categorical. However, in Barcelona the norm is to use either Catalan or Castilian categorically, and conversational codeswitching is minimal and often discouraged by social forces. Therefore it seems in the case of Eugenio that any deviation towards codeswitching or mixing is categorically perceived as "mixed" and linguistically unidentifiable.

Two questions arise about this phenomenon, and these are addressed in the following analysis. First, it is of interest to know what it is that Eugenio does to create the impression that "you can't tell what language he's speaking", given that the two languages are not equally represented in his speech. Secondly, I wish to consider why this should be so funny and lead to such enormous public success. What social message did Eugenio's code manipulations create that was so appealing to so many people at that time and place?

Data and Analysis

There are several commercial cassettes of Eugenio's jokes available. This analysis is based on the first tape, the one that carried him to local fame. The tape is 51 minutes long and contains 55 different jokes, varying in length from four-second one liners to shaggy dog stories lasting 3 minutes and 40 seconds. The jokes were recorded before a live audience, and laughter, applause, and other audience responses are mostly preserved on the tape. It is not certain that all the jokes were taped on the same night or that they constitute an entire sequential performance. Much of it flows smoothly from one joke to another, and deliberate rapid sequencing is apparent, but a few splices are also obvious. Nonetheless, it does appear that most of the jokes came from the same performance, and there is clear linkage between the beginning of the performance and the last joke, which refers back to an initial comment from the audience. In any case, the tape itself became a public event to which listeners who had never seen Eugenio responded as a whole performance, and it is reasonable to analyze it as such.

While the greater part of Eugenio's performance is identifiably Castilian in lexicon, morphology and even phonology, five factors create the reasonable perception of extensive language-mixing. These are some phonological shibboleths of Catalan "accent"; characteristic Catalan prosodic patterns; morpho-syntactic "interference"; the repeated use of a small set of Catalan formulaic phrases and single lexical items (primarily terms of address) that might be viewed either as borrowings or switches; and finally innovative or "fresh" codeswitching. The first four I will discuss only briefly, in order to concentrate on the last, which is peculiar to Eugenio's performance.

Phonology

While Catalan and Castilian are closely related Romance languages, phonology is one of the principal systems in which they differ. In speaking Castilian, Eugenio shows the influence of Catalan in the vowel system. He tends to reduce unstressed vowels, to make monophthongs of Castilian diphthongs, and to use 'open' versions of 'o' and 'e' where they would be found in Catalan equivalents of Castilian words. Catalan influence leads Eugenio to velarize 'l' before back vowels. And finally he forms characteristic Catalan liaisons between words in Castilian utterances by eliding un-stressed vowels and assimilating voiceless consonants to following voiced segments:

(1)   Dice que es un tio . . .   [diθe kɛzun tiu]

(2)   . . . el mono me ha puesto . . .   [. . . ma pwɛsto . . .]

However, all of these phonological traits are quite typical of the Castilian normally spoken by many Catalans in Barcelona. Tuson reports (personal communication) that such Catalan charac-teristics as vowel reduction could be heard even from monolingual Castilian-speaking adolescents as they complained about their inability to understand Catalan. In daily life, these widespread phonological features rarely elicited from Barcelona residents the comment that you can't tell what language the speaker is using.

Prosody

Eugenio uses certain tell-tale Catalan intonation patterns in his jokes even when speaking Castilian, as in the typical high-falling tone of yes-no questions, (which by Catalan convention are also marked by the particle *que*):

(3)   Que hay
                  más?   'There's more?'

(4)   Que tienen alpar
                  gatas?   'Do you have espadrilles?'

Again, this salient construction and accompanying prosodic pattern are often found, in fact are nearly normative, in Barcelona Castilian, as well as Catalan.[3]

Loanwords

Eugenio also introduces single lexical items of Catalan origin into Castilian clauses. Some of these are marked morphologically as Castilian, and thus can be considered clear cases of loanwords, integrated into the receiving system:

> (5) Eso embolicado bién . . .   (Cat. **embolicat**, inf. **embolicar**)
>   'This, well wrapped . . . '
>   Standard Castilian: Eso envuelto bién . . .

Other single items or formulaic phrases retain Catalan phonology and/or morphology, and thus it is not clear that they should be considered borrowings rather than true codeswitches. However, many are colloquial terms of address: **maco** ('beautiful'); **home** ('man'), **nano** ('kid'), appearing consistently in Eugenio's talk and with some frequency in colloquial Castilian around Barcelona. These and formulaic phrases such as si **us plau** ('please') and **molt maco** ('very nice') undoubtedly have exaggerated frequency in Eugenio's narrative style as compared to everyday speech, but they might well be considered as integrated parts of his Castilian, similar to Gumperz' (1982) claims about single lexical items in the English of Yiddish and Spanish speakers in the United States.

Morpho-syntactic interference

There are indeed ways in which it is difficult to know what language Eugenio is speaking. For example, the following clause is prescriptively neither Catalan nor Castilian:

> (6) *Estabas a Igualada*   'You were in Igualada'
>   Standard Castilian would be:
>   Estabas en Igualada
>   And prescriptively correct Catalan would be:
>   **Eres a Igualada**.

However, these prepositions, *en/a*, and the *ser/estar* verb distinction, which are distributed differently across semantic space in Catalan than in Castilian, suffer considerable interference in the speech of the general population. In the context of discourse clearly marked as belonging to one of the languages, utterance (6) would not create any confusion about what language a person is speaking, although it might draw correction from language purists of either stripe. It is only because of other elements in the context that Eugenio provides that this kind of interference creates ambiguity; its interpretation is influenced by occasions when he clearly does switch languages. Elements that ordinarily would be taken as Castilian pronounced with a Catalan accent or with morphological interference are reanalyzable as Catalan when we find that they have provided a bridge from unambiguous Castilian to unambiguous Catalan. [4]

These phonological, prosodic, lexical, and morphological cues are partially responsible for the characteristic impression Eugenio creates. But the fact that they have such a high incidence in ordinary popular speech makes it difficult to explain why they would arouse so much commentary on his language patterns. It is possible that Eugenio's speech is indeed representative of Barcelona, and that it provokes comment not because it is unusual, but because it is heard on a public stage; perhaps audiences are accustomed to more movement toward standard in public performers. This explanation is not generally borne out, however, by the Castilian heard from many political leaders and figures appearing on radio and television at the time, often marked by weak or strong Catalan accents.

Codeswitching proper, rather than just "interference" and borrowing, is the one variable that Eugenio does use to a much greater extent than the general population, and it is this phenomenon which gives force to his other Catalanizing strategies and lends salience to his style. There are many examples of codeswitches into Catalan in his performance, of both the inter- and intra-sentential variety. These switches are clear at central points although the borders are often fuzzy; it is sometimes possible to know that a codeswitch has taken place but quite literally not be able to identify where it began.

For example, his trademark joke introduction, so typical of Eugenio that it was taken as the title of his second cassette, is:

(7)   El *saben* <u>aquel</u> . . .   'Do you know the one . . . '

There is a predictable pause after every occurrence of this phrase, and it consistently evokes some laughter. *Saben* (third person plural or distant/polite second person plural of *saber*, 'to know'), is both a Catalan and a Castilian verb. The two differ only in the phonetic realization of the second vowel, which is reduced to schwa in Catalan. However, many Catalans often reduce their unstressed vowels in both languages. The important point is that the linguistic affiliation of the verb is ambiguous, and Eugenio takes advantage of this fact. El is the Catalan masculine object pronoun (Castilian <u>lo</u>), while <u>aquel</u> is a Castilian demonstrative pronoun (Catalan **aquell**, ending in a palatal lateral).

Thus the phrase clearly begins in Catalan, and the first two words could be considered Catalan. But the third element is clearly Castilian, leading us to reanalyze the verb, which could also be Castilian. The phrase is perfectly balanced, partaking equally of both systems through the double valence of the central element. Quite literally, from this phrase alone one cannot tell what language Eugenio is speaking. From the pauses that often occur after this phrase, and the fact that it was adopted as the title of the cassette, we might infer that in this construction Eugenio is consciously exploiting the close linguistic relationship of Catalan and Castilian.

Eugenio introduces unambiguously Catalan segments into every joke he tells. This would seem quite promiscuous language behavior by community standards. However, his promiscuity is not without discretion. Some of the switches are so systematic as to be virtually categorical. Most significant of these is the distribution of the Catalan and Castilian third person singular forms of 'say' (**diu** and <u>dice</u>, respectively), an item which crops up with great frequency in stand-up jokes.

The impression created in my circle of friends in Barcelona was that these forms were frequently juxtaposed: "<u>dice</u>, **diu**, <u>dice</u>, **diu** . . ." was a catch phrase we used to index inside references to his jokes. A few listeners (including myself) would have sworn that this was the second most characteristic phrase in Eugenio's delivery. But in fact, in the entire 55 jokes, the immediate juxtaposition of these two verb forms occurs only once, although **diu** occurs 410 times and <u>dice</u> 62 times.

What analysis shows instead is a functional division of labor between the two forms when they are examined in terms of the discourse structure. Eugenio has taken advantage of his bilingual repertoire to create different markers for different parts of his comedic narrative. His standard framing device for the preamble to each joke is roughly 'Do you know the one that says . . .", Here, he uses the Castilian form invariantly:

(8) <u>Dice que hay un tío</u> . . .   'Says there's this guy . . . '

(9) <u>Dice que era</u> . . .   'Says there was . . . '

The Catalan form, **diu**, on the other hand, is used for a very different discourse purpose. It occurs later in most narratives, after the expository preamble introduced by <u>dice</u>, and it indicates that quotation of a character's speech will follow (most of the complication of the jokes is developed through direct speech):

(10) <u>Dice que hay un tío que va al medico</u>,
     y **diu**, "<u>Hace una temporada</u> . . . "
     'Says there was this guy who goes to the doctor,
     and he says, "For a while now . . . "

It is repeated often, and interjected frequently into the reporting of the speech:

(11) **Li diu, diu,** "<u>Oiga</u>", **diu,** "<u>le vendo un reloj.</u>"
     'He says to him, he says,
     "Listen", he says, "I'll sell you a watch." '

The use of **diu** indicates nothing about the language of the quote to follow; sometimes it is Catalan and more often Castilian. **Diu** simply indicates that speech is about to be reported.

Exceptions to this rule are extremely rare. In only four instances does <u>dice</u> stand immediately before a direct character quotation. In two of these, the narrative frames are collapsed. These are not jokes that begin with a general exposition and then go on to develop action and verbal exchange. Rather, the joke is a representation of three turns of speech, with no introductory exposition:

> (12) Dice, "Oiga, padre," diu,
> "Usted es él que aparta a las mujeres del mal?"
> Diu, "Si, hijo, si."
> Diu, "Apártame dos para el sábado, si us plau.
> Says, "Listen, Father, " he says,
> "are you the one who saves women from sin?"
> He says, "Yes, son, yes."
> He says, "Save me two for Saturday, please."

We can see in this joke that Eugenio does not use the two language forms to distinguish different speakers, but rather always uses the same form − **diu** − for the same narrative function of introducing a quote, regardless of the number of characters. The collapse of the narrative frames here enables and induces the apparent violation of the division of linguistic labor that I have posited. This is confirmed by the second of the three anomalous occurrences of dice before a quote, in which we see an identical collapse of the expository and quoting narrative frames:

> (13) Dice, "Oiga", **diu**, "Usted domina el inglés?"
> "Pues, sí, si es bajito y se deja."
> 'Says, "Listen", he says, "Do you control (the) English?"
> "Well, yes, if he's short and he allows it." '

That there is a nearly categorical rule for **diu** before quotations appears to be confirmed by the other construction which occurs occasionally. In nine instances, dice is used to introduce a character's speech, but a noun phrase intervenes between the verb and the quotation:

> (14) Dice el portugués, "Qué dices, . . . "
> 'The Portuguese says, "What are you saying, . . . " '

(15) <u>La madre dice a los hijos,</u> "**Fills meus.** . . . "
'The mother says to the children, "My children" . . . '

In seven other cases, not only does a noun phrase intervene, but the Catalan **diu** is then used as the immediate introduction to the quote:

(16) <u>Dice el otro,</u> **diu,** "*Mira* . . . "
'The other says, he says, "Look . . ." '

(17) <u>Dice el medico,</u> **diu,** "*Uy!* . . . "
'The doctor says, he says, "Uy!" '

On the few occasions when another layer is added to the narrative and a character is represented as quoting himself or another, Eugenio again uses his bilingual repertoire as well as a change in tense to separate discourse levels, and to distinguish himself from the internal, fictional narrator. For narrative-internal quotes, the past tense of the Castilian form is used:

(18) " 'Buho', hijo, dije, 'buho' ". " "Owl", son, I said "owl." "

(19) <u>Me dijeron que</u> *estabas a Igualada.*
'They told me that you were in Igualada.'

The categorical assignment of a particular discourse function to Catalan, that of indicating that a character's speech is about to be reported, accounts for all the codeswitches into Catalan in 12 of the jokes (over 25%). In five more jokes, the entire presence of Catalan is accounted for by **diu** + indirect object pronoun: **li diu** ('he says to him'). And in ten more jokes, the use of Catalan is accounted for by (**li**) **diu** and one formulaic phrase or term of address. In all, the use of Catalan in half of the jokes is restricted to these simple and quite predictable devices. Calculated in terms of switch points, "diu" accounts for an even greater proportion of the Catalan present. Seventy percent of the switches into Catalan occur at a verb, and nearly all of these verb forms are "diu."

This extremely simple yet systematic codeswitching strategy does much to establish Eugenio's dual linguistic claim, in spite of the relatively minor presence of Catalan lexicon, because a salient part of the narrative frame is executed in each language. One slot is much higher in frequency than the other, allowing many Catalan tokens for one type, but both slots are structurally salient, thus creating the impression of juxtaposition and balance between the two languages.

No other codeswitch is as categorical or predictable as that just described. But there are other structures that are staples of Eugenio's narrative style, flexible formulas that crop up often in one form or another. These show a great propensity for code-switching. Outstanding among these forms is any construction involving the formula "one . . . to the other". The most common is "one says to the other", and it naturally interacts with the use of Catalan for 'says' in this position. Often the entire clause, except for the following quote which constitutes the verb comple-ment, is affected. But as can be seen in the examples from the tape given below, it appears that almost any switch point is permis-sible, underlining the almost morpheme for morpheme equi-valence of Catalan and Castilian syntax and supporting Poplack's hypothesized syntactic equivalence constraint:

(20   a) <u>uno</u> **li** <u>dice al otro</u>
        b) <u>uno</u> **li diu** *al* <u>otro</u>
        c) **un li diu** *al* <u>otro</u>
        d) <u>uno</u> **li diu al altre**
        e) **un li diu al altre**

Repetition and parallel structures are characteristic stylistic devices in many of Eugenio's jokes. Seven stories on the tape rely to some extent on repetition to set the scene and build anticipa-tion for the punchline. In six of these, switching to Catalan occurs in the repeated phrases. In the seventh, codeswitching does not occur. In this joke, repetition is not simply the set-up for the punchline, it also <u>is</u> the punchline. Codeswitching is avoided in this case where exact repetition makes the punchline effective.

In all of the parallel structures where codeswitching is used, the first occurrence is in Castilian, and only in successive mentions is Catalan introduced. This underlines the point that Castilian is the primary language of most of the narration, and that Catalan is most often called into play as a special device to accomplish particular discourse tasks or for playful embellishment in structural slots that do not carry a significant load of new information:

21. Y al pasar por este lado de mejilla la hace un corte. Pasa al <u>otro lado</u> **de la galta,** <u>le hace otro corte</u>.
    'And going over this side of the cheek, he cuts it. He goes over to the other side of the cheek, he cuts him again.'

22. . . . <u>cierto día se le acerca un individuo</u> . . .
    . . . <u>al día siguiente,</u> *un* **altre tio que se li acosta** . . .
    . . . <u>el tercer</u> *dia un altro* **tio** **que se li** <u>acerca</u> . . .
    . . . one day an individual comes up to him . . .
    . . . the next day another guy comes up to him . . .
    . . . the third day another guy comes up to him . . . '

One we have extracted these strategies for switching to Catalan, one of them nearly categorical, the others fairly regular if not entirely predictable, almost no Catalan remains to explain in the majority of jokes. Eugenio creates the effect of rampant language mixture primarily through the use of a small number of devices.

However, there are three stories on the tape that involve considerable use of Catalan in unpredictable positions; positions, moreover, where some information may actually be lost for those who don't understand Catalan. In these jokes the switches are extensive, but even here Catalan does not constitute more than 35 % of the narrative.

In these three stories, Catalan is used both for descriptive exposition and for character speech, although there is more of this last. (Probably simply because the jokes in general involve more quoted speech than description or reported action.) In none of these jokes is Catalan associated exclusively with one character while Castilian is used for the other, in either speech or description, although this might be our expectation from knowledge of dialect jokes elsewhere. Catalan is not used to tag or identify a character, except perhaps in one joke which involves a Catalan peasant, who is always referred to with the Catalan form, **el pagès**. But even here, Catalan is used extensively in describing the other character, who is a German tourist.

Systematic patterning of these extended switches is not readily apparent in the way that it is for the predominating switches discussed above. Although a certain amount of headway can be made by looking at these more elaborate switches in terms of discourse functions such as summarization or elaboration of preceding information, such a tactic is not particularly fruitful overall. There is however, one very important generalization that can be made at a relatively broad level of discourse analysis: codeswitching to Catalan does not appear in the punchline of the jokes. I believe that this generalization can lead us to an understanding of the social meaning of Eugenio's popularity. Before further discussing the switching pattern, then, I will briefly consider some sources of bilingual and interethnic humor, and their appropriateness to this case.

Other studies of intergroup humor have focused on joking as an expression of social conflict or social control (e.g. Burma 1946, Zujderveld 1968). However, that kind of analysis derives from jokes which specifically stereotype and usually denigrate an ethnic or linguistic outgroup. In this performance, Eugenio rarely draws on ethnic stereotypes to create his humorous effects. There are only two such jokes in the repertoire, one aimed at the Andalusian (the main working class immigrant group in Barcelona) and one at the Catalan. Only one joke pokes fun at language attitudes or patterns *per se*, and the target of this one is the Gallego, an Iberian ethnicity not well represented in Barcelona.

Nor is Eugenio telling "dialect jokes" about Catalans. He rarely if ever sketches a Catalan character by mimicking his speech for comic effect, although he shows that this is a tactic he is capable of when he imitates Germans, Russians, Gallegos, and in one case, Andalusians. Many of Eugenio's jokes are puns, but they are not bilingual puns and do not depend on knowledge of the two languages for their humor.

We might entertain the hypothesis that the use of Catalan itself is comic, that as a minority language it sounds funny and has the comic associations discussed by Weinreich (1974). However, because of the high prestige enjoyed by Catalan, this seems unlikely and indeed does not seem to be the case. Since audience response and laughter are captured on the tape, I was able to check for the effect of the introduction of Catalan. In almost no case is there laughter after a Catalanism or a Catalan word. This occurs in only two places on the tape, and thus seems more likely to be coincidence than indicative of a patterned source of humor. Except for these two occasions, no codeswitch draws immediate laughter, even when there are pauses that would accommodate it.

Most of these are a stand-up comedian's classic punch-line dependent jokes. People hold in their laughter throughout the exposition, waiting expectantly for the real humor. And here lies the most socially significant point about the distribution of Catalan across the narrative structure. Of the 55 jokes, the punch-line comes in Catalan only one time. And the exception proves the rule: in the introduction to that one story, Eugenio explicitly disclaims it as a joke, calling it instead a fable that the audience may interpret as it wishes. Moreover, when the punchline does come in this "fable", laughter is only moderate, even though this is a favorite story that was requested by more than one audience member at the beginning of the session.

It is useful to compare this finding to Barbara Kirshenblatt-Gimblett's study of English-Yiddish codeswitching in humorous narratives told in the Jewish community of Ontario (1972). Her primary generalization is the exact opposite of what is found in Eugenio's stories. Kirshenblatt-Gimblett discovered that in her collection, if switching to Yiddish occurred at all, it was most likely to happen in the punchline. If one generalization can be made about the present corpus, it is that switching to Catalan will not occur in the punchline.

The difference in the discourse slotting of switches in these two corpora is directly related to the difference in the social functions of switching. In the Yiddish case, codeswitching is a test of ingroup membership. Kirshenblatt-Gimblett reports that speakers in the Ontario community are proud of their command of Yiddish and use it in structural slots that carry a high information load as a way of testing the competence of others who claim full member-ship in the community of Yiddish speakers. This is appropriate to what we know about codeswitching from most other socio-linguistic analyses, where it is an ingroup phenomenon restricted to those who share the same expectations and rules of interpreta-tion for the use of the two languages. Codeswitching is thus usually seen as a device used to affirm participants' claims to

membership and the solidarity of the group in contrast to outsiders.

From this significant difference in the distribution of code-
switching across the punchline, we can identify the important
differences in the meaning of the speech event in the two communities. In Eugenio's performances, codeswitching is used for
boundary-levelling rather than boundary-maintaining purposes,
and is popular for exactly that reason. The use of the two languages in a way that doesn't obscure critical information for
any listeners eases rather than emphasizes group boundaries in
Barcelona, and allows the widest possible audience to participate
(cf. Tuson, n.d.).

Eugenio demonstrates a use of the two languages that is different from their use in the community, and one that breaks down
two of the most tension-creating associations in the socio-political
context of the time: the identification of language choice with
ethnic boundaries (i.e., Catalan for native Catalans only), and the
entrenched but besieged norm of selecting Castilian for public
uses. It is not an absence of reference to group boundaries through
language use, but the explicit *overriding* of them that is appealing.
A bilingual Catalan and a monolingual Castilian can equally participate in the event and not lose any enjoyment of the humor,
appreciating these punchline-dependent jokes fully. They could do
this in Castilian, as well. But the actual use of both languages and
their varying distribution across characters is an important denial
of the boundary-identifying force of the two languages.

There is, of course, ambiguity in the appeal, which is also an
essential ingredient in Eugenio's success. Catalans can get special
enjoyment from his jokes because they are hearing their own
suppressed language used in front of a broad public audience. This
use is not at their expense as would be the case in dialect jokes,
nor is it associated here with the old-fashioned, the quaint, or the
"corny" – Eugenio is a hip young comedian whose material is
spiced with references to drugs and sex. On the other hand, a
Castilian can enjoy the performance because he is listening to
Catalan and "getting it", not being excluded from a (usually
prestigious) Catalan ingroup event (cf. Heller 1982, Auer 1984
discussed in Gal 1986, for other uses of codeswitching for boundary-levelling rather than maintaining purposes.)

Most importantly, in Eugenio's jokes, a fictional world is model-
led where the two languages have found a peaceful coexistence.
Neither one has had to disappear; they are both in use, side by
side, but there is no battle line between them like that encountered in the real world. The last story on the tape brings home the
social symbolism that seems to be at work in Eugenio's overall
performance. This is the story that members of the audience
request from the very beginning of the recorded show, and that
Eugenio finally gives them at the end. It is also the one joke in
which the punchline is delivered in Catalan. However, Eugenio
explicitly disclaims it as a joke in his introduction, calling the
story a fable, an allegory, and inviting the audience to interpret it.
I thus feel entitled to do so.

The tale is a shaggy dog story, or rather a talking pigeon story.
It was no doubt once a punchline-dependent joke — the joke being
that the pigeon is an hour late for a date because it was such a nice
day that he decided to walk. But Eugenio spins out and elaborates
the exposition — this is the longest story on the tape — then rushes
the punchline in a way most untypical of his usual splendid
timing. What we are left with is the touching story of a man and a
pigeon who meet in the central square of the city, discover that
each can talk and that they can converse, and become intimate
friends in spite of disbelief and disdain from the man's family; this
is a friendship that puts his sanity in question at home, but he
insists on inviting the pigeon to dinner. Both the pigeon, Amadeu,
and the fellow, Cirili, speak Catalan and Castilian equally well,
and they switch back and forth between the two.

Here we have the ultimate assertion that communication across
group boundaries is not only possible but worthwhile. The group
boundary in this case is that between humans and birds; the
illustration may be humorous but the point is pertinent (Levi-
Strauss 1969 explains the frequent appearance of birds in
mythology as deriving from a view that the bird world is an
inverted image of human society).[5] There is a message in this
seemingly silly story that people might have been relieved and
happy to hear in this city where linguistic and ethnic tensions
threatened to break out. This message is both enacted and encoded,
the bilingual form itself indexing the cross-boundary action, in the
following bilingual exchange from the "fable":

(23) Amadeu: *"Hola, maco"*.
     Cirili: "Caray! Que hablas, tú!?"
     Amadeu: **"Clar que parlo.** No hablas tú, tambien?"
     Amadeu: "Hi goodlooking."
     Cirili: "Geez! You can speak?"
     Amadeu: "Of course I can speak. Don't you speak too?"

From this initial exchange, the friendship grows, and Amadeu and Cirili delight in each other's company and conversation. Not all of Eugenio's jokes illustrate the overriding of social boundaries quite so graphically, and I make no claim that the teller was conscious of the bilingual yet boundary-free world he created. Nonetheless, in his codeswitching performances, Eugenio gave many of the people of Barcelona something that was at once amusingly abnormal and of enormous and easy appeal: a world in which the two languages could peacefully but meaningfully coexist, at no cost to anyone.[6]

Conclusions

I have argued that, as has often been shown to be the case in studies of codeswitching, the juxtasposition of two languages in Eugenio's performance conveys a social message, a message as important as the literal content in determining the comedian's success. What we have seen, however, is that the link between switched utterance and social effect is not the direct one that has been described for many codeswitching situations. In this case, codeswitching does not index a direct association between certain topics or social realms and a specific language. Nor do Eugenio's codeswitches have the direct effect of metaphorical codeswitching, where the use of a particular language adds a connotation of, e.g. intimacy, distancing, mitigation or authority to the switched utterance itself. In the material analyzed here, the social message is not one that exploits the social contrasts between two languages or language groups to achieve rhetorical effects.

However, this is not to say that the social meaning of the event derives simply from the fact that the two languages are used, and that they could be used randomly. As we have seen, the placement of the two languages is neither random nor unimportant, and this is best appreciated if we take as the unit of analysis neither the sentence nor the whole public performance as a speech or interaction event, but rather the narrative structure of the individual joke. We find that certain structural slots either demand switching to Catalan or create enabling conditions, while other structural slots in the narrative categorically constrain switching to Catalan. Although uses of Catalan are not especially frequent, they are judicious and occupy salient positions that nonetheless bear a low information load.

On the other hand, these performances have an audience with an unequal distribution of knowledge of the two languages and importantly, an increasingly anomic vision of the social distribution of the two languages. I have argued that the relatively predictable distribution of codeswitching across the narrative structure of the joke interacts with this distribution of the languages across social groups to produce in a more indirect way the social meaning of the codeswitching event. The symbolic social message, that the two languages and thus language communities can co-exist and interact peacefully, is indeed contained in the whole event rather than specifically in any of its switched parts. But it is very much a product of those specific parts, and the same social effect would not result from a different distribution of the two languages.

Notes

Acknowledgments. The research on which this article is based was funded by a doctoral research grant from the Social Science Research Council. While I am indebted to the Council for its support, the analysis and opinions expressed here in no way reflect those of the Council. This work has benefitted from comments made on earlier versions presented at the American Anthropology Association meetings, the University of Michigan Linguistics Department, and the UCSD Communications Department. This version was previously published in Papers in Pragmatics, 1987. Juliana Flower carried out some of the counts and calculations reported here, for which I certainly thank her. Thanks also to Sue Gal, Pep Soler, Bambi Schieffelin, Amparo Tuson, and especially Monica Heller for helpful comments.

1. Throughout the paper, Castilian forms that are cited will be underlined and Catalan forms will appear in boldface. At transition points between the two languages, words whose affiliation is ambiguous or uncertain will be italicized.
2. The proportions for Catalan and Castilian given here are based on a word count of the entire corpus. Words that are of Catalan origin but morphologically integrated into Castilian are counted as borrowings, and therefore Castilian, not codeswitches, but unintegrated words (which may well also be standard community borrowings) are counted as codeswitches.

   Many words throughout the transcript are of ambiguous affiliation and conceivably could be either Catalan or Castilian. The method followed here was to count a word as Castilian if it was both preceded and followed by Castilian words; similarly, it was counted as Catalan if preceded and followed by clearly Catalan words. However, at a transition point between Castilian and Catalan, and vice versa, words that could belong to either language were counted in a separate category as "ambiguous". While an interesting category, it is numerically relatively insignificant because of the definition used.
3. This construction is so common in Barcelona Castilian that it can cause problems for native Castilian speakers from other regions. A Castilian speaker from Valencia reported that she had to ask a Barcelona resident to help her out in an interchange with a waiter. On sitting down at a cafe table, she inquired "¿Qué se puede comer?" – "What can one eat?" – and the reply came back, "Sí" – "Yes", obviously in response to a different question, "¿Que se puede comer?" – "(Is it the case) that one can eat?" The interrogative pronoun and coordinate conjunction are pronounced identically in Castilian.
4. Because the two languages in question are so closely related, the distinction drawn by Auer and Di Luzio between codeswitching and codeshifting does not apply here. They found that abrupt alternation – switching – occurred between languages, while gradual transition – shifting – occurred only among the varieties within a language. Eugenio's deployment of Catalan and Castilian resembles their notion of codeshifting perhaps more than switching.
5. Hervé Varenne first pointed out to me the relevance here of Levi-Strauss' observation.
6. In the course of preparing this article I met a young Catalan man named Amadeu whose personal experience demonstrates the extent to which Eugenio's story captured the popular imagination in Barcelona. Returning in 1980 from his stint of military service in the southern Spanish province of Granada, Amadeu bought a copy of *La Vanguardia* newspaper at the train station and arrived at home with it under his arm, to find family and

friends rolling with laughter. Never having heard of Eugenio while in the south, he didn't know about the famous pigeon Amadeu, who turned up at Cirili's house with *La Vanguardia* under a wing, but he quickly learned from repeated recountings about his well-known namesake.

References

Argente, Joan et al.
    1979 Una nació sense estat, un poble sense llengua? *Els Marges* 15:
          3–15.
Auer, J. C. P. and Aldo Di Luzio
    1983 Three types of linguistic variation and their interpretation. In
          Dabene, L., Flasaquier, M., and Lyons, J., eds., *Status of Migrants'
          Mother Tongues.* European Science Foundation. 67–100.
Blom, Jan-Peter and John J. Gumperz
    1972 Social meaning in linguistic structures: codeswitching in Norway.
          In J. J. Gumperz and D. Hymes, eds., *Directions in Sociolinguistics.*
          NY: Holt, Rinehart & Winston. 407–434.
Burma, John, H.
    1946 Humor as a technique in race conflict. *American Sociological
          Review* 11: 710–715.
Calsamiglia, Helena and Amparo Tuson
    1980 Us i alternança de llengües en grups de joves d'un barri de
          Barcelona. *Treballs de sociolingüística catalana* 3: 11–82.
Gal, Susan
    1986 Codeswitching in history. Paper presented at the annual meetings
          of the American Anthropological Association, Philadelphia, PA.
Gumperz, John J.
    1982 *Discourse Strategies.* Cambridge: Cambridge University Press.
Gumperz, John J. and E. Hernandez-Chavez
    1978 Bilingualism, bidialectalism, and classroom interaction. In M. Lourie
          and N. Conklin, eds., *A Pluralistic Nation.* Rowley, MA: Newbury
          House. 275–294.
Heller, Monica
    1982 'Bonjour, hello?': negotiations of language choice in Montréal. In:
          J. Gumperz (ed.), *Language and Social Identity*, Cambridge:
          Cambridge University Press, pp. 108–118.
Kirshenblatt-Gimblett, Barbara
    1972 Traditional storytelling in the Toronto Jewish community. Ph. D.
          dissertation, Indiana University.

Labov, William
  1966   *The Social Stratification of English in New York City.* Washington, D.C.: Center for Applied Linguistics.
Poplack, Shana
  1980   Sometimes I'll start a sentence in English y termino en español. *Linguistics* 18: 581–618.
Sankoff, Gillian
  1980   *The Social Life of Language.* Philadelphia: University of Pennsylvania Press.
Scotton, Carol
  1983   Negotiation of identities in conversation: A theory of markedness and code choice. *Int'l. J. Soc. Lang.* 44: 115–135.
Tuson, Amparo
  n.d.   When codeswitching becomes an allegory. Manuscript.
Weinreich, Uriel
  1974   *Languages in Contact.* The Hague: Mouton.
Woolard, Kathryn A.
  1984   A formal measure of language attitudes in Barcelona: a note from work in progress. *Int'l. J. Soc. Lang.* 47: 63–71.
  1985   Language variation and cultural hegemony: toward an integration of sociolinguistic and social theory. *American Ethnologist* 12 (4): 738–748.
  1986   The "crisis in the concept of identity" in contemporary Catalonia, 1976–1982. In G.W. McDonogh, ed., *Conflict in Catalonia: Images of an Urban Society.* Gainesville: U. of Florida Press, pp. 54–71.
  forth- *The Politics of language and ethnicity in Barcelona.* Stanford
  com-   University Press.
  ing
Woolford, Ellen
  1983   Bilingual codeswitching and syntactic theory. *Linguistics* 13: 520–536.
Zentella, Ana Celia
  1981   Tá bién, you could answer me en cualquier idioma. In Richard Duran, ed., *Latino Language and Communicative Behaviour.* Norwood, NJ: Ablex.
Zijderveld, Anton C.
  1968   Jokes and their relation to social reality. *Social Research* 35: 286–311.

Strategic ambiguity: code-switching in the management of conflict[1]

Monica Heller
Ontario Institute for Studies in Education

Code-switching has often been described as a conversational strategy. Sometimes this strategy is discussed in terms of stylistic effects, that is, in terms of its use in aggravating or mitigating such conversational acts as requests, denials, topic shifts, elaborations or comments, validations, or clarifications (Gal 1979; Gumperz and Hernandez-Chavez 1971; Gumperz 1982a, b; Zentella 1981; Valdés 1981; McClure 1981; Genishi 1981). Examples of such stylistic uses include:

1. From Gal (1979: 115–111). Here, code-switching is used to convey anger, to escalate an argument. Hungarian husband, wife and daughter in a bilingual (German-Hungarian) Austrian town. The wife usually fetches beer for her husband, but on this occasion she is drinking coffee with her daughter and refuses to go. The husband gets his beer himself. When he returns his wife asks for a sip:

H	Wife:	ide, itt tessik	'here, here please'
H	Husband:	hojne	'oh sure'
H	Wife:	ja, hát add oda	'come on, give it here'
H	Husband:	hojne, ott csek idd e kávet (laughs) niksz	'oh sure, just drink your coffee there, no'
H	Daughter:	ne addsz! ne addsz!	'don't give her any, don't give her'
H	Husband:	fë nëm hoznyi, de mëginnya, o ho, oaszt nëm	'you won't bring it up but you want to drink it, oh, no, you don't'
H	Wife:	nëm is kë mer ha kë le mënëk osztá hozok	'I don't even want it because if I wanted some I'd just go down and get some'
H	Husband:	niksz oh ho nem szabad neked	'oh no no you're not allowed'

H	Wife:	nem nem szoruktam ra	'I don't I don't have to
		hoj te adzs nekem	depend on you to give me'
H	Husband:	nekem nëm hozu fë	'if you don't bring it up
		magadnag akko nem	for me then you can't
		szabad inna	drink it yourself'
H	Wife:	in akkor iszok mikor	'I drink when I want to
*G		in akarok	
		deis vird niks	I don't even want it
		kbrak	I don't even want it'
		das vird niks	
		kbrakt	

It seems that the argument had escalated to such a point that, in order to defuse it, the daughter had to start making silly noises, to get people laughing.

2. From McClure (1981: 83). Here, code-switching is used to attract the addressee's attention, to focus. M. is a Spanish-English bilingual nine-year-old in the southwest of the United States:

E	M:	Now let me do it. Put your feets down.	
*S		¡Mira!	'look!'
E		It's Leti's turn again! Hi Leti!	

The discourse effects depend on the interlocutors' inference of anger or seriousness, humour, deference, distance, solidarity and so on. These inferences can be made solely on the basis of participants' knowledge of the social context: they need to know how they stand with respect to one another in the activity in progress, and where that set of relations fits within the wider community (cf. Gal 1979: 91, 129; Gumperz 1982b: 84[2]). A clear example of this would be the choice of specific languages in addressing interlocutors seen to prefer or to be more competent in those languages (Genishi 1981; McClure 1981; Calsamiglia and Tuson 1980; Woolard 1983): in such cases speakers clearly operate with notions of how to assign people to certain social categories which are associated with the use of specific languages, and with notions of where their relationship to those people fits into that system of social categorization. (It is interesting in this regard that even very young children are able to do this). This categorization extends to third parties (audience, indirect addressees):

3. From Genishi (1981: 147—148). Code-switching used to include a third party. A bilingual (Spanish-English) boy, Arturo, is telling on his Spanish monolingual classmate, Miguel, to teacher, Liz (in California):

S	A (to M.):	mire que hiciste	'look what you did'
S	A (to L.):	Leez!	
*E/S		Lookit que hizo M. el rayo mi papel con la tinta	'. . . what M. did he put lines on my paper with ink'
	(to M.):	mira M. que hizo aqui	'look M. what he did here'

Thus the association of language and social relationship is usefully exploited in the management of social relationships, often through the management of conversation. This is particularly evident when unmarked associations are violated by code-switching:

4. From Calsamiglia and Tuson (1980: 70). Monolingual Castilian teenagers are talking to bilingual Catalan speakers in informal conversation in a Barcelona neighbourhood. Code-switching here is used to mitigate the swearing:

Cs	Oye, chaval, ¡no seas pesao!	'listen, buddy, don't be a drag!
*Ct	Ves-t'en a la merda!	go to hell!
Cs	Anda ya, ¡no fastidies!	go on already, don't be a pain!'

Here, the swearing is attenuated, since the speaker has chosen the language of the interlocutor; the speaker realigns his relationship to his interlocutor as ingroup, thereby permitting him to say things only an ingroup member can get away with. By the same token, he can avoid some of the responsibility for having said it which would have been his had he spoken in his own language. Code-switching here constitutes claims on the rights of ingroup membership in the other group, and avoidance of the obligations of membership in one's own group. This inference depends on the knowledge of context that interlocutors have; they know who is who and what is expected of them. The very same code-switch can mean very different things depending on the exact context operating in an interaction. What does not change is the act of making claims about the rights and obligations the interlocutors bear to each other as a function of all of the levels of their relationship, from the most personal to the most socially constrained: Example 5 constitutes another case where code-switching achieves such a claim, directly this time, since the code-switch conveys the nature of the relationship and the feelings that flow from events that occur in a relationship of that type.

> 5. From Gumperz (1982b: 93). Code-switching used to comment on the nature of the relationship between the speaker and the person he is talking about. Hindi-speaking informants judged this version to indicate that the date was casual and the speaker not upset. An all-Hindi version, however, was seen to indicate that the speaker was annoyed because an important obligation was not met. Here, a Hindi-speaking man tells how a friend (a member of the same group) failed to meet him at the bus stop to accompany him on a trip to town:

H	Man:	Timarpur ki bǝs samne khǝri thi	'the Timarpur bus was standing before me'
*E		then I thought I might as well take it	

Thus stylistic and conversation management code-switching strategies, while they relate on one level to the accomplishment of the task at hand and to the management of interpersonal relationships in a particular activity at a precise moment (Scotton 1976; Heller 1982), derive their effect from background knowledge regarding the unmarked association of languages with social relationships. Those social relationships are formed on the basis of participation in social networks defined by overlapping and cross-cutting criteria on many levels simultaneously, including the superordinate level of linguistic group membership. Style, conversation management and social significance are intimately bound to each other.

It is, perhaps, best to reiterate that code-switching operates in a multi-levelled context, and that the analyst of code-switching must take all these levels into account. To my knowledge all the existing ethnographic descriptions of the social context of code-switching reveal a separation somewhere of domains of language use, be it the home, the public arena, rural vs. urban life, or anything else (cf., e.g., Blom and Gumperz 1972; Woolard 1983; Heller 1982; Scotton 1976; Poplack 1980; Gumperz 1982a; Eckert 1980).

Thus at least some speakers in the community operate in a context where in *some* domains, in *some* ways, the languages are separate: this renders code-switching meaningful and available. Other speakers may operate exclusively within the domain of *one* language: for them, code-switching is unavailable and meaningless (this will be further explored below). One level of meaning derives, then, from the social organization of language use in the community.

The second level of meaning derives from the interpersonal relationship between speakers in the particular context of the activity in which they are engaged. In this case, the analyst's ability to impute meaning (be it social, interpersonal, or stylistic) to code-switching resides in his or her knowledge of all the various levels of context operating during an interaction, in observation of the conversational and social consequences of code-switching, and in his or her knowledge of speakers' background knowledge regarding conventions of language use.

A third level of meaning, the semantic content of specific instances of switching, concerns us less here. At this level the semantic content of what is switched may or may not be directly connected to the association of a language and the domain of its use: this is something which may occur, but which does not have to occur for code-switching to have stylistic, interpersonal and/or social significance.

The goal of this paper is to discuss reasons why code-switching may work as a strategy in both situations of certainty and of uncertainty, that is, (a) in situations where there are clear unmarked conventions of language choice; and (b) in situations where no such conventions may exist OR where there may be competing conventions.

My hypotheses are based on the idea that code-switching creates ambiguity primarily on the first two of the three levels of meaning discussed above. By creating ambiguity, code switching offers opportunities for the interpretation of social action that would otherwise be unavailable. My first hypothesis concerns the way in which ambiguity is created by code-switching, the second concerns the social consequences of code-switching (and so the inferences regarding social organization that can be made through an analysis of the distribution of code-switching in a community).

It is my first hypothesis that code-switching creates ambiguity either by violating conventional associations (without redefining them), or by refusing to define them (where they do not exist), or by refusing to choose among them (where several frames of reference are in competition). Some reasons code-switching seems so attractive as a strategy, where it is available, are that it permits people (a) to "suggest inferences without actually putting (themselves) on record and risking loss of face" (Gumperz 1982b: 98), (b) to ". . . neutralize those potentially salient attributes of one variety which may have an unfavourable value" (Scotton 1976: 919), or (c) to ". . . gain access to roles in situations defined by (a) norm" without claiming the social identity that conventionally is associated with those roles (either because they are not really entitled to them or because the cost is too high) (Heller 1981: 11). It can allow the simultaneous accomplishment of tasks through conversation and the management of conversation and of personal relationships through the avoidance of the conflict which categorical language choice would entail. Or it can allow the avoidance of tasks and a different form of conversation management through creating conflict where categorical language choice would be the norm. By creating ambiguity at the level of unmarked language choice, ambiguity is created for all levels of interpersonal interaction embedded within the superordinate category of language group membership.

It is my second hypothesis that code-switching is attractive as a strategy in situations where unilateral choice entails claims regarding group membership (and so definitions of rights and obligations) for which a speaker does not want to be held responsible or cannot be held responsible. For different reasons code-switching may also be attractive where to speak a language other than the unmarked one implies claims on group membership (and so rights and obligations) to which one is not considered entitled. In other words, code-switching can be used both to create conflict and to neutralize it.

The actual concrete situations in which these two possibilities will be realized will depend entirely on the actual constellation of language and social groups in the community. While based on some notion of unmarked association of language and social group, the stability of group boundaries, the power relations obtaining between groups, the arenas available for intergroup interaction, and the criteria of access to those arenas will all affect whether (and where) code-switching is to be found.

Code-switching is clearly NOT always available in multilingual communities, nor is it available to everyone even in those communities where it is used. For example, in some situations of certainty, code-switching is available as an ingroup strategy, based on the semantic associations of language and domain of language use and on the we/they ingroup/outgroup distinction. Code-switching can be used to appeal to the shared understanding characteristic of co-membership, or to create distance by associating oneself, momentarily, with the out-group. However, in others, code-switching is unavailable because group boundaries are so permeable that it is impossible to know for sure which individuals to assign to the mutually-exclusive domains. Categorical language choice may be the only way to define social identity and group membership. Similarly, in intergroup interactions, code-switching may be rejected as an option since it is seen to constitute a claim on co-membership which no participant may want. Finally, some members of multilingual communities may themselves be monolingual and so unable to code-switch or understand code-switching.

I will first consider some concrete cases where code-switching is used in ingroup and intergroup interactions, and in situations of certainty and uncertainty. The analysis of these cases will be used to elucidate the ways in which code-switching may create ambiguity and so achieve stylistic, conversation management and social effects. I will then build on these cases to hypothesize what factors might predict the presence or absence of code-switching in multilingual communities. The data which I will discuss here are drawn from two studies, one a study of the process of language shift from English to French in a large company in Montreal, the second a study of the social meaning of French and English for students enrolled in a French-language minority (i.e. NOT immersion) elementary school in Toronto.

The Montreal study is a case of breakdown of old conventions of interaction, a case of social, economic and political change producing changes in the basis of ethnic organization, in the basis of the boundary between English and French (details of the background can be found in Heller et al. 1982, Heller 1982 and Clift and Arnopoulos 1979). Private enterprise was (and is) the frontier of change in Quebec, the arena in which change in ethnic boundaries is being carried out. The company studied here is typical of the change in that, while it used to be an English business with anglophone management and francophone labour, at the time of the study many anglophone mangers had been transferred to branches in other Canadian provinces or had retired. They were being replaced by young francophones. Further, the new language law, supporting the general social movement, had decreed that the language of work be French.

Two patterns of code-switching stand out in this company. The first is a cross-over effect of the use of code-switched routines, especially opening and closing routines. Here, it seemed that the older francophones in low management positions who had worked for the company for a long time, tended to use English routines in ingroup conversation, while anglophones used French routines in both ingroup and intergroup interaction (the base language for most intergroup interaction being English unless the anglophones were in the minority). Younger francophones never used English routines in ingroup interaction, although they sometimes used English routines as a deference strategy with structurally superior anglophones (thus the direction of asymmetry in group relations can be offset by the opposite direction in personal relations).

6. English routines used in ingroup interaction by older francophones:

F M:	bonjour Mme Grégoire comment allez-vous?	'hello . . . how are you?'
F G:	très bien merci et vous?	'very well thank you and you?'
F M:	très bien merci	'very well thank you'
*E G:	*good*	
F M:	bonjour	'goodbye'
F G:	bonjour	'goodbye'

7. French routines used by anglophones in intergroup interaction; openings:

*F Bob:	bonjour ma fleur comment ça va?	'hello my flower how is it going?'

F	Denise:	bonjour monsieur	'hello mister MacDonald
		MacDonald bien et vous?	well and you?'
F	Bob:	ça va merci	'fine thanks'
E	Denise:	*well you won't say that*	
		when I (unint) you this	

Also: Bonjour Hélène *how's the suntan?*
     Bonjour tout le monde *how's everything?*
     Bonjour *good morning* tout le monde!

8. French routines used by anglophones in intergroup interaction; closings:

E:	Anne:	*you need the par number (unint)*	
E:	Bob:	*(unint) that's the par number*	
		there two eight nine eight	
E:	Anne:	*ah okay I have no choice okay*	
		(sighs)	
*F:	Bob:	tragique	'tragic'
E:	Anne:	tragique hein? (unint)	'tragic eh?'
F:	Bob:	quel numéro? *oh that's the*	'what number? . . .'
		work order number	
F:	Anne:	oui okay	'yes okay'
F:	Bob:	okay mon amie?	'okay my friend?'
E:	Anne:	*thank you*	
*F:	Bob:	merci	'thank you'

9. French routines used by anglophones in ingroup interactions; closings:

E	M:	*so I'll come back at about two o'clock?*
*F	H:	parfait c'est bien

10. English routine used by young francophones with older anglophone boss; ethnic status offset by hierarchical status within the company:

*E	Denis:	*sure you don't want a seat*	
		before you look at this?	
E	Mgr.:	*not gonna do any good to sit ah*	
*F	Denis:	hm nous sommes à un et demi	'hm we're at one
		icitte	and a half here'
F	Mgr:	toute la bière qu'ils ont pris	'all the beer that
		ils ont mis ça dans les (unint)	they took they
			put that in the (unint)'

My observations in other domains lead me to believe that there are two new phenomena here: the use of French routines by anglophones in ingroup interaction, and the absence of English routines by younger francophones, in ingroup or intergroup interaction. Why is this happening? In this company it is the use of French that now legitimates one's presence, whereas until very recently the language of power in private enterprise was English. Francophones thus have an interest in defining themselves as such. To use English is to evoke the conventions of the old regime when the English were in power. These code-switching routines seem to symbolize a claim to the right of the speaker to participate in situations defined by the use of the other language, without necessitating or entailing a claim on the part of the speaker to that identity (the reasons anglophones do not wish to pass can be attributed to the continued advantages of being English in the North American business world). By violating the expectation that a speaker will choose a language in accordance with his or her identity he or she manages to claim both identities at the same time (or neither). Since that is impossible, another interpretation is necessitated, namely, that it is not the identity that matters but rather the rights and obligations that constitute that identity. By code-switching in this way the speaker signals a claim on some of the rights and obligations attached to the roles in question, but not all of them. This enables a speaker to do things he or she would otherwise not be able to do: in the case of this company gain access to situations to which the criterion of access is ability to speak French, without actually having to be French. By the same token it is possible to avoid some of the responsibilities of categorical language choice through this kind of code-switching.

This is notably the case with a small group of anglophones who have been recently recruited. Not only did they accept their jobs in the awareness of (and in some ways desirous of) the condition that they work in French, they themselves are not part of the long-established Montreal anglophone community and so have nothing invested in the local ethnolinguistic struggle. They came from other provinces, several are married to francophones, and one was actually of francophone origin although he had lost the language. Thus they need to avoid the categorical alignment with one group or the other that categorical language choice would represent. For this reason I call them "marginals". For them code-switching represents a way of maintaining access to both networks without having to take on the responsibilities associated with full membership in one or the other (such as commitment to a career in Quebec or geographical career mobility).

11. Two marginals use code-switching with each other:

F	Charles:	bonjour Henri	'hello Henri'
F	Henry:	bonjour	'hello'
F	Charles:	comment ça va?	'how's it going?'
F	Henry:	bien toi?	'fine you?'
F	Charles:	ça va bien j'ai une question pour toi	'it's going fine I have a question for you'
F	Henry:	oui?	'yes'
*E	Charles:	*what are the specs for . . .*	

Another outstanding pattern of code-switching is that which occurs in intergroup interaction at the management level, the frontier of change. Here, such official interactions as department meetings are supposed to occur in French. However, some young newly promoted francophones find themselves presiding over meetings where there are older anglophones, who were originally in line for promotion but who were blocked because they do not speak French, and older francophones who are used to working in English. There are often also other young francophones present. What to do? If the francophones only speak French they will seem hostile to the anglophones, since they will have deliberately erected a language barrier which will prevent anglophones from participating (and everyone knows that the francophones are able to speak English). Yet the francophones like these anglophones, they are friends; furthermore, they consider themselves to be nice people who would never deliberately be nasty to somebody else. Finally, they recognize their need for the expertise and experience that the anglophones have; the anglophones are, after all, generally senior to these young francophones (and this adds the dimension of respect for elders to the picture). If the francophones speak only English, however, their legitimacy is undermined: their rapid promotion was based not only on their technical ability but also on the principle of francophone control of private enterprise. Answer: code-switch, and thereby do neither, permitting the accomplishment of the task at hand (to take care of the order of business), the management of personal relations (maintaining good relationships with anglophones) and the maintenance of the legitimacy of one's status as a francophone manager. Similarly, the anglophones must legitimate their presence through some use of French.

12. Albert, the young new francophone manager, uses English to talk to Bob, an anglophone who is junior in rank to Albert but his senior in age and experience, and French to open the meeting:

E	Albert:	*he would have got*	
E	Bob:	*he's twenty-one years of age*	
E	Albert:	*yeah twenty-one years of age*	
*E		(pause) bon mais vous	'good but you can
		pouvez fermer la porte	close the door
		c'est tout ce qu'on va	that's all we're
		avoir aujourd' hui	going to have today'

13. Claude, an older francophone used to working in English, reads his report in English, but directs comments on the report in French to Albert:

Claude: oui uh vacation staff Roland Masse George Kovacs cette seminare la semaine prochaine Roland Masse George Kovacs *again* uh uh temp Denis Blais *he's on the lubrication survey* Leo Charrette uh *working on the expense budget but he's going off for two weeks hein?* il prend deux semaines de vacances ça je l'avais donné ça y a un bout de temps
'eh? he's taking two week's vacation that I gave that a while ago'

14. Bob uses French routines or short phrases in otherwise English episodes:

a)	E	Albert:	*oh Monday afternoon we have a*
			meeting with Daniel Vincent
	E	Bob:	*what time is it?*
		Albert:	*uh*
	E	Claude:	*right signs*

	F	Albert:	douze heures	'twelve o'clock'
	E		*signs*	
	*F	Bob:	quelle place	'what place?'
	E	Albert:	*I think it's my office*	
b)	E	Albert:	*uh it's like passing the buck to*	
			somebody but uh (laughs) can you	
			spend some time some time with	
			Pierre (unint) Monday it could	
			be a good thing	
	*F	Bob:	avec plaisir	'with pleasure'

It is noteworthy that Bob can even use code-switching to defuse an argument between Claude and Albert:

15. Bob uses code-switching to de-escalate an argument between Claude and Albert in which he has been called in to arbitrate:

	E	Bob:	*okay good but I think I'm just not sure*	
			if Claude I got the complete message	
			clearly as I understand it Albert will	
			look for from you in the hand-written	
			form the one you'll pass over to him	
			will have breakdowns as opposed to	
			your full sheet going to him	
	E	Claude:	*no I don't need to prepare that because*	
			I already got it	
	E	Bob:	*okay good*	
	E	Claude:	*I'm only summarizing*	
	*F	Bob:	*mm fine* fini?	'finished?'
	*F	Claude:	vendu	'sold'
(pause)				
	E	Albert:	*do you see that? Gaz Naturel?*	
			increase in price?	

In the meeting discussed here there was a fourth person present, a young francophone who had no personal ties to anyone in the group, and who occupied a position in which the use of English was largely unnecessary. He never spoke English during the meeting: there was no reason for him to do so, his position with respect to the French/English boundary being such that his distance from it rendered code-switching meaningless. Aside from this fourth person, code-switching in this situation accomplishes the ambiguity of not choosing frames of reference. Once the participants use code-switching to neutralize the tension between French and English, they can all participate in the meeting. Further, code-switching becomes available as a conversation management device (Albert uses English to include Bob, Bob uses French to enter the conversation, Claude uses French to gain his boss' ear) and as a device for managing interpresonal relations (Bob uses French to make peace between Claude and Albert).

The Toronto situation is similar to that of the marginals in the Montreal company. Here are a group of students in Grades 7 and 8 in an elementary school in anglophone Toronto established for the purpose of teaching francophone children in their language, and for the purpose of maintaining French language and culture in Ontario (Choquette 1975; Mougeon and Heller 1986). The presence of students at such a school can be legitimized only by the use of French as a symbol of French ethnic identity. The school insists explicitly, regularly and vocally on the use of French on school grounds. However, for reasons too lengthy to go into detail about here (cf. Heller 1984), the school population is not exclusively francophone. Only 30% of the families have only French as a mother tongue (and in many French is not necessarily the regular language of communication). 52% claim between two and four mother tongues. Further, the students are bussed to school from all over the western half of Toronto: when they go home in the afternoon they play not with their schoolmates but with the English- or Italian-speaking children on the block. At least half of their lives is conducted in English. These students are caught at school between the English and French halves of their lives in a situation that demands the use of French. But for the students to do so would be to make a claim regarding their social identity that some of them CANNOT make and that many of them do not want to make. This is reflected in their patterns of language choice and in their use of code-switching.

There are some students who may attempt to alter their choice of language depending on the interlocutor, but who never code-switch. These are students who do not speak the other language well enough to code-switch (some are francophone and some are anglophone), and/or who are so sure of their identity that code-switching is meaningless for them (most of these are francophones from Quebec who view their stay in Toronto, sometimes realistically and sometimes not, as temporary). The others, whether French-dominant or English-dominant, are caught between two identities. Their French identity, derived from school and sometimes from home, pulls them in one direction, while their English (and other) identity, derived from neighbourhood and sometimes from home, pull them in another. Most of the students speak English to each other at school, although they do some code-switching, and they speak French in the presence of and to their teachers. Their use of code-switching is limited to a few situations, all of them in the presence of teacher(s) AND classmates, and so usually in the classroom. For example, in formal presentations in class side comments will often be in English (e.g. "gimme a minute", "um, okay", "I'm getting there"; cf. also Valdés 1981: 84 and Zentella 1981: 123). Students speaking in French to teachers in front of other students may make side comments in English:

16. A student from another class comes to the door and asks the teacher for some sports equipment:

Student: uh monsieur je m'excuse de vous déranger *I know I better be* mais est-ce que je pourrais avoir le poids rond?
(uh sir I'm sorry to disturb you . . . but may I have the round weight?)

Students will also code-switch with teachers or to other students in the presence of teachers:

17. One student explaining to another how a science competition is being run (in the classroom):

Yes but they're not all aussi bien, *they're not all at the same* niveau *(. . . . . . . equally good . . . . level)*

18. Another student makes a suggestion to the teacher regarding individual student speeches at graduation:

Student: monsieur, elle peut dire par   'sir she could say
          exemple "Eh, Marie, avez-vous   for example "eh,
          entendu *the latest*   Marie, have you
          gossip?"   heard . . ."'

It seems that code-switching here is a refusal to commit oneself to all the obligations of being French, while maintaining one's right to be at this school. It is a way of mediating the conflicting pressures felt by these students from different parts of their social network, and of maintaining access to both. It only matters, however, in the presence of representatives of conflicting groups, or in situations where access to both has to be maintained, otherwise categorical language choice is not dangerous.

In each of these cases — in the Montreal company and the Toronto school — it is possible to predict where code-switching occurs on the basis of an understanding of the nature and dynamic of the language boundary involved. There are going to be certain people structurally involved at the boundary who are likely to be bilingual and for whom the creation of ambiguity through code-switching is likely to be a useful thing. The boundary may be stable or in transition, but it is there. The exact nature and meaning of code-switching is only derivable from an understanding of the larger social context and of the exact nature of the social situation and the social relationships involved. Since these are not always clear, the meaning of a code-switch may be ambiguous itself (or rather, the meaning is always ambiguous but it is usually possible to decide on a meaning). The interpretive choice interlocutors make can then in turn serve to define the relationship and the identity of the interlocutors. If interlocutors share background knowledge then narrowing down the options of what code-switching might mean is less tricky; where interlocutors do not share this knowledge the code-switching can actually backfire, when each interlocutor chooses a different possible meaning, or when it is not clear which of many possible meanings is dominant. For example, I have participated in several such tricky situations. In one case, a francophone academic whom I have known for years, my senior in age and rank, was discussing with me (in French) in a collegial way a paper he was writing for a conference. After complaining at length about how hard it was to get it done by the deadline, he said: "C'est très très difficile" with an English accent (sej tɹej tɹej difisijʌl). I had a choice between two different interpretations. If I saw the context as ingroup, then he was probably distancing himself from his academic role, in effect, making fun of himself for taking these silly papers so seriously. If, however, I took the context as intergroup, then I could only interpret the switch as making fun of *me*, that is, teasing me that I speak French with an English accent. In another case, I found myself in a long-term working relationship with a francophone woman of about my age and status who frequently code-switched. Again the interpretation of the code-switch as solidary or distancing depending entirely on whether *I* thought *she* thought we were co-members of a group, and I had no idea which context operated.

In Barcelona (see Woolard, this volume) there is another type of tricky situation. There, two contexts always operate: the Castilian federal context and the Catalan regional/provincial context. To code-switch is to violate one or the other frame of reference, one directly contradictory to the other: the problem is that often one has no way of knowing which it is that is operating.

In all these cases code-switching cannot operate to refuse to choose: we need to know which the relevant frame is, or which the two *are* that are in competition. In Barcelona the two exist at all times, and somehow the balance must be maintained between them. The code-switching will be available at the boundary, but often there are danger zones which may block the use of code-switching. Code-switching can backfire if interlocutors do not share frames of reference, since it is only on the basis of shared background knowledge that strategies are successfully deployed. Lack of shared knowledge may arise because interlocutors are unsure of their relationship to each other (and this is important, since power relations at that level can offset power relations at higher levels, cf. example 10). Lack of shared knowledge can also arise from the constant existence of mutually contradictory frames of reference, between which it is both impossible to choose and to mediate, at least for people with clearly defined group memberships in contact with each other.

Thus code-switching works where there is ambiguity to be created or exploited in a situation where participants agree as to what the ambiguity is. It permits people to say and do, indeed to *be*, two or more things where normally a choice is expected. It allows people to take refuge in the voice of the other, in order to do or say things that normally they would not be able to get away with. Or it allows them to assert their own voice to claim new roles, new rights and obligations.

94   *Monica Heller*

By appealing to the notions of rights and obligations and of ambiguity of frame of reference it has been possible to form a general concept of the strategic use of code-switching in which stylistic, conversation management and social significance effects can all be seen to be embedded in one another. It is necessary to situate code-switching at the level of face-to-face interaction in order to accomplish this, since that is where the many levels of social relations, the many levels of context, are defined and acted out, and so it is there that it becomes possible to exploit this strategic resource, in the hope, of course, that it doesn't blow up in one's face.

Notes

1. This paper is based on two studies. The first was conducted in Montreal in 1979–1980, and was funded by the Ministry of Cultural Development, Government of Quebec, and by the Social Sciences and Humanities Research Council of Canada. The second was conducted in Toronto in 1983, through a post-doctoral fellowship at the Modern Language Centre, Ontario Institute for Studies in Education, as part of the Development of Bilingual Proficiency Project (J. P. B. Allen, J. Cummins, R. Mougeon and M. Swain, principal investigators; funded by the Social Sciences and Humanities Research Council of Canada). I gratefully acknowledge this support. The content of the paper, of course, does not necessarily reflect the views of the funding agencies or of the principal investigators of the Development of Bilingual Proficiency Project.

   I also wish to acknowledge the support of the staff of both research sites and of the students and parents of the Toronto school.

   Sheila Embleton, Guy Ewing, Timothy Kaiser, Shana Poplack, David Sankoff and Nina Spada have all provided valuable comments. The point of view presented here is, of course, my own.
2. "Choice of styles or languages is seen as a strategy on the part of speakers, trying, for instance, to present themselves as individuals with particular socially-defined qualities, or, as another example, trying to convey a particular attitude or impression concerning a topic of conversation" (Gal 1979: 91).

   ". . . while conversational language switching, like style-shifting, is used for expressing momentary intents in an interaction, the invariable choice of one language conveys the speaker's claim to a social identity" (Gal 1979: 129).

"The ultimate semantic effect of the message . . . derives from a complex interpretive process in which the code juxtaposition is in turn evaluated in relation to the propositional content of component sentences and to speakers' background knowledge, social presuppositions and contextual constraints" (Gumperz 1982b: 87).

References

Blom, J.-P. and J. Gumperz
    1972   "Social meaning in linguistic structures: code-switching in Norway," in: J. Gumperz and D. Hymes (eds.), *Directions in Sociolinguistics: the Ethnography of Communication*, N.Y.: Holt, Rinehart and Winston, pp. 407–434.

Calsamiglia, H. and E. Tuson
    1980   "Us i alternança de llengües en grups de joves d'un barri de Barcelona: Sant Andreu de Palomar," *Treballs de sociolinguistica catalana*, Valencia, pp. 11–82.

Choquette, R.
    1975   *Language and Religion: A History of English-French Conflict in Ontario*, Ottawa: University of Ottawa Press.

Clift, D. and S. Arnopoulos
    1979   *Le fait anglais au Québec*, Montréal: Éditions Libre Expression.

Eckert, P.
    1980   "Diglossia: separate and unequal," *Linguistics* 19: 1053–1064.

Gal, S.
    1979   *Language Shift: Social Determinants of Linguistic Change in Bilingual Austria*, N.Y.: Academic Press.

Genishi, C.
    1981   "Code-switching in Chicano six-year-olds," in: R. Durán (ed.), *Latino Language and Communicative Behaviour*, Norwood, N.J.: Ablex, pp. 133–152.

Gumperz, J.
    1982a   "Social network and language shift," in: J. Gumperz, *Discourse Strategies*, Cambridge: Cambridge University Press, pp. 38–58.
    1982b   "Conversational code-switching," in J. Gumperz, *op. cit.*, pp. 59–99.

Gumperz, J. and E. Hernández-Chavez
    1971   "Bilingualism, bidialectalism and classroom interaction," in: J. Gumperz, *Language in Social Groups*, Stanford: Stanford University Press, pp. 311–339.

Heller, M.
   1981   "Language shift in Montreal: verbal strategies in the workplace,"
          paper presented at the 80th Annual Meeting of the American
          Anthropological Association, Los Angeles, California.
   1982   *Language, Ethnicity and Politics in Quebec*, unpublished Ph. D.
          thesis, Dept. of Linguistics, University of California, Berkeley.
   1984   "Language and ethnic identity in a Toronto French-Language
          School," *Canadian Ethnic Studies* 16 (2): 1–10.
Heller, M., J.-P. Bartholomot, L. Lévy and L. Ostiguy
   1982   *Le processus de francisation dans une entreprise montréalaise: une
          analyse sociolinguistique*, Québec: L'Éditeur Officiel.
McClure, E.
   1981   "Formal and functional aspects of code-switched discourse of
          bilingual children, " in: R. Durán (ed.), *op. cit.*, pp. 69–94.
Mougeon, R. and M. Heller
   1986   "The social and historical context of minority French language
          education in Ontario," *Journal of Multilingual and Multicultural
          Development* 7 (2 and 3): 199–228.
Poplack, S.
   1980   "Sometimes I'll start a sentence in Spanish Y TERMINO EN
          ESPAÑOL: towards a typology of code-switching," *Linguistics* 18:
          581–618.
Scotton, C. M.
   1976   "Strategies of neutrality: Language choice in uncertain situations,"
          Language 52 (4): 919–941.
Valdés, G.
   1981   "Code-switching as a deliberate verbal strategy: a microanalysis
          of direct and indirect requests" in: R. Durán (ed.), *op. cit.*,
          pp. 95–107.
Woolard, K.
   1983   *The Politics of Language and Ethnicity in Barcelona*, unpublished
          Ph. D. thesis, Dept. of Anthropology, University of California,
          Berkeley.
Zentella, A.
   1981   "Tá bien, you could answer me in cualquier idioma," in: R. Durán
          (ed.), *op. cit.*, pp. 109–131.

MIX – IM – UP:
Aboriginal code-switching, old and new

Patrick McConvell
University College of the Northern Territory

Introduction

This paper is about code-switching amongst Gurindji Aborigines of the Victoria River District of the Northern Territory of Australia. It proposes a theory of social meaning in code-switching, based on the work of Gumperz and associates, and Scotton and Ury (1977), modified in terms of analysis of triangular kin-terms in Gurindji (McConvell 1982) and Warlpiri (Laughren 1982). The theory is tested using examples of code-switching drawn from a film[1] of Gurindji men butchering a cow. Examples of switching between dialects of Gurindji, and between Kriol and Gurindji[2] are analysed.

Most current speech[3] amongst Gurindji speakers themselves involves regular code-switching between Gurindji, the Aboriginal vernacular of the Pama-Nyungan family, and an English-based variety along a continuum between basilectal Creole/Pidgin and acrolectal 'Aboriginal English'. This is well recognised and is termed 'mix' or 'mikijimap' (mix-im-up). No distinction is drawn by most speakers between Creole/Pidgin varieties and English; 'mix' is considered to be a mixture of Gurindji and English. Amongst people of age about 20–60, 'mix-im-up' is predominant. This may involve intersentential code-switching, and intrasentential code-switching of both types, i.e. a basic Kriol/English structure with Gurindji items inserted or vice-versa. Sampling of the text analysed here indicates around one third fully Gurindji sentences, one third Creole and/or English and of the remaining 'mixed' third, approximately half of each type. I would estimate that this type of distribution would be fairly common in everyday discourse, based on several years of observation of Gurindji people conversing.

This situation is common in Northern Australia, and is recognised as a mixing or code-switching phenomenon. Ron Day (1982) writes of the situation on Mer:

The speaker commences the sentences in very good, if sometimes simple Meriam Mir, but suddenly switches and ends in Pidgin. Let's take this question for example:

| Ma pe nako pe ma nali | iu go kam tu? |
| How about you | will you come too? |

Such 'mixed' or 'half-and-half' speech styles currently in use by Australian Aborigines and Torres Strait Islanders are referred to by many authors. The location of groups referred to in the work below is shown on the map. The inset map shows the position of

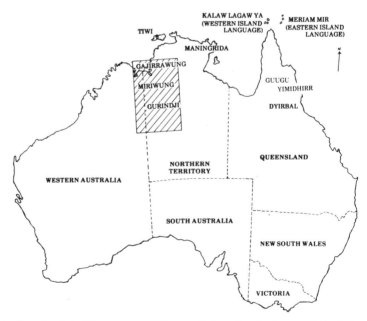

Australia: aboriginal languages of the north (see detailed map of shaded area).

the Gurindji dialects and neighbouring languages in more detail (from McConvell 1981).

In parts of the Western Torres Strait, a style of speaking called Ap-ne-ap (Half-and-half) involving pervasive switching between Torres Strait Pidgin and Kalaw Lagaw Ya has become the norm for younger people (Bani 1976), and Haviland (1982) describes frequent switching between English and Guugu Yimidhirr as the 'unmarked register of discourse' at Hopevale. On Bathurst Island, where the traditional language Tiwi has undergone drastic changes in the present generation, code-switching between Tiwi and English is widespread (Lee 1983). Amongst the Miriwung and Gajir-rawung, of the Kununurra area, Western Australia, Shaw's descrip-

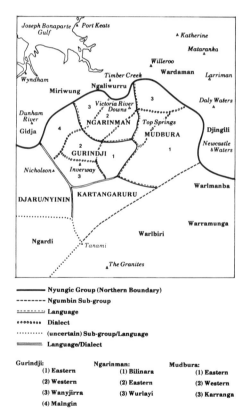

Aboriginal languages and dialects referred to in the text.

tion of the insertion of the traditional languages into Aboriginal English (Shaw 1982) coincides with an apparent language shift to Kriol or Aboriginal English, as with the Gurindji and other language groups in the area. In this area, I have also often observed switching between different traditional languages and dialects, e.g. between Ngarinyman and Ngaliwurru, Miriwung and Gija. Code-switching between traditional languages, and between these and English, is to be heard at Maningrida (Elwell 1982), but in this case, no language shift to English is apparent or likely to occur in the near future.

However, Dixon (1980: 82–84) notes the lack of actual analytical studies of code-switching in Australian Aboriginal situations. He provides his own data on Dyirbal code-switching, but explanations of only a few of the insertions of English into the Dyirbal conversation could be given, on the basis that they were referring to 'European artifacts or typically European activities' and repetition in English 'for emphasis'. For other insertions, Dixon 'can hazard no explanation'.

In recent studies it is the social factors which have received most attention in attempting to explain instances of code-switching. Some attention is devoted to instances of switching where linguistic differences are of major importance (cf. McConvell 1985). Nevertheless, these factors are rarely, if ever, the sole explanatory factor in a switch: all code-switching must be considered within the framework of a social theory.

Social theories of bilingual code-switching have been plagued by a compulsion to construct dichotomies of types of code-switching. Since each dichotomy proposed divides the phenomenon in a different way, the potential for confusion is great, and growing.

Gumperz and Hernandez-Chavez (1971) have broken through this type of confusion to some extent in separating the 'wide variety of contextual meanings – degree of involvement, anger, emphasis, change in focus' from the 'basic meaning inclusion (we) versus exclusion (they)', and in likening the meaning of code-switching to lexical meaning. A linguistic form with social meaning is meaningful because a choice (between languages) is involved.

This paper intends to follow this lead given by Gumperz and associates in relating the various subtle meanings of switches between languages and dialects by the Gurindji to assignment of people and events to more or less inclusive social arenas linked to social groups, by the speakers. The approach here de-emphasizes probabilistic accounts of levels of correlation between supposedly fixed social determinants in the environment of the speech event and language varieties, in favour of a more direct approach to the meaning of switches, without even using the 'situational' – 'metaphorical' dichotomy.

Scotton (this volume) has pointed out some problems with Gumperz' use of the term 'metaphorical' in contradistinction to 'situational'. In some of Gumperz' work, the distinction 'situational' : 'non-situational' appears to be identified with 'unmarked' : 'marked'. A linguistic form, "in a new context, becomes socially marked" (Gumperz 1972). In Scotton's current use of the term, 'unmarked' can be used to describe the pattern of using two varieties in the same conversation, where speakers have two social identities or profiles. This is the kind of situation I shall be illustrating in the Gurindji data below, and one which I suspect would account for a large proportion of the other cases of Australian Aboriginal code-switching referred to.

However, Scotton (this volume) also speaks of individual switches within such 'unmarked' codeswitching speech as not necessarily having a special significance, and the whole speech style as expressing 'merged' social identities. I have not followed this trend and have continued to seek evidence of social meaning in each switch analysed. I believe that there is such meaning in a significant number of the switches in the Gurindji data. Further in the elaboration of Scotton und Ury's social arenas concept (1977), I have attempted to construct a means whereby models of the configuration of social arenas within particular speech communities can be built. The expression of social identity or standpoint through switching results from the disposition by the speaker of elements in the discourse in different positions in the social arenas configuration. As I argue, even rapid switching can result from confusion about which identity to choose, or an attempt to use more than one standpoint virtually simultaneously. The social arenas model does not change in such cases: social identities are not merged in the sense of arenas being collapsed, so that the speaker's choice of language or dialect remains potentially meaningful.

The Social Arenas — Trirelational Model

The theory being developed here takes as its departure point the theory of Scotton und Ury (1977) on the social functions of code-switching, which itself builds on earlier work by Gumperz and associates, and Brown and Gilman (1968). Scotton und Ury's study does not formally break with the situational/metaphorical dichotomy of Blom and Gumperz (1972), but it does launch a new approach to the social functions of code-switching, through the concepts of strategy and social arena, which actually transcends the dichotomy.

The situational and metaphorical classifications are useful because they describe how and when code-switching occurs. But to know that a code-switch signals change in topic or lends emphasis to a topic still does not tell *why* a speaker code-switches. To explain the 'why' of code-switching means to explain the switch as an extension of the speaker. It means to explain the relationships between the subject of discourse and the participants of an interaction and the societal norms which give a language choice a meaning (Scotton and Ury, 1977).

It is suggested that a speaker switches codes for the following reasons:

1. To redefine the interaction as appropriate to a different social arena, or
2. to avoid, through continual code-switching, defining the interaction in terms of any social arena.

The approach to code-switching in this paper is similar to that of Scotton and Ury in the following respects:

1. It dispenses with the situational/non-situational and the switching/mixing dichotomies;
2. It adopts the idea of the speaker employing strategy in discourse;
3. It adopts the idea that code-switching is primarily connected to the definition of social arena.

The present approach differs from that of Scotton and Ury in a number of ways:

1. The speaker may not only use conscious strategies of code-switching to a particular goal, but may also be unconsciously influenced by his viewpoint towards the social arena (as partially admitted by Scotton and Ury, p. 6). It follows that explicit reasons for switches cannot always be elicited from participants (as against their methodology).
2. Scotton und Ury define the social arenas as universally three: identity, power, and transactional. The present approach prefers not to define the social arenas a priori, but to discover them on the basis of local social formations, their linguistic composition and local ideologies.
3. If the function of code-switching in 'redefining the interaction' refers only to the interaction between speaker and interlocutors, then it appears too narrow; switching may also redefine the relationship between speaker and/or interlocutor, and an element in the discourse.
4. This element in the discourse may be a person, but it may also be an animal, an inanimate object, a relationship, an event, etc. A connection between a person and an object is not 'social' in itself, but may be associated with a social arena

Scotton and Ury diagram their model of 'social arenas' as follows:

Identity arena   Transactional arena   Power arena

Figure 1. Social Arenas in Code-switching (after Scotton & Ury)

A & B are 'participants'; X is 'the discourse'. The length of the line joining A and B represents their 'social distance', which is 'the separation which exists between A and B, participants, in terms of their mutual relationship to X, the discourse'.

Although a triangular model is used, 'any number of participants could be involved, either clustered, or at individual points in a figure of any geometric shape'.

Rather than try to explicate Scotton and Ury's model, I will now compare the above to a model constructed by Laughren (1982) to deal with trirelational kinship terms (also called 'triangular' and 'shared' in the same volume). I have sketched the elements of such a system among the Gurindji (McConvell 1982) and pointed out its relevance to both the social arena model and the Gurindji codeswitching data (McConvell 1985). Here I shall further explore this new model of social arenas among the Gurindji and use it to generate hypotheses about the meaning of their codeswitching.

Triangular kinship terms have a wide distribution among Australian Aboriginal groups, but have frequently gone unnoticed in ethnographic descriptions. Before the volume edited by Heath, Merlan and Rumsey (1982), few studies had paid much attention to them (exceptions are O'Grady and Mooney (1973), and Hansen (1974)). Heath (Heath, Merlan and Rumsey eds. 1982, p. 1) characterises these terms as follows:

These are terms which simultaneously relate the designated referent to the speaker and to another person, commonly the addressee, so that three (rather than just one) relationships are indexed by a single term (speaker-referent, addressee-referent, speaker-addressee), though usually any two of these relationships make the third predictable.

The relevance of these terms to the theory of social meaning in code-switching is that the triangular terms index the relationship between the speaker and the primary referent and the speaker and another person linked to the referent, as well as indexing the referent of the term himself or herself. In a similar way, the use of a particular language or dialect in codeswitching can index the speaker's view of his or her own links with the referent (or perhaps 'topic'[4]) and with a particular social group or arena associated with it, as well as indexing the referent itself, through its normal lexical meaning. Both types of selection of varieties provide a means for the speaker to define the 'us' and 'them' that he or she is talking about at a particular time, in addition to the socially neutral meanings of the words and phrases.

In the type of code-switching I shall be dealing with, the selection of language or dialect is not simply made in accordance with the identity of the addressee. As with triangular terms, the speaker defines by code selection primarily his relationship to the main referent or topic, and secondarily implies thereby what the relationship of another person or persons to the referent and to himself should be, in his view. The other person, whose position is parallel with that of the propositus in kin terms, I call here the participant.

In this paper the advantages of the two models of language/lexical item choice (the social arenas model of Scotton and Ury 1977 and the trirelational model of Laughren 1982) will be combined to produce the model to be used here. The vague elements of the triangle in Scotton and Ury's model ('the participants' X and Y and 'the discourse' X) are replaced by the terms of Laughren model S (peaker); P (here interpreted as 'participant' rather than 'propositus'); R(eferent). The social arenas model (absent in the kinterm model) is adopted but the purported universal arenas (personal, power and transactional) are to be replaced by arenas which are to be defined on the basis of local organization and

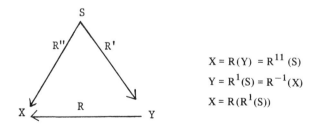

$$X = R(Y) = R^{11}(S)$$
$$Y = R^{1}(S) = R^{-1}(X)$$
$$X = R(R^{1}(S))$$

R = relation; R^{-1} = inverse or reciprocal of relation R;
S = speaker;   X and Y are two referents.

Figure 2. Trirelational Model (after Laughren 1982:73)

ideology, and which bear a relationship to each other within an integrated framework.

Putting the triangle of discourse relations into the context of a social arena is an essential step in expanding the triangular kinterm model to account for the variety of social relations indexed by code-switching. But the social arenas must have a definite and definable content and should exhibit some relationship between them which is also definite and definable. Some attempts to apply this model are to be found in the following section.

The model applied to the situation

It is not possible within the confines of this paper to explore all the possible types, combinations and configurations of social arenas relevant to a study of social meaning in code-switching. What I shall do is to elaborate a preliminary model of social arenas in the Gurindji context, relevant to the code-switching data I shall be presenting below.

The configuration of social arenas in the Gurindji case is one in which several arenas are nested within each other, or to put it another way, each social arena properly includes those 'below' it, or more 'exclusive' than it (the terms 'inclusive' and 'exclusive' are there used in a different sense from their use in relation to the 'us' pronoun). It is not suggested, however, that this is the only possible configuration which produces code-switching, nor that the particular configuration and rules which are proposed for the Gurindji situation can be transferred without alteration to other situations. To name only two, the bilingual Canadian situation (Heller, this volume) and the various East African situations (described by Scotton, this volume) seem to me to require different social arena configurations from the type described here; I do not intend to pursue this further here. To the extent that the relevant social formations and their ideologies are similar to the Gurindji case, though, one might expect to find a roughly analogous configuration.

There is, however, one case which provides some illuminating parallels with this situation on a structural level. Sauris (Denison

1971) is a trilingual community in Italy, where people speak a German dialect; Friulian, a regional Romance dialect; and Italian. The homology with the Gurindji situation lies in the fact that the social arenas/language speaker-sets are organised in nested layers, (three in this case), each of which properly includes the next one down: the national language group (Italian) has a proper sub-set, the regional language group (Friulian) which in turn has a proper sub-set, the local language group (German). This situation can be represented by a Venn Diagram:

The 'triangular model' of discourse elements can be super-imposed on such a social arenas model to provide a model of particular instances of language use. For instance, the three examples of the use of 'we' in different languages in Sauris, given above, could be diagrammed as in Fig. 4.

Here S stands for speaker and P the 'participant' which is equivalent to the propositus in the kinterm model, or the non-speaker participant in the Scotton and Ury model. P is normally the addressee.

In the cases at hand, R is the 'referent'. It is the change of the nature of R, the referent, which shifts the social arena and there-fore shifts the appropriate code. S and P remain the same through-out; both members of the village, and trilingual, basically of German mother tongue. The referent R in these cases consists of

Figure 3.
Sociolinguistic Arenas in Sauris

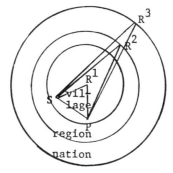

Figure 4. The Triangular-Nested
Social Arena Model (for Sauris)

the members of the set 'us' other than the participant: R_1 are members of the village, R_2 people of the region, and R_3 people of Italy as a whole.

This is clearly not a model which necessarily prescribes determination of code by 'fixed' identities of statuses of interlocutors, since three different codes can be chosen despite S and P being in the same position for each.

Setting, the second major factor said to be involved in 'situational' code-switching, rarely figures in strict or unique correlation with language selections in Sauris (Denison 1971):

other ingredients of the situation, especially the roles of the participants have greater priority than physical setting in diatypic selection.

Nor is it a model in which 'topic' is necessarily determinant either; it is not implied by Denison that in Sauris, for example, the affairs of the Italian state *must* be discussed in Italian; one could well imagine national matters being discussed in a local dialect (with, of course, a social effect different from discussing them in the national language). In this model, R^n, the referent, represents largely a standpoint adopted by the speaker, by identifying with an element in a particular social arena.

The example of Sauris is relevant to the Gurindji situation in that the Gurindji too conceive of certain social arenas relevant to languages as embedded within each other. The Gurindji situation may be briefly characterized as follows: a numerically relatively small (about 500) group of classless former hunter-gatherers, Gurindji speakers inhabit a large area with groups linked through residence or descent to smaller areas within the larger area, some of which groups speak identifiable dialects of the main language. The language has been somewhat standardized by the concentration of people in non-traditional centers (a large cattle station and a government settlement) for some decades. They have been, for about one hundred years, progressively and acceleratingly absorbed into the colonizing society and economy, which in their area is mainly represented by cattle stations (where they work as stockmen) and governmental and missionary institutions, which function to assimilate them to a western way of life and cultural values. The language of these institutions is exclusively Standard

Australian English. Traditionally, links with some neighbouring non-Gurindji groups were strong, through trade, ritual, intermarriage etc.; communication was mainly possible through widespread multilingualism. Today contacts with other Aboriginal groups are more frequent and widespread, and carried out using a Pidgin English which developed on the cattle stations. This Pidgin/Creole (Kriol) is also used today (switching with Gurindji) among older Gurindji speakers and has become the first language of the younger generation.

Some of the embedding of social arenas is, then, in part traditional in nature: the position of locally-based dialect groups within a wider speech community of Gurindji speakers. However the current manifestation of this departs from its traditional form in having been moulded by European contact: 'standard' Gurindji has largely grown up by a fusion of different dialects first on Wave Hill Station, then at Wave Hill Settlement and Daguragu, whereas local origin dialectal groups now are based more on smaller stations (e.g. Wanyjirra at Inverway) than strictly on traditional estate or foraging range. The other arenas of the model presented in Fig. 5 are more direct results of contact: the wide network of Aboriginal people who speak Pidgin/Kriol either as a first or second language, and the wider Australian society for which English is the standard language.

These are categories which are widely known and used amongst Gurindji people, and there is a recognized association of each with particular language codes. They are also generally associated with different patterns of kinship ties and forms of address.

Fig. 5 is centred on the Wanyjirra local group because it is the group clearly represented by the two older dialect-speaking interlocutors, J and G in the text supplied. The younger Gurindji speakers, C, N and R are less identified (in this context at any rate) with a particular local origin group, and speak a more 'standardised' Wave Hill variety of Gurindji. Although perhaps on some grounds to be considered by descent as outside the Regional Speech Community, and simply as a 'cattle station Aboriginal', K has nevertheless spent a long time within the broader Gurindji community, and understands and speaks Gurindji. The composition of the group of interlocutors (the butchers) is symbolized on Fig. 5 as the area within the dotted line.

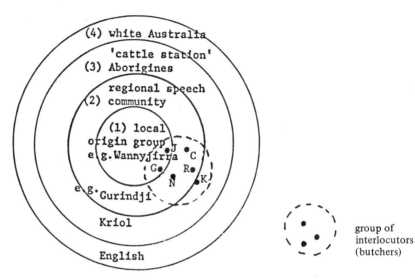

Figure 5. Model of Gurindji Social Arenas

Also of relevance in assessing the speech behaviour of the inter-locutors is the kinship relationship between them, which also includes some non-participants referred to. It has already been mentioned that the relationship between J and G could be, in terms of the 'rules', one of respect and avoidance. However, because of the practicalities of G's having to live with his mother-in-law, J's classificatory 'sister', in one house, the extreme form of avoidance has been relaxed between them. Moreover, since J and G's mother-in-law are not full siblings, and because J and G have to work together closely in cattle station work, in which J is, in European terms, G's boss, the relationship has departed even more from avoidance 'norms'. It has not been reinterpreted in a fixed way, however, so it is a relationship in which there is uncertainty and ambiguity, which, as we shall see below, is reflected in a con-tinuing wavering and redefinition of the relationship in linguistic terms.

A number of the interlocutors and people referred to by them are in a type of relationship which is at the opposite extreme from that of avoidance: the 'joking relationship' of classificatory mother's brother-sister's son, in which the norm is light-hearted swearing and abuse (for details, see McConvell 1982). G at one point tries to use the same tone with J, but is curbed by G.

In fact, the case of J and G is only a slightly more obvious example of a principle that needs to be recognised for any study of the correlation of kinship relations and linguistic and other behaviour. While appropriate 'rules' are often formulated, either rules themselves or the kin relations according to which they apply can be ambiguous, or the 'rules' can be deliberately 'bent' or ignored to cope with particular circumstances. A person can be related to another one not just through one tie, but through a network of different ties, and may choose to emphasize a particular tie or a particular aspect of a tie and de-emphasize others in his dealings with that person to achieve particular effects, at particular times. This may be done by using sociolinguistic devices, such as the indexing of a relationship through the use of triangular kinterms, or by different degrees of avoidance or joking registers. On a different plane, different aspects of a relationship may be stressed by code-switching between dialects or languages indexing different social arenas in which the relationship can be viewed.

The text from which examples are drawn is the transcript of film footage shot at Daguragu for the Australian Institute of Aboriginal Studies (AIAS) by Kim MacKenzie and myself in 1977. The particular sequence used was tentatively titled "Killer", and is a record of a group of Daguragu stockmen butchering a cow in a bush paddock. It lasts about 30 minutes (unedited). The transcript is about 15 pages of typescript, which is impractical to reproduce here in full. Transcription of the soundtrack was done with the assistance of C, who also commented on the use of the code-switching (J added some comments as well).

The presence of two *kartiya* (white men: Kim MacKenzie filming and myself recording sound) may have had some influence on the choice of language at some points, but I believe this was minimal. The men asked me before the filming started if they should talk in English, and I said no, talk just as you would normally —— which is, on most occasions a 'mix' of Gurindji and Kriol, as in the present text. More significantly, the butchering had to be done very quickly as it was the middle of the day in full sun. Everyone was working hard and had little time to relate to the whites observing them or to carefully monitor their speech. The result is a fairly natural and typical piece of modern Gurindji conversation.

For the purposes of studying code-switching of a 'non-situational' type, the butchering sequence is well-suited in a number of ways. Firstly, all present were adult bilingual speakers of Gurindji and Kriol; differences in depth of knowledge certainly exist, but not great enough to make speakers switch languages solely because of the competence or lack of competence of any participants in either language. The additional presence of Wanyjirra speakers provided an interesting sidelight on code-switching between Gurindji dialects; Wanyjirra is sufficiently close to standard Gurindji to be understood, in most cases, by all the participants. As we shall see, the use of Wanyjirra is not determined simply by the speaker, or addressee, or both being Wanyjirra speakers, but by other 'non-situational' factors. One factor which may perhaps be seen as 'interlocutor'-determined 'situational code-switching' is the tendency to use Kriol more than Gurindji when speaking to younger people. However this is evidently not a firm rule, and may not even account for the majority of utterances of older to younger men, which are in both languages.

'Situational' factors of interlocutor play a limited role; factors of 'setting/place' and 'topic' are clearly even less relevant to code-switching here. 'Setting' remains constant throughout: butchering a cow in a bush paddock. 'Topic' is similarly very limited: the great majority of the talk is about either the detail of butchering the animal or about the distribution of the meat. There are some joking references to other people and places. Since switches happen in the middle of talking about one of the two major topics, and switches often do not happen when changing from one to the other or inserting jokes, we can conclude that there is no strong connection between 'topic' (at least in the superficial sense) and the pattern of code-switching.

Since the obvious 'situational' factors are almost completely absent here, the text provides a good testing-ground for the theory of code-switching which is being developed in this paper. There is not space enough to analyze the whole text, so reference will be made to particular examples of code-switching, set in a brief discourse context. Some examples of code-switching which I believe to be motivated at least in part by contrast in lexico-semantic organization between Gurindji, Kriol and English are also present in the text. Some of these are briefly examined in McConvell (1985).

Code-switching between Gurindji dialects

We can now tackle the problem which is central to our present endeavour: the analysis of code-switching in terms of its social meaning. For the most part, to avoid confusion with 'linguistically motivated' code-switching, we shall be looking at cases in which both languages could equally well express the basic information, in a similar length of speech, and using a similar or identical semantic organisation. The choice of language is not determined by the content of the basic message, but adds, in terms of the position argued for here, another dimension of meaning to the utterance.

Before analyzing some of the cases of code-switching between Gurindji and Kriol/English in the text, we shall examine first code-switching between standard (eastern) Gurindji and the Wanyjirra (south-western) dialect. Since these are dialects the differences are not great.

Code-switching in conversation between Aboriginal dialects and languages occurs frequently. In the Victoria River District, I have often observed frequent switching back and forth between Gurindji and Mudbura, Ngarinyman and Ngaliwurru etc., and in the Western Desert area between different Western Desert dialects, and between Western Desert dialects and neighbouring languages e.g. Nyangumarta, Walmajarri, Jaru etc. In traditional situations such switching would have been used and is used mainly 'stylistically', to express *meanings* about social situations. As with other types of code-switching discussed, very little of it is amenable to analysis in terms of *determination* by situation, whether this is defined as including person, setting, topic or any combination of them, unless determination is seen in some vague, probabilistic way. In the modern situation, this type of traditional code-switching is often combined with code-switching between vernacular and a creole and/or a form of English.

In the butchering text from which examples are drawn, the two older men J and G are associated with the South-Western area, and are basically Wanyjirra (W) speakers. Both of them more often use Standard Eastern Gurindji (SEG) forms when they are at Daguragu or Wave Hill, as in the present text. Although there is a tendency for them to use Wanyjirra when speaking to other Wanyjirra speakers, this does not always occur, as we shall see in examples below. On occasion, J and G both use Standard Eastern Gurindji to each other, as well as Wanyjirra, to convey specific social meanings, as I argue. Although they mainly speak in Standard Eastern Gurindji, J and G also sometimes use Wanyjirra when speaking to the group of interlocutors in general, again to convey social meaning. The younger men are all Standard Eastern Gurindji speakers who also use a lot of Kriol. They generally do not use Wanyjirra, but in rare instances C does use Wanyjirra forms for a particular social effect, often with a touch of humour.

The social meanings being played upon in Standard Eastern Gurindji/Wanjirra code-switching concern only the two inner circles of the model in Gurindji social arenas (Figure 5). The position of the interlocutors in these two concentric circles is to be interpreted in this way: J and G belong potentially to both the more exclusive Wanyjirra local origin group arena, and to the wider more inclusive Gurindji speech community; for present purposes, the other interlocutors belong to the Gurindji speech community arena, not to the Wanyjirra arena. The social meaning in the dialect selection of J and G arises from them defining events or relationships involving the referent (R) as falling within either (a) the local origin arena; or (b) the wider community arena. They do this by speaking (a) Wanyjirra, or (b) Standard Eastern Gurindji, respectively. In terms of the model, the choice (a) places the referent R in the inner circle, and (b) places R in the second circle within which the first circle is nested.

Actual examples of these two options are given below in example (1) and diagrammed in Figures 10 and 11. Before beginning to analyze textual examples, however, it may be valuable to look at some of the other ways in which the SPR triangle can fit into the nested social arenas configuration involving only two circles, using the Wanyjirra local origin group/South Eastern Gurindji speech community configuration as an example. There are eight logically possible ways in which the triangle can be positioned within the two concentric circles. Perhaps the simplest cases sociolinguistically are those in which all three elements (Speaker, Referent, and Participant) are in the same circle: a Wanyjirra speaker is talking Wanyjirra with Wanyjirra people; or non-Wanyjirra SEG speakers talk in SEG with SEG speakers. In these and subsequent examples, P, the participant, is assumed to be the addressee.

Figures 6 and 7 represent cases which I hypothesize are not found. If such things were possible, 6 would mean that a Wanyjirra speaker is using Wanyjirra to talk to an SEG speaker; and 7 that an SEG speaker is using Wanyjirra to talk to another SEG speaker.

The impossibility of 6 and 7 is based on a hypothesized constraint (Constraint I below) which is proposed as a property of nested social arena configurations.

Constraint I:P can only be interpreted as being in the arena delimited by R.

In reading this it must be borne in mind that P in the first, more exlusive circle is in fact also in the second, more inclusive circle in a nested configuration. On the other hand, the position of R, the

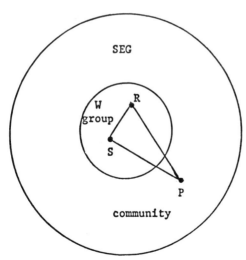

Figure 6.

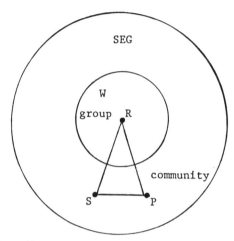

Figure 7.

referent, delimits the most inclusive arena with which the referent, and the code in which it is expressed, can be associated. For this reason the situation of a Wanyjirra or SEG person using SEG to a Wanyjirra person discussed above, which is common, does not contravene the constraint. This asymmetry between the functions of the two dialects reflects their relative position within the nested social arenas configuration.

It might be objected that situations 6 and 7, while highly marked, cannot be ruled out entirely. 6 could result from the speaker artificially including a non-member in his exclusive 'us' group; 7 could involve the speaker mimicking another dialect or pretending that he, his intended audience or both were members of a group to which they do not belong in fact.

Both these situations differ from the normal situation based on shared perceptions of social arenas and their membership. In the new case, the speaker is trying to create an artificial situation which goes against the accepted nature of the situation. To deal with such cases it is necessary to introduce an extension of the model introduced. The triangle with solid lines is retained to represent the actual position of S, P and R in the arenas, but a second triangle of broken lines can also be added to represent the artificial situation being created. This broken line triangle can share S and R with the first triangle, as in Figure 8, which shows

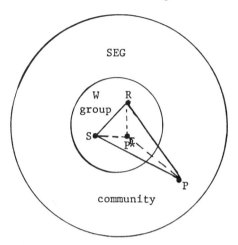

Figure 8.

the first artificial situation described above in relation to Figure 6, or it can share only R as in Figure 9, which is the case of the speaker pretending both he and the audience are members of another group, described above in relation to 7. The created positions of Speaker and Participant are shown as S* and P* respectively and are joined to the actual S and P by a broken line arrow.

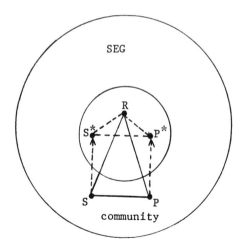

Figure 9.

The four other possible ways in which SPR triangle fits into the two social arenas, and a couple of more complex structures, are diagrammed below together with examples from the Gurindji butchering text which illustrate them.

Many of the exchanges between the butchers during their work concern the distribution of meat. Sometimes these exchanges are of a joking nature, sometimes more serious. For a number of reasons, the killing and distribution of cattle stands at the heart of a number of socio-economic contradictions in which the Gurindji find themselves. Although this aspect deserves separate treatment, I will only mention one or two factors as background. Since 1975 the Gurindji have owned Daguragu Station in Australian law. Some of their white advisors want them to run the station according to a particular concept of an 'economic basis', which involves restricting as much as possible the people to whom beef is given without payment. On the other side, it has been traditional hunting practice to distribute meat killed in hunting on the basis of kinship obligations. Neither traditional lore nor 'modern' station practice give unambiguous answers to questions about meat distribution. On many white-owned stations, at least some of the resident white people get free beef, often according to a varying combination of factors of staff and sometimes family position. Who are staff and who are family in the Daguragu situation where everyone is kin of some kind? (This contradiction is reflected in the 'working-fellas' — 'camp people' distinction, as we shall see later). Who is the 'boss' who makes the decisions (in European terms), or the 'hunter' who controls the meat (in Aboriginal terms), in this new situation? If there is such a person or people, what criteria do they use to assign cuts of meat to people?

In this context there are obviously competing interests. It is not common for proponents of such interests to argue for them explicitly, but more common for subtle verbal cues (such as code-switching) to be used to place an issue in the particular framework in which they would like it to be viewed.

Consider the passage (1) (specifically SEG forms which contrast with W forms are underlined; specifically W forms are in bold. Kriol continuum elements are in capitals. Code-switches are indicated by a vertical line. The same conventions are followed in the translation below the example (beneath the broken line and in all textual examples henceforth)).

(1) G: MINE | **pampirla** | THERE AGAIN, OLD MAN |
  | shoulder | |

  pampirla, waku nyarra?
  shoulder or which way

  kankurla-pala-nginyi   ngu – yi – n | **kuma**-wu
  above   ACROSS SOURCE AUX   1sO   2sA | cut   FUT

J: | Laja   -ma | ngartji ma-ni   W-rlu
  | shoulder   TOPIC | choose get PAST   ERG

G: | **Nganinga-** | ma
  | my | TOPIC

G: **The shoulder** | THERE IS MINE TOO, OLD MAN | **the shoulder, or what?**
  You can **cut** it for me from across the top

J: W – picked out | the shoulder

G: (It's) | **mine**

G begins in Kriol, but switches to Wanyjirra to emphasize the close local bond between himself and J, in relation to J's giving him the shoulder. and the cutting action which will provide G with the shoulder. J however responds by shifting back on to the wider community arena by using SEG, and emphasizing the rights of a non-Wanyjirra community member. G reasserts his claim within the narrower arena by using the W term for 'mine'.

The latter two switches (G going into Wanyjirra, and J going into SEG) are represented by Figures 10 and 11 respectively in the social-arenas/triangular model. By Constraint I above, the interpretation of 10 is that the referent (the shoulder, and its destination, in both cases) belongs to the local origin group aspect of the speaker and participant's identities (the more exclusive arena, in which R is located); in 11 that it belongs to the wider community aspect of their identities (the more inclusive arena, to which R has been shifted by code-switching). The fact that S and P (G and J, and vice-versa) remain in the same exclusive arena in both cases means that they both potentially have dual roles, because of the nested configuration, and it is this distinction which is indexed by

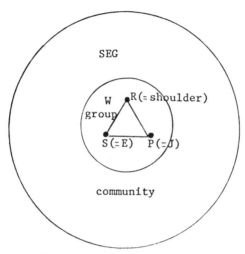

Figure 10. (for (1), Line 1)

switching. The fact that the referent or topic is also the same object, but is encoded differently, supports the position that neither interlocutor nor topic is determinant in dialect choice. This same 'shoulder' also recurs later in the text, but there has a more complex social semantic structure (see below example 7 and Figure 12).

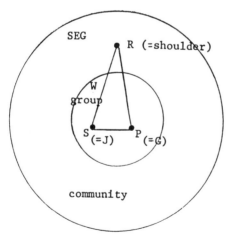

Figure 11. (for (1), Line 3)

Note too that while speaking Kriol, G calls J 'old man'. Normally this term or its vernacular equivalents are used to address a (classificatory) mother's brother. It has already been noted that J and G are supposedly in a *malirlang* (mother-in-law's brother-sister's son-in-law) relationship. G on several occasions seems to want to push this tendency to informality further and establish his relationship to J as being like a nephew to his maternal uncle (whether because of a secondary kinship tie, I am not certain). A nephew can make strong demands on his maternal uncle, and the relationship has a lot of licence for joking and swearing, quite at the opposite extreme from the *malirlang* relationship. However, in the above case, the use of the term 'old man' in a Kriol context (the less local Aboriginal arena) probably means that it is not to be so strictly interpreted as deriving from a kinship tie.

When G appears to take the fictive Mo Br/Si So relationship between J and him more literally, and apparently make jokes about him being circumcised[4], J reacts against this, and G responds in a confused way.

(2) C (to N): YOU LITTLE BIT BAD HAND, YOU MIGHT CUT-IM' IM . . .

    G: . . . | ngumparna   -marnany
                   | brother-in-law   your

    J: Ngantu-ku-yi **kuma-rnana?**
           who ERG 1s0 cut   PRES

    G: Wayi-rna-nga | BLOODY NEAR | **karr-iya** | TODAY | **-mali**
        AUX 1 sS DOUBT | | be IRR | | FOCUS

        nyununga-nyja patati   -rla | OLD MAN, ONLY | lani
        your   LOC initiation LOC | | frightened
                        ground

        | NOW |

        ngu-rna | TOO MUCH | tarlarlap-kaji | INTIT K-?
        AUX 1sS | | shaking NOM |

- -

    C (to N): YOU'VE GOT A BIT OF BAD HAND, YOU MIGHT CUT...
    G: . . . **your** brother-in-law
    J: Who's **cutting** me? (**or** for me)
    G: I **was** | NEARLY (circumcisor) TODAY | at **your** (son's) initiation, | OLD MAN, ONLY | I was too **frightened** and shasky | WASN'T I, K-?

The code-switching aspects of this interchange are particularly interesting. The initial utterance is between young men on a neutral work level, in Kriol. G interjects a joke, in SEG, since on the one hand it is more on the level of community identity concerning kinship relations and joking relationships and on the other it concerns the whole group present, not pointed at the more local W group. However it was intended, J takes it as possibly referring to himself. In the previous case G speaks W and J, SEG; in this case it is reversed: J responds in W specifically to speak more directly to J (although the question is not only addressed to him) and to bring the social arena down to the level of the W local group, within which G's relationship to him does not entitle J to joke at his expense in this fashion. Playing on the ambiguity of J's response, G replies using a jumbled mixture of Kriol and Wanyjirra. This puts one in mind particularly of Scotton and Ury's second reason for code-switching: to 'avoid, through continual code-switching, defining the interaction in terms of any social arena'. G is probably here simultaneously trying to distance himself from the SEG 'joke in poor taste', through the use of 'impersonal' Kriol, and to emphasize his intimacy and solidarity with J, through the use of W.

There is continuing ambiguity throughout the text about the assignment by J and G of the giving or receiving of meat, to the local group arena or to the wider community arena, and as a result, continual code-switching between W and SEG when talking about it. J and G each speak in both dialects, at different times, even where the addressees are the same, and the other elements of the situation the same. In a number of instances, one begins in one dialect and the other deliberately switches to the other to effect a change in social arena standpoint, but no overall generalization can be made about who will start, and which dialect they will use; this depends on the interaction of the social meaning of the switch with the basic meaning of the utterance.

3)   J: Nyila-ma   kanyju   **nganinga**
         That TOPIC under   mine

     G: |Nyununy, wayi?
         yours   eh

J: | Nyawa-ma   ngu-rna-yina kangku   pilirli-**ngu**-rra-wu
     This   TOPIC AUX 1sA 3p0 takeFUT MoMo your p1 DAT

J: That (meat) undemeath is **mine**

G: | <u>Yours</u>, eh

J: | I'm going to take this to **your** "grannies" (who are my "aunties")

Here J at first makes the 'we' of discourse the Wanyjirra group specifically, thus especially drawing G's attention to his claim to a certain cut of meat. G switches to SEG to bring the decision into the wider social arena, presumably to disassociate himself from 'collusion' on J's previous statement. J counters by putting the transaction in the context of G and J's *shared* kin (J's relationship indicated by the triangular term *pilirli*), to whom he is going to take the meat, and re-emphasizes the close kinship solidarity he wishes to impute to the event by using the W second person kin possessive suffix *-ngu*, rather than SEG *-marnany*.

Elsewhere too J uses the same strategy of switching to W, combined with invoking shared kin through triangular terms, to reinforce requests to G:

(4) J (to G): nyila niyan **kuma**-yi,   pilirli-**ngu**-wu
                that flesh cut   1s0 Mo Mo your   DAT

                <u>parra-rla kankurlu-rra</u>
                cut   3sI0 above   ALL

   J (to G): **cut** that meat for me, <u>cut</u> for **your** "granny" (my "aunty") towards the top

In the following example, it is G who first switches to W; J switches back to SEG.

(5) G: Kula-rlaa   warlu julyurrk yuwa-rru |
         NEG lindpA fire pile up <u>put</u>   FUT |

        CUT-IM UP, CUT-IM ALL THE BONE LONGA 'IS HEAD, PUT IN THE CAR AND GO, FIND-IM GOOD SHADE.

        CHUCK-IM HERE | ngumayi-rla | THAT | **langka**

   J: | Nyila-ma <u>ngayiny</u>
         that TOPIC   mine

G: | **Langka yirra**-yi
head   put   1sO

G: We can't put the firewood in one pile | CUT IT UP,
CUT ALL THE BONES AROUND ITS HEAD, PUT IT IN THE CAR
AND GO; FIND SOME GOOD SHADE. CHUCK THAT | **head**
behind

J: | That's <u>mine</u>

G: | **Put** the **head** in for me

G starts in SEG, making a general statement (in the inclusive
first person) about a detail of work of the whole group, moving
into Kriol (somewhat acrolectal in parts) in giving more long range
orders, or suggestions (a type of switch discussed in the following
section), but then finally switching to the W term for 'head'
to signal local solidarity with J (and therefore expectation of
approval from J of the claim to the head). J rejects the local
solidarity viewpoint and himself claims the head on the basis of
the wider community viewpoint (perhaps his position as head
stockman). G reverts to W to in effect reiterate his appeal to J,
while overtly giving an order to someone else.

A third example of the same theme involves both J using SEG
and G using both Kriol and SEG at first, then J switching to W to
claim a cut as part of an interaction with G as co-members of
the local group, followed by G using both Kriol, in a relatively
impersonal way, and SEG in relation to the other interlocutors, to
stake his own claim.

(6) G: PUT-IM HERE

J: | kaa-rni-mpa   partaj <u>yuwa</u>- rra-rla
| east up area   climb put   IMP 3sIo

C: | I BIN PUT-IM LONGA 'IM BUSHES

G: | Nyawa-ma   -rna | DINNER | <u>paya</u>-wu
| this   TOPIC 1sA | | bite FUT

J: Nyawa-ma   ngu-yi | **nganinga**
this   TOPIC AUX 1sO   mine

G: | I WANT 'IM THIS SKIRT

K: WHAT ABOUT THE WIRE?

G: | Kujarra | THERE | ngayiny-ma   Jangari
   | two | | mine TOPIC   =K

- -

G: PUT IT HERE

J: | Put it up in the higher east (of the truck) for him

C: | I PUT LEAFY BRANCHES ON IT

G: | I'm going to eat this for | DINNER.

J: This is | **mine**

G: | I WANT THIS SKIRT (meat)

K: WHAT ABOUT THE WIRE?

G: | There are two of mine there, Jangari (K)

Indexing the social arena by means of code-switching need not simply result from manipulation of a situation to advantage, by the speaker trying to influence the framework within which the thing or event is perceived. Use of a particular language for an item, phrase etc. can be used to denote the kind of circumstances under which the particular item is normally raised, or has been raised in the discourse. This can be close to the use of quotation to refer back to a part of an utterance; in this case of an item which is in a code-switching paradigm it is not only the fact that it was spoken by a particular person which is recalled, but the social meaning intended in the context. An example of this in the text concerns the shoulder, which G earlier in example (1) called (in W) *pampirla*, and J (in SEG) *laja*. Finally, the shoulder is again mentioned by J who tells R to cut it. Although speaking to an SEG speaker, and using mainly SEG, the word *pampirla* is used to refer not to J's own viewpoint on the social arena in which the shoulder enters discourse, but rather to refer to G's earlier use of the W word, and G's viewpoint about the relevant social area. In fact *pampirla* here could be glossed 'the shoulder which G asked to be an issue between J and G only, as joint local group members'.

(7) J: HERE, R-, CUT-IM, GIVE IT LONGA 'IM | nyila **pampirla**
                                                        tnat shoulder

| parra kataj   NOW
  cut   IMP cut

Ngu-rna kang -ku   parntara-rni,   ngantu-wu-warla?
AUX 1sA take FUT whole   ONLY who   DAT FOCUS

J: HERE, R-, CUT IT, GIVE HIM IT | cut that
  shoulder | NOW | I'm going to take the whole lot; whose is it?

The type of quotation of code-switching variants sometimes comes close to mimicry and parody: the above example has more than a touch of humour in it. When C engages in the following exchange, which involves him (not a W speaker) using the W verb *yirra-* 'put', it may be that he is trying to show deference to J, or that he is asserting some identity with J's group (he is J's sister's son). However, given that C is a known joker and mimic, and that C and J are in the approved joking relationship, some humour is almost certainly intended too.

(8) C (to N): Ngapu, kataj parra-yi   kanyju-pal
                     father cut cut   1s0 below ACROSS

   J: | PUT-IM | jimpiri
                          | hole

   C: Jimpiri **yirra**-yi   wartarn-ta   jamana-rla
                     hole   put 1s0 arm   LOC leg   LOC

C (to N): Daddy, cut it across the bottom for me
                  (could also mean 'cut me across the bottom')

   J: | PUT | a hole (in it)

   C: **Put** a hole in the foreleg and hindleg for me
                     (could also mean 'put a hole in my hand and foot')

The examples of code-switching between SEG and Wanyjirra in most cases reflect an attempt by the speaker to 'shift ground' — to locate the discourse in a different social framework. In terms of our social arenas/triangular model, this is expressed by saying that R moves from one code expressing a social arena, to another, expressing a different arena. R is the referent in the discourse which links together the speaker S and P, who is, in most of the examples used so far, the unique participant who is a joint member of the Wanyjirra group. In the latter two examples, however, the situation is somewhat different. It is still possible though, to describe such examples in terms of the proposed model.

In the case of example (7), J is, as it were, embedding one triangle of social meaning, where G is the speaker, within the actual triangle operating with J as speaker, much as a subordinate clause is embedded in a main clause in syntax. J is recalling G's attitude to the shoulder, rather than directly expressing his own. In the diagram of example (7), Figure 12, I have represented the embedded triangle as a broken line triangle sharing the R node (the shoulder) with the triangle of actual relations. At this stage this is an informal treatment; more work will be needed to properly incorporate such examples into the theory.

With (8) one might attempt to diagram the situation simply as Figure 13, representing a person in a more inclusive group using a more exclusive group's language or dialect to talk to members of the latter. This may occur, without a particularly marked inter-pretation, and I do not intend to invoke any constraints like Constraint I to rule it out. In many such cases, however, there is an implied claim (serious or otherwise) to membership of the more

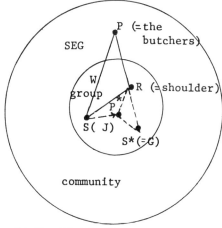

Figure 12. (for (7), Line 1)

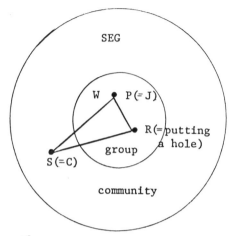

Figure 13.

exclusive group, in this use of switching, so that a more complex structure involving broken lines is more appropriate. This is the case in (8), which is not so much a matter of quotation, as of C insinuating, whether jokingly or not, that he is a member of the Wanyjirra group and therefore using the appropriate dialect form. Figure 14 therefore shows a created situation in which the speaker C, is shifted into the inner circle.

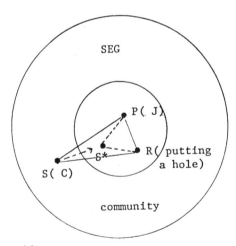

Figure 14.

We have now looked at seven of the basic eight ways in which the SPR triangle can fit into the two-tier configuration. For the sake of completeness, consider the case of a non-Wanyjirra SEG speaker talking in SEG to Wanyjirra participants. This is a situation commonly found in the text and is generally unmarked as a pattern, unlike 13 which is relatively rare. This asymmetry is probably accounted for by the proper inclusion property of the arenas model, and perhaps something akin to Constraint I on the interpretation of Participant should be added for Speaker.

Whatever further connotations may be created by individuals, or through discourse, there is a common core of feeling about the difference between a local dialect and the standard language Gurindji. Judging by the above examples, a major element in this is overall closeness of kinship ties in the local group arena, and a commensurate lack of value placed on non-kinship roles and relations, such as position in the cattle station workforce, Council etc. in that arena. It is for this reason that triangular kinterms are frequently associated with local dialect use, and that local dialect is used to reinforce adherence to traditional avoidance practice, on the basis of actual kin relations, as opposed to a looser 'matiness' of co-workers. Most importantly, it is this set of kin-based values which ensures that requests or claims for meat or assistance are most appropriately expressed in a shared local dialect, where this is possible. Sharing and help between kin is an obligation, and the closer the tie, the more pressing the obligation. 'Asking' for something (*yangki panu* and other verbs) is predicated on such ties, which are most significant in the local group.

Kinship ties of various kinds also exist, of course, among most people in the wider speech community. Fewer such ties are close, actual kinship links than in the local origin group, and more are distant and classificatory. Such links are therefore less intimate in general, and less strong in conferring rights and duties to others in terms of sharing food, and rendering other assistance. Also other types of relations, of a political or ritual nature within or between large communities or involving work relationships, etc. come into play more strongly, whereas in the local origin group context these are overshadowed by close kinship ties. It is for this reason that a switch to SEG from a local dialect indicates a less personal and more distant relationship, one in which larger numbers of people are involved, at the level of community, or cattle station. It is the dialect appropriate to questioning, or detaching oneself, from claims made on the basis of kinship ties, in the local dialect.

Code-switching between Gurindji and Kriol

A switch from W to SEG only takes the discourse one step up the in the hierarchy of social arenas, by transferring R into the second circle of the model, and thereby defining the S-P role relationship as being (at least temporarily) enacted at the wider speech community level. But there are further steps up the hierarchy of social arenas.

All Gurindji speakers also have Kriol as part of speech repertoire. For the youngest speakers it is their first language, Gurindji being acquired more slowly, and mostly as a passive competence. Most of the younger speakers have a better passive command of standard English than the older people, and actively control a more acrolectal Kriol (as well as basilectal), and, in some cases, fairly standard English too.

Kriol, in the model proposed here, is, for middle aged Gurindji at least, the language of the next higher social arena, which is equated here with Aborigines in general, of which the Gurindji community is a small part. There is of course a limit to the range of Aborigines with whom the Gurindji actually interact and use Kriol as a medium of expression. For most of them this would only include people in the cattle station belt of the central-west of the Northern Territory, and the Eastern Kimberleys of Western Australia; actual delimitation of this group is not particularly important.

In what follows there is little discussion of the variation within the local Kriol between forms which are closer to standard English, and those which are farther removed from it. Examples of this type of variation do occur in the text, and could well be regarded, in some cases, as a type of code-switching with social meaning (e.g. GET THE ... in (12) below). Neither the form nor the function of such variation/switching has been thoroughly studied, however, so it will only rate a brief mention here. For the most part switches will be referred to as between Gurindji (G) and

Kriol (K) without detailing the Kriol lect involved. Since there is no standard English in this text, switching involving Standard English (which does occur elsewhere) will not be discussed either. Since Standard English is not available to many speakers or frequently used and such speakers do not often distinguish between Kriol and Standard English, Kriol discourse usually covers a social arena which includes not only Aboriginal matters beyond the community level, but also many other matters relating to a wider social arena of the majority (English-speaking) culture and the social, economic and cultural systems associated with it.

From what has been said about the social functions of W/SEG switching, it might be hypothesized that K will bear a relation to G analogous to that which SEG bears to W, but on a higher level of generality, impersonality and social distance. This is what I intend to argue here, by looking at examples of K/G and G/K switching taken from the same 'butchering' text from which the W/SEG examples were drawn.

It has often been pointed out that code is switched to a more 'familiar' language or dialect when joking, swearing etc. occurs (Hatch 1976). There are a number of examples of a switch from K to G in order to make some joking or uncomplimentary remark about someone else, in the butchering text.

(9)   G: I'LL TAKE-IM BOTTOM AND GO BACK; | ngalking-ku

       | greedy   DAT

       kungulu-yawung
       blood   **PROP**

    J: I'LL HAVE-IM | kungulu-yawung. Nyuntu marntaj
                    | blood   **PROP**   you   all right

    G: I'LL TAKE THE BOTTOM AND GO BACK; | the bloody meat
                                         | is for greedy ones.

    J: | I'LL HAVE | the bloody meat. You're right.

This second part of G's contribution is a referent to J, who has just expressed a liking for bloody meat; *ngalking* 'greedy' can be interpreted as being fairly abusive. The different style of the two parts of both the above utterances is typical of K and G switches;

K often encodes statements about the speakers' intentions or attitude, or about the situation, which are relatively impersonal in the sense that they do not refer to another person (interlocutor or other referent). The contrasting G utterance directly (and often bluntly) refers to an interlocutor.

There are other examples of a K/G switch arising from a switch to a 'joking' mode of expression (that is, the more or less abusive type of joking characteristic of joking relationships). This switch can occur within a single speaker's utterance, or between two speakers, as in the following two examples, the first of which was already quoted as part of an example of SEG/W switching (example (2); see also Note 4).

(10) C (to N): YOU LITTLE BIT BAD HAND, YOU MIGHT CUT-IM
                 'IM . . .

    G: . . . | ngumparna   -marnany
          | brother-in-law your
_____

    C (to N): YOU'VE GOT A BIT OF A BAD HAND, YOU MIGHT
              CUT . . .

    G: . . . | your brother-in-law

---

(11) K: THIS ONE MINE

    G: | Ngalking ngana, warri-warri!
       | greedy   who   sorry
_____

    K: THIS IS MINE

    G: | Someone's greedy! sorry!

In both cases G is making a joking comment on someone he is not strictly in a joking relationship with. In the first case, J pulls him up in W; in the second G avoids direct abuse of his 'brother-in-law' K by saying 'someone' and using the conventional formula for sympathy usually used by someone else when their relation is abused.

Another joking interchange with a K/G switch is somewhat different:

(12)   C: GET THE | wirlka | NUMBER FOUR!
                | axe |

      J: | Nyampa-wu-rna   purlka   karri-nyangu-ku
          | WHAT   DAT 1sS grey hair   be PROG FUT

     C: GET THE | axe | NUMBER FOUR! |

     J: | What's the good of me going grey?

Here C is using parody. Here he is acting like a white man
(*kartiya*); this is shown by the style of giving the order, the grammar (GET THE . . . rather than K CATCH-IM . . . [kejim]), and the
form of direct address using a station nickname, 'Number Four',
unusual in Gurindji terms where subsection or kin terms are
usually used for address. J reacts by bringing the discourse well
back into Gurindji terms, by indirect reference to C's kinship
relation to J (*purlka* is a term for Mother's Brother), and jokingly
rejecting the idea of being ordered around (by a young man or a
white man).

    Other examples of K-G switching do not involve joking directed
at individual interlocutors, but semi-humorous comments on the
butchering situation as a whole.

(13)   G: THIS ONE MINE

      J: CUT-IM | nyawa | LITTLE BIT | wanyji-ka-warla |
                | this | | where LOC FOCUS |

        | RIB BONE FIRST
          TIME?

      G: | Kayili-yin   ngutji- ngutji- rla   yan-ku-rra-ngala
          north ABL haggle REDUP LOC go   FUT HORT linc1p0

    G: THIS ONE MINE

    J: CUT | this | A LITTLE BIT | where's | THE RIB BONE FIRST?

    G: | Let (the helicopter) from north come and see us haggling
        (over meat)

Here G injects an elements from the *kartiya* (white man's)
world into the discussion (the helicopter from the neighbouring
station which had been flying around) to throw the butchering
scene into relief, as it were. The helicopter is viewed as an out-

side presence here from the point of view of solidarity with the Gurindji people on the ground (cf. *-ngala*, inclusive 'we' used), and this is reinforced by choice of the Gurindji language.

The following example also contrasts the 'us' of the butchers, with a 'they', but the latter is a rather different group from that of the last example:

(14) J: CUT-IM RUMP, ROAST, CHUCK | **ngara** -ngala   -ngkulu
                                       LEST linc1p0 3pa

                                       yarriyi marnana
                                       say   PRES
- -
     J: CUT THE RUMP, ROAST AND CHUCK | so they don't grumble
     about us.

The first part has J well in the role of head stockman imperson-ally issuing orders, on the pattern of a white man, and using Eng-lish terms for cuts of meat. The switch indicates a more personal concern about the relationship between the people in the camp (*ngurra-ngarna*, camp people) and the butchers, about whether they will be satisfied with what they are given (a community level concern). It is interesting to note that a W form is used here (*ngara*) despite the fact that all the butchers are included in 'us': this, it seems indexes the fact that J and G (the W speakers) are the senior men present and the higher ranking ones in station work, so that most of the blame for any dissatisfaction would come to them, rather than to the SEG speakers.

J talking to all the butchers as head stockman also starts the next example in K but then switches to G (SEG) apart from a brief insertion in K.

(15) J: WE GOTTA GREENHIDE HERE YET | karla-rni-yin   yala-ngurlu
                                     | west UP ABL there ABL

       yuwa-rra. Kula-nta kaputa-rla   pan-ana.   Karla-yin | TOO
       put   IMP NEG 2pS night   LOC cut PRES West ABL |

       SKIN-IM | parntara-rni.   Kula kaputa nyawa-ma
                | whole   ONLY NEG night this   TOPIC

C: Ngayu karta   ngu-rna | TEA | kampa-wu, kaput . . .
    me MOD AUX 1sS | | cook   FUT morning

    YOU SEE-IM | jangkarni
              | big

J: WE'VE GOT A GREENHIDE HERE YET | Put it away from
   there, away from the upper west. You mob aren't
   butchering at night. | SKIN IT TOO | the whole lot, from
   the west | This isn't night-time.

C: I suppose I'll make the | TEA | in the morning . . . YOU CAN
   SEE | (the cow) is big.

J starts on the level of impersonal description of the situation in
K; for the order to an individual to do something about this situation, there is a switch to G. This contrasts with earlier examples of
J giving orders in K, but this may be because of the necessity to
switch 'down' a level for an instruction to an individual especially
as it involves a directional term. The next comment ('you mob
aren't butchering at night') indicates that there is no excuse
for the job to be hurried and left half done. The comment is
semi-humorous; the use of G also takes the edge off the chiding by
putting it in the context of solidarity of Aboriginal stockmen in
the self-regulation of their work, and of kinship-related joking
routines. C takes up the comment about 'night-time' to joke
further in G, that the stockmen might be butchering all night
because of the size of the cow.

A further example once again shows a K-G switch which follows
the shift from a general impersonal enquiry about a knife, to an
enquiry directed at the group of butchers.

(16) G: WHERE 'NOTHER KNIFE | walima | POCKET-KNIFE |
                              | any | |

      | karrwa-rnana?
      | have PRES

      G: WHERE'S THE OTHER KNIFE? | Does anyone have a | POCKET
      KNIFE? |

Similarly an impersonal enquiry about the state of the knife is
in K, but the joke directed at a joking partner which follows from
it is in G:

(17) G: 'IM SHARP?

J:		Marntaj; marntaj ngu mulu-ngku Ng- pija -ma . . .
		All right all right AUX this ERG foreskin TOPIC

G: IS IT SHARP?

J: | It's all right, sharp enough for N's foreskin.

We have seen how K-G switches represent moves from relatively impersonal statements or orders to more personal, affective utterances linked to solidarity on a local community basis (joking relationships, traditional or semi-traditional obligations, shared identity vis-à-vis other Aborigines or whites). Switches from G to K demonstrate the same kind of differences, moving in the opposite direction.

Sometimes the code contrast is used to point up group differences even within the community, by using K to give a relatively 'detached' external view of such differences. We have seen, in example (7), how a switch to G (and W) was used when mentioning the community back in the camp: an 'internal' view of a community difference. In the following example, (which is a continuation of example (7) above), J switches to K in the last sentence in order to make a distinction between 'camp-people' (*ngurra-ngarna*) and 'working fellas', and, half-jokingly, include C in the former category.

(18) J: HERE, R-, CUT-IM, GIVE IT LONGA 'IM | nyila **pampirla**
                                                            | that   shoulder

parra   kataj | NOW | Ngu-rna kang-ku   parntara-rni,
cut IMP cut | | AUX 1sS take FUT   whole ONLY

ngant-wu-warla?
who DAT FOCUS

G: Ngantu-ku?
   Who   ERG

C: ngayiny
   me DAT

J: | NO, YOU | ngurra-ngarna
              | camp   NOM

J: HERE, R-, CUT IT AND GIVE IT TO HIM | cut that **shoulder** |
    NOW | I'll take the whole lot, who is it for?

G: Who'll take it?

C: For me

J: | NO, YOU ARE A | camp-person

The original switch by J into G reflects a move from the impersonal head-stockman to a discussion of meat distribution within the community (the use of W *pampirla* here has already been discussed). When J wishes to rebut C's direct claim to the meat, J does it on the basis that he is not a 'working-fellow' i.e. not regularly officially employed by the station at the time, and therefore, although he is actually helping with the butchering, he is to be regarded as a 'camp-person'. These sentiments are very much in line with *kartiya* (white man) values about the running of a cattle station. As such this statement is at least partially a joke, but one which reflects a real contradiction discussed above about limiting the distribution of meat. Since a *kartiya* or general societal viewpoint is much in evidence, the language is switched 'up' to K, although the actual term for 'camp-people' is in Gurindji, as in some of its uses it reflects a division also as seen from the community level.

C takes up this same point in a joking way later in example (19) below, again switching into K to do so.

It must be noted that no particular rhetorical category is necessarily correlated with a particular language. We have seen examples of switching into G to make jokes, but G does not have the monopoly on jokes. Speakers also switch from G into K to make jokes; the jokes however, are of a different kind.

(19) C: Nyawa-ma   jutany   ngu man-ku   murlu-ngku . . .
         this   TOPIC neckbone AUX get   FUT   this ERG

      J: J^2 - tu
         ERG

      C: | M - **kuya**-wula
         REL   2dS

      G: CHICKEN . . . FOWL | -u | THEY WANT-IM NECK BEEF
                        | DAT |

J: | Punyu?
   good?

G: | YEAH, 'IM FEED-IM CHOOKY-CHOOKIES

C: FOWL LONGA FOWL-SHED GOOD WORKER; HE'LL WAKE-IM
   UP YOU EVERY MORNING.

C: This neck bone will be got by . . .

J: J²-

C: M's **wife**

G: | THEY WANT THE NECK BEEF FOR THE FOWLS

J: | Good?

G: | YEAH, IT FEEDS THE CHOOKS

C: THE FOWLS IN THE FOWL-SHED ARE GOOD WORKERS;
   THEY WAKE YOU UP EVERY MORNING.

C is talking about meat distribution, in Gurindji, the normal language for this. J interposes a joke against his joking partner, J². After C throws in a joke in Wanyjirra (cf. example (6)), G, as he frequently does, switches up to K to make a more general comment about the use of the neck beef, unrelated to kinship considerations and more in the context of the modern activity of keeping chickens. C then makes a joke on the basis of the worker/non-worker distinction; the chickens are getting beef because they are supposedly good station workers, whereas he is having it withheld because he is supposedly not a 'worker', although he is working. Such a play on concepts relies heavily on being within the type of discourse associated with the economics of 'modern' cattle station operations, for which K is more appropriate.

In speaking of a cow, J switches to K from G:

(20) J: Nyawa-warluk parra | NOT BELONGING TO THIS COUNTRY
        This   FIRST CutIMP |

    J: Cut this first | (That cow) DOESN'T BELONG TO THIS
       COUNTRY.

As with the talk of workers and camp-people above, the choice of K here indicates that the framework here is of cattle-stations and stockwork, that this cow has strayed from another station.

A direct translation into Gurindji, using the Gurindji word for 'country' would probably suggest more a statement about traditional ownership of land than modern station boundaries.

In the proposed model of the Gurindji situation, two or more social arenas are available to every speaker, and events may be defined as belonging to more than one of these virtually simultaneously. In the following examples (of which (21) has been already partly analysed as example (4)), the same underlying assertion (a claim by the speaker to a particular cut of meat) which we have encountered in different forms several times already, is phrased in three different codes successively. In all three cases the order of codes is Wanyjirra, Kriol then Standard Eastern Gurindji. This order does show an increase in 'social distance' in the first switch. On the basis of these examples I could not claim that this order is particularly significant generally; it is motivated by the speaker's strategy as analysed below.

(21) J: Nyawa-ma   ngu-yi **nganinga**
        This   TOPIC AUX 1s0   mine

    G: | I WANT-IM THIS SKIRT

    K: WHAT ABOUT THE WIRE?

    G: | Kujarra | THERE | ngayiny-ma,   Jangari
        two | | mine   TOPIC   =K

    J: This is **mine**

    G: | I WANT THIS SKIRT (meat)

    K: WHAT ABOUT THE WIRE?

    G: There are two | THERE | that are mine, Jangari (K)

Here J's use of W indicates foregrounding of the relationship between him and G (as discussed earlier). G makes his claim first (in a way which is far removed from this mode), by reporting it as a property of his feelings (I WANT-IM), apparently devoid of social connotations. Gurindji does not have an equivalent of English/Kriol *'want'*, in fact, and Kriol seems to be the medium for expressing what are in fact claims of a share in a particular group's goods as statements about one's self (I want, I like ... etc.), overtly devoid of social context. In the last sentence, however, G makes his claim more straightforwardly in terms of the butchering group using SEG and addressing K by a subsection term.

The next passage, spoken entirely by G, follows a similar pattern: a direct claim in W, a statement of personal preference in K, followed by an enquiry about the distribution of meat in terms of the butchers and community, in SEG.

(22) G: **Nganinga, nganinga** | I LIKE-IM FAT OUTSIDE AND |
        mine   mine

niyan nywawa nyata?
flesh this   which way?

— —

    G: **Mine, mine** | I LIKE FAT OUTSIDE AND | where's this meat going?

I have not attempted to apply the social arenas/triangular model in detail to the case of three nested arenas, although the main lines of how this more complex model would work can be discerned from the earlier two-arena configuration. Without detailed comment I present Figure 15, representing the use of Kriol in example 21. In Figure 15, the appeal is to a wider perspective than the actual P, the butchers, and by constraint I, the

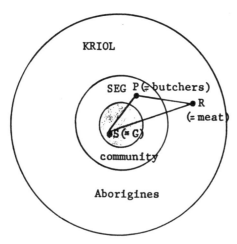

Figure 15.

interpretation of P is that this group are to be regarded in the wider more inclusive group associated with Kriol.

We have seen that the uses of K in contrast to G in this text can be seen as positive and negative. In its positive form, the use of K stresses that the matter spoken of is viewed from a non-community, non-traditional outlook (such as that of a head stockman or manager in a European model of this role). In its negative form, the use of K indicates that factors associated with the G social arenas (speech community and local origin group) such as pervasive kinship rights and duties, are being ignored or played down. The two may seem to be merely two facets of the same function; it seems important to distinguish them because they reflect the question of markedness of the codes. In this particular text, as has been noted, K and G are about evenly distributed. If K is mainly viewed *negatively* though, it is the *unmarked* code in this type of discourse: it is the neutral language used when there is no particular reason for choosing otherwise. K's position of association with the wider, overarching social arena which includes the smaller community groups, would tend to make it the unmarked form. There is some indication that this is the case for the younger speakers in the present text. They certainly use Kriol slightly more frequently, and they may use it in circumstances where the older ones do not. What is harder to say is whether this may partly result from a gradual change in the field of discourse, as well as in code; perhaps the younger people actually talk less in terms of the kinship and local group ideologies than older people do, and it is partly for this reason that they use less Gurindji.

Conclusions

In the model adopted here the speaker decides in which social arena the referent R is to be placed; that decision is not, in most cases, made for him by the type of discourse topic or other aspects of the situation. In the preceding extracts from the text we have seen many examples where the choice of language is not dependent on fixed attributes of the interlocutors, situation or topic. Many such examples can, however, be analyzed in terms of the social arenas in which the speaker *wishes to place* his relation to the interlocutor, and/or another referent, for the purposes of the discourse. In this way, *point of view* towards a person, thing or event can be expressed.

Shifting social arenas in discourse can be indexed by language choice amongst the Gurindji as kinship relations between speaker and referents can be indexed by the use of triangular kinship terms. The use of different dialects of Gurindji, and the use of Kriol instead of Gurindji, or Gurindji instead of Kriol, each carries with it a social meaning in terms of the background arena against which the elements of discourse are to be viewed. Such language-related arenas may not be absolutely and rigidly definable, but the differences between them in relative terms is apparent.

The social arenas/triangular model which I have advanced here is a way of showing how social meanings are organised in code-switching. It is based mainly on the work of Scotton and Ury (1977), but has significant differences from that model. In the present model, social arenas are defined on the basis of local ideology; the need for a configuration which shows the relations between arenas is insisted upon; and the points of the triangle are defined as speaker, participant and referent. One form of the model, involving two nested social arenas, and one constraint on interpretation of the position of R, has been extensively illustrated and shown to be useful in the Gurindji case. Some further variations and extensions of the model to deal with more than two arenas, and with cases of quasi-quotation and the creation of artificial situations, using secondary triangles, have been introduced.

The meaning bearing function of code-switching is what has been our main concern here. This function is not to be considered necessarily secondary or metaphorical in relation to 'situational' code-switching, nor is it in any way less important than 'macro-linguistic' concerns about 'domain' (Fishman 1972), or questions of the markedness of code-switching. Code-switching can certainly be seen as more or less marked relative to an accompanying social situation. For instance, the idea that the use of Kriol is a relatively unmarked option in more and more situations may be a way of characterising the progress of language shift among the Gurindji.

This brings us to the question of the evolving language situation among the Gurindji. Can our approach to code-switching tell us about the future of Gurindji and Kriol in this area? Can we develop a more satisfactory model of the language changes which are having profound effects on this and most other surviving Aboriginal languages? If we can, will it help us to apply this knowledge to assist the Aboriginal groups who are concerned about these changes?

I have elsewhere (McConvell 1983, 1985) explored some other aspects of this set of important problems. Here I wish to conclude by making a few brief remarks about the possible contribution of the model of code-switching advanced here.

Studies of language decay and death have pointed to decline in the functional range of the subordinate language as a symptom of its pathological stage. The functional range may be considered in relation to the factors of situation or 'domain' already discussed: interlocutors, place or setting, and topic. Certainly in many language shift situations, one might find e.g. use of the minority language first declining and finally disappearing in public functions, and this process only happening later in the home. (This is not always the pattern; it may be the reverse).

From our present perspective, such generalizations could be of less interest than the analysis of the actual use of different languages within a single 'domain' or across 'domains'. It is unlikely that the shift ever takes place in a single step from Language A, entirely, to Language B, entirely. An interim period involving code-switching is likely to occur. If the examples of 'non-situational' code-switching we have discussed have more general validity, then this 'transitional' code-switching too will involve expressions of 'social meanings' not determined by 'situational factors' in the above sense.

It is quite possible, indeed likely, that there are changes in the patterns of code-switching involved in this process of language shift, and that these changing patterns represent changes in the assignment of social meaning to the different languages involved. Thus in the case we have been examining, the Gurindji situation, there is an apparent shift in progress between Gurindji and Kriol. Not much of this change seems to be related specifically to language domain or function, and even if some statement could be made about this, it would not be particularly enlightening about most of the changes in the use of the two languages. As we have seen, the use of Kriol at a certain stage, as against Gurindji, can signify that an event or relationship being talked about is being seen from a more general, less local and less kin-based viewpoint (perhaps deriving from its original lingua franca status). At a later stage, or among a younger group, the use of Kriol could lose these specific connotations and take on some of the 'social meanings' previously associated with Gurindji. Concurrently, Gurindji would become more highly 'marked' and restricted in the social meanings of solidarity etc. which it expresses.

Such changes could be formulated, in terms of the triangular social arenas model advanced here, as changes in the scope and configuration of the social arenas associated with languages, relative to each other. In terms of an additional 'social-situational markedness' theory associated with the model, use of a particular code could change its markedness value and this could eventually lead to a change in the language-social arena configuration itself. This is in line with a theory of change of social meaning in codeswitching which parallels a theory of change in lexical meaning, in which 'marked' occurrence of lexical items in new environments may precede a change in substantive meaning of the item.

Thus in the Gurindji case, the use of Kriol in an intimate group could be changing from a marked one of detachment, certain types of jokes, talking 'down' to a younger person etc. to a more neutral one lacking that special set of meanings. Conversely, Gurindji could be becoming more marked as an indicator of arenas of certain traditional relations, involving ritual etc. The roles of the languages could then be redefined in terms of social arenas. Ultimately such a process would end in total language shift if these small shifts continued in the same direction. At no intermediate stage would the shift necessarily be obvious as the total loss or gain of a 'domain' for either language.

Notes

1. I did linguistic fieldwork on the Gurindji and Mudbura languages between 1974 and 1977 at Daguragu station, Northern Territory, Australia as a

Research Fellow in Linguistics with the Australian Institute of Aboriginal Studies. During this period I lived with the Gurindji people and was an observer and participant-observer of many hours of conversation between them, and between Gurindji and other nearby groups (Mudbura, Ngarinyman, Warlpiri etc.). The film referred to was made towards the end of this period, when I was already familiar with the Eastern Gurindji and Wanyjirra dialects, and with various speech styles ('mix-im-up', avoidance, joking, etc.). The film was not made with the specific intention of studying code-switching, but simply as an ethnographic document. Transcription was done originally with the aim of subtitling the film in English, and it was during the work of transcription aided by C and J that my attention began to focus on code-switching. Until then, I had followed the linguist's usual path of trying to record the grammar and lexicon of the traditional languages in their pristine form. The film brought to my attention forcefully what I had previously observed but neglected to study: the pervasive code-switching which is the unmarked style of speech of Aboriginal people in the area today. The film has not been fully edited or subtitled, and is lodged with the Australian Institute of Aboriginal Studies, Canberra. An earlier version of this paper was presented to the Applied Linguistics Association of Australia conference in Melbourne (1983).

2. Kriol is the name given by Sandefur (1982) to an English-based Creole widely spoken by Aborigines in the North-central cattle station belt of the Northern Territory and in neighbouring parts of Western Australia and Queensland. It has been more commonly known to Aborigines as 'Pidgin English', 'Broken English' and 'Blackfella English'. Although introduced into the Wave Hill area (where Gurindji is spoken) in the late nineteenth and early twentieth century, it was for some time used only as a second (often third or fourth) language of wider communication with Whites (*kartiya*) and Aborigines who were outside the usual multilingual speech community in the area. In the last thirty years it has begun to replace the traditional languages of the area as the first language. Many older speakers find this situation confusing and disturbing. Discussion of the possible relations between the type of code-switching discussed in this paper, and the apparent language shift in progress is to be found in McConvell (1985).

In this paper I have used a transcription of Kriol which retains English spelling for words which are of English origin (almost all). This is not in accord with Sandefur's practice of using a phonemic spelling, which has also been adopted by schools in which Kriol is used e.g. Bamyili. I have decided on this in order to make it easier for the reader to read the Kriol parts of the text, and because phonetic or phonemic accuracy is not particularly important for present purposes. The orthography used for Gurindji is the same as that used for Warlpiri, Walmajarri (Hudson 1980) and other languages, and in Gurindji books published by the Summer Institute of Linguistics.

3. 'Topic' may be interpreted to reflect the notion of 'topic' as the item around which other information is assembled in the sentence. In this sense, 'John' is the topic in 'John was left behind by the others', indicating that 'What happened to John?' is the most prominent presupposed question. This type of function has overt marking in Gurindji: the suffix -*ma*. However, topic in this sense may change very frequently from sentence to sentence (as can be seen from the shifting placement of -*ma* in the text), without much bearing on language choice.

What is usually intended is a broader notion, which perhaps may be answered by the question 'what are they talking about?, about a longer stretch of discourse. The answer to such a question is not always easy to give, as many different strands may be interwoven in even a short conversation. The conversation we are to analyze may appear to be exceptionally homogeneous in this regard: the interlocutors are butchering a cow, and the great majority of their utterances could be classed as being about the topic 'butchering a cow'. We shall see how deceptive such an answer is, and how little it tells us about the underlying social relations which are also mentioned, often parenthetically, and therefore what little help such a concept of topic gives us in analysing the code-switching which takes place.

While the term 'topic' does not appear at first sight to be useful here in these two senses, or in any of the numerous other ways in which it is used, it may be able to be more rigorously defined and to play a role in the theory of code-switching. Where whole phrases, sentences or longer passages appear in a language, the identity of the 'referent' which is central to the switch must be definable within the theory, and some explanation given of its relation to the other material which is switched along with it. It seems likely that such a relation would be definable in terms of information structure, rather than grammatical structure, and the notion 'topic' could well come in here. This is not further investigated here.

4. Circumcision (*marntiwa* and other associated rites, known as 'making young man' in Aboriginal English) is one of the main rituals of the Gurindji and neighbouring groups. Boys generally go through this ceremony in early puberty. Suggesting that someone is not circumcised and should be is a stock part of the teasing repertoire in a joking relationship. Circumcision also creates special ties between the circumciser and the initiand and his family, some of which involve avoidance practices: this aspect is raised by G in the text following passage (11).

References

Alatis, J. E. ed.
  1970 *Bilingualism and language contact.* Monograph series on language
        and linguistics, 23. Washington D.C.: Georgetown University Press.
Ardener, E. ed.
  1971 *Social Anthropology and Language.* ASA Monograph 10, London,
        Tavistock.
Baetens Beardsmore, H.
  1982 *Bilingualism: basic principles.* Clevedon: Tieto.
Bani, E.
  1976 The language situation in the Torres Strait, in Sutton ed.
Blom J. P. and J. J. Gumperz
  1972 Some social determinants of verbal behaviour, in Gumperz and
        Hymes eds.
Brown, R. and A. Gilman
  1960 The pronouns of power and solidarity in Sebeok ed. pp. 253–276.
Cazden, C. B., V. P. John and D. Hymes eds.
  1972 *Functions of language in the classroom.* New York: Teachers'
        College Press.
Clyne, M. ed.
  1985 *Australia – – Meeting Place of Languages.* Canberra: Pacific
        Linguistics.
Day, R.
  1983 The language situation on Mer, *Ngali*, Batchelor: School of Austra-
        lian Linguistics.
Denison, N.
  1971 Some observations of language variety and plurilingualism, in
        Ardener ed. pp. 157–184.
Dil, A. S. ed.
  1972 *Language in Sociocultural Change.* Stanford University Press.
Dixon, R. M. W.
  1980 *The Languages of Australia.* Cambridge University Press.
Elwell, V.
  1982 Some factors affecting multilingualism among Aboriginal Austra-
        lians. *IJSL*, 36, pp. 83–104.
Fishman, J. A.
  1972 The relationship between micro- and macro-linguistics in the study
        of who speaks what to whom and when, in Dil ed.
Gumperz, J. J. and E. Hernandez-Chavez
  1972 Bilingualism, bidialectalism and classroom interaction, in Cazden
        et al. eds.

Gumperz, J.J. and D.Hymes eds.
1972   *Directions in Sociolinguistics.* New York: Holt.

Hansen, K.
1974   *Pintubi Kinship.* Alice Springs: Institute for Aboriginal Development.

Hatch, E.
1976   Studies in language switching and mixing, in McCormack and Wurm, eds. pp.201–214.

Hathaway, L.H.
1982   Style shifting as a metaphorical change in point of view. *Chicago Linguistic Society* 18, pp.185–190.

Haviland, J.
1982   Kin and country at Wakooka Outstation: an exercise in rich interpretation. *IJSL*, 36.

Heath, J., F. Merlan and A. Rumsey eds.
1982   *Languages of kinship in Aboriginal Australia.* Oceania Linguistic Monograph 24: University of Sydney.

Hudson, J.
1980   *The Core of Walmajarri Grammar.* Canberra: Australian Institute of Aboriginal Studies.

Lambert, R.D. and B.F.Freed eds.
1982   *The Loss of Language Skills.* Rowley: Newbury House.

Laughren, M.
1982   Warlpiri Kinship Structure, in Heath et al. eds. 72–85.

Lee, J.
1983   *Tiwi Today.* Ph.D. thesis, Canberra: Australian National University.

McConvell, P.
1980   Hierarchical Variation in Pronominal Clitic Attachment in the Eastern Ngumbin Languages, in Rigsby and Sutton eds. pp.31–117.
1982   Neutralisation and degree of respect in Gurindji, in Heath et al. eds. pp.86–106.
1983   Domains and Domination. *Aboriginal Languages Association Newsletter* 5.
1985   Domains and Code-switching among bilingual Aborigines, in Clyne ed. 95–125.

McCormack, W.C. and S.A.Wurm
1976   *Language and Man: Anthropological Issues.* The Hague: Mouton.

McKay, G.R. ed.
1982   Australian Aborigines: Sociolinguistic Studies. *IJSL* 36.

O'Grady, G. K. N. and K. Mooney
  1973 Nyangumarda Kinship Terminology. *Anthropological Linguistics* 15, pp. 1−23
Rigsby, B. and Sutton eds.
  1980 Papers in Australian Linguistics: Contributions to Australian Linguistics. *Pacific Linguistics* A 59.
Sandefur, J.
  1982 Kriol and the question of decreolisation. *IJSL* 36, pp. 5−13
Scotton, C. M.
  1976 Strategies of neutrality: language choice in uncertain situations. *Language*, 52.4, pp. 919−941.
Scotton, C. M. and W. Ury
  1977 Bilingual strategies: the social functions of code-switching. *IJSL*, 13.
Sebeok, T. A. ed.
  1960 *Style in language.* Cambridge: MIT Press.
Sutton, P. ed.
  1976 *Languages of Cape York.* Canberra: Australian Institute of Aboriginal Studies.
Wierzbicka, A.
  1980 *Lingua Mentalis: the Semantics of Natural Language.* New York: Academic Press.

Code switching as indexical of social negotiations

Carol Myers Scotton
University of South Carolina

Introduction

This paper provides an overall explanation of code switching, using primarily an East African data base.[1] A number of previous studies have dealt with code switching in East African contexts. Their emphasis, however, has been different (Abdulaziz-Mkilifi 1972; Abdulaziz 1982; Whiteley 1974; and Scotton 1982a), or their explanations have not been comprehensive (Parkin 1974; Scotton 1976; Scotton and Ury 1977). Some of these studies will be mentioned in the synthesis attempted here.

The model developed here focuses on social consequences as motivating linguistic code choices and how speakers use conversational implicatures to arrive at the intended consequences. In this sense, it extends the markedness model of Scotton (1983), proposed to explain code choice in general, but its focus is more specific. The premise of Scotton (1983) is that in addition to relying on a cooperative principle, its associated maxims, and the conversational implicatures which they generate in understanding the content of what is said (Grice 1975), speakers use a complementary negotiation principle to arrive at the relational import of a conversation. The negotiation principle directs the speaker to 'choose the form of your conversational contribution such that it symbolizes the set of rights and obligations which you wish to be in force between speaker and addressee for the current exchange' (Scotton 1983: 116). A set of maxims referring to the choice of one linguistic variety rather than another relates to this principle, and the speaker's following or flouting the maxims generates implicatures about proposed interpersonal relationships.

While conveying referential information is often the overt purpose of conversation, all talk also always is a negotiation of rights and obligations between speaker and addressee. Referential content – what the conversation is about – obviously contributes to the social relationships of participants, but with content kept constant, different relational outcomes may result. This is because the particular linguistic variety used in an exchange carries social meaning. This model assumes that all linguistic code choices are indexical of a set of rights and obligations holding between participants in the conversational exchange. That is, any code choice points to a particular interpersonal balance, and it is partly because of their indexical qualities that different languages, dialects, and styles are maintained in a community.

Speakers have tacit knowledge of this indexicality as part of their communicative competence (Hymes 1972). They have a natural theory of markedness. The result is that all speakers have mental representations of a matching between code choices and rights and obligations sets. That is, they know that for a particular conventionalized exchange, a certain code choice will be the unmarked realization of an expected rights and obligations set between participants. They also know that other possible choices are more or less marked because they are indexical of other than the expected rights and obligations set. Their reference to other sets depends on their association with other conventionalized exchanges for which they are unmarked choices. While the theory is universal, actual associations are speech community specific, with speakers knowing what code choice is unmarked and which others are marked for exchanges conventionalized in the community.

A conventionalized exchange is any interaction for which speech community members have a sense of 'script'. They have this sense because such exchanges are frequent in the community to the extent that at least their medium is routinized. That is, the variety used or even specific phonological or syntactic patterns or lexical items employed are predictable. In many speech communities, service exchanges, peer to peer informal talks, doctor patient visits, or job interviews are examples of conventionalized exchanges.

Exchanges themselves are realized as speech events consisting of specific participants, a code choice and a rights and obligations balance between the participants. The rights and obligations balance for a speech event is derived from whatever situational features are salient to the exchange, such as status of participants, topic, etc. The salient features will not be the same across all types of exchanges; they are, however, relatively constant across speech events under a single type of exchange. The following example shows a change in feature salience as the exchange type changes from an interaction between strangers to an interaction as ethnic brethren. Initial interactions with security guards at places of business in Nairobi constitute a conventionalized exchange in the speech community. The most salient feature in this exchange is the visitor's appearance of being a Kenyan African or not. If the visitor is apparently a local African, the unmarked choice is Swahili, a relatively ethnically neutral lingua franca widely used across the Kenyan populace. (Observations at a number of Nairobi places of business showed that Swahili indeed is the unmarked choice across a number of different speech events realizing this type of exchange.) However, if the conversation develops so that shared ethnic group membership is recognized, then the interaction is perceived as a speech event under a different conventionalized exchange type. It is not an exchange between strangers who are Africans, but an exchange between strangers who share ethnic identity. In this case the most salient of their social features is the shared ethnicity and the unmarked choice for such an exchange is the shared mother tongue. The following example illustrates changes in the salience of the social features of the situation. It also shows that the same uninterrupted sequence of conversational turns can constitute more than one exchange type.

(Entrance to the IBM Nairobi head office. The visitor, who is a school principal in the Luyia area of Western Kenya, approaches. He speaks English and Swahili fluently in addition to his first language, a Luyia variety.)

Security Guard (Swahili): Unataka kumwona nani? 'Whom do you want to see?'
Visitor (Swahili): Napenda kumwona Solomon Inyama. 'I want to see Solomon Inyama.'

Guard (Swahili): Unamjua kweli? Tunaye Solomon Amuhaya — nadhani ndio yule. 'Do you really know him? We have a Solomon Amuhaya — I think that's the one you mean.'

Visitor (Swahili): Yule anayetoka Tiriki — yaani Mluyia. 'The one who comes from Tiriki — that is, a Luyia person.'

Guard (smiles) (switches to Luyia). Solomon mwenuyu wakhumanya vulahi? 'Does Solomon know you?'

Visitor (Luyia): Yivi mulole umovolere ndi Shem Lusimba yenyanga khukhulola. 'You see him and tell him that Shem Lusimba wants to see you.'

Guard (Luyia): Yikhala yalia ulindi. 'Sit here and wait.'

(At this point another visitor comes in.)

Visitor II (Swahili): Bwana Kamidi yuko hapa? 'Is Mr. Kamidi here?'

Guard (Swahili): Ndio yuko — anafanya kazi saa hii. Hawezi kuiacha mpaka iwe imekwisha. Kwa hivyo utaketi hapa mpaka aje. Utangoja kwa dakika kama kumi tano hivi. 'Yes, he's here — he is doing something right now. He can't leave until he finishes. Therefore you will wait here until he comes. You will wait about five or ten minutes.'

(Then Guard goes to look for Solomon Amuhaya.)

Speech events among white collar office personnel constitute another type of conventionalized exchange in Nairobi. In this case, educational attainment is a more salient feature than simply being a Kenyan African or not. English is a frequent unmarked choice in such speech events, extensive observation indicated. An example follows:

(The conversation takes place in a downtown office building. Herman, a young man who has finished secondary school and who comes from Western Kenya, is visiting a relative of his. They first converse alone in their shared mother tongue. Then, the relative switches to English as he shows him around within earshot of fellow workers.)

Relative (to Herman): And, you, are you looking for employment or have you got a job already? You look very smart as someone who is working.

Herman: I haven't got a job yet. I'm still looking for one.

Fellow worker of relative: So you have visitors. I can see you're showing someone around.

Relative: Yes, these are my visitors.

While I speak of an unmarked choice, the singular is used only as a convenience. The model calls for a markedness continuum:

speakers operate with degrees of markedness, not categorical distinctions. They perceive one or more choices are more unmarked than others; and among marked choices some are more marked than others. Further, the same choice is not necessarily unmarked for all participants in the same exchange. For example, structured observations in many Nairobi offices showed that English and Swahili are both unmarked choices for conversation among fellow workers, although each one seems more unmarked under different conditions (see Scotton 1982b).

Of course far from all exchanges are conventionalized. Very often, situations arise for which norms of behaviour are not established, or conflicting norms apply, and an unmarked choice is not clear. In such cases, community members have no communal sense of how individual participants are expected to carry out such an exchange, no sense of 'script'. Non-conventionalized exchanges typically include such situations as lengthy conversations with strangers (if their social identities remain unknown), interactions as the superior of a former peer, or conversation as a peer with someone of a much older generation. In such cases, both speaker and addressee recognize that any linguistic choice is exploratory, intended as a candidate to become the index of a mutually acceptable relationship — to become the unmarked choice.

Speaking of choices as marked or not assumes that they take place in a normative framework. Yet, norms do not determine choices. Rather, norms determine the relative markedness of a linguistic code for a particular exchange, given the association of the code with a specific rights and obligations set. What the norms do, then, is give all speakers a grammar of consequences. Speakers are free to make any choices, but how their choices will be interpreted is not free. The mental representations of the 'histories' of possible choices (and their associated rights and obligations sets) is the backdrop against which the choosing of one linguistic variety rather than another is played out. (This sets up a three-way association between the speaker, the addressee, and the speech event).

The choices themselves are negotiations in the sense that, given the normative framework, speakers make their choices as goal-oriented actors. They weigh the relative costs and rewards of their choices in seeking a good outcome (Thibaut and Kelley

1959; Brown and Levinson 1978). In this way, choices are creative and 'localize' the construction of a speech event.

Three main types of choices are possible. Making the unmarked choice in a conventionalized exchange is a negotiation to recognize the status quo as the basis for the present speech event, since it is indexical of the rights and obligations balance which is expected, given the salient situational factors. But speakers also can make marked choices in conventionalized exchanges. Such a choice is a dis-identification with the expected. It is a call for some balance other than the expected one since it indexes a rights and obligations set which is unexpected, given the salient situational factors. Finally, far from all exchanges are conventionalized and choices in such cases are seen as the nominating of some rights and obligations set as in effect for the present exchange, as the unmarked basis pro temp.

It can be seen, then, that there is an interplay between societal factors and more dynamic, individual considerations in the choice of linguistic varieties as media for conversational exchanges. The mentally-represented normative framework is the primary source of the consequences of choices. It makes speakers aware of the relative markedness of choices for a given exchange and likely outcomes. Speakers, however, are free to assert their individual motivations since, whatever their markedness, all choices are open to them. Finally, another dynamic aspect is that all choices, unmarked or not, are basically negotiations, requiring reciprocity from the addressee, making the construction of any speech event an ultimately cooperative enterprise.

Specifically in reference to code switching, this markedness model has some of the same concerns as Scotton and Ury (1977). That is, both models stress switching as simultaneously a tool and an index. For the speaker, switching is a tool, a means of doing something (by affecting the rights and obligations balance). For the listener, switching is an index, a symbol of the speaker's intentions. Switching, therefore, is both a means and a message. The model developed in the 1977 paper, however, treated all switching as a strategy to change social relationships. Within the terms of the markedness model, attempting to change relationships involves making a marked choice, but it is only one possible motivation for switching. The markedness model predicts switching as a realization of one of three negotiations: in conventionalized exchanges, switching may be an unmarked choice between bilingual peers, or with any participants it may be a marked choice; in non-conventionalized exchanges, switching is an exploratory choice presenting multiple identities.

The psychological reality of switching as encoding such negotiations has been demonstrated empirically in two studies of reactions of local speech community members to switching in contexts familiar to them (Scotton and Ury 1977, Scotton 1982a). In both studies, facsimile audio recordings of actual conversations were played to subjects. Local persons served as amateur actors, with the identities of the original participants masked. Subjects were told they would hear possible conversations taking place in Western Kenya, their home area. They were told they would be asked questions 'about the relationships' of the people in the conversation, but their attention was not drawn to the code switching, or even language usage in general.

Results were consistent with the explanations proposed here and were significant, according to certain statistical tests.[2] Also of interest is that subjects regularly attributed to speakers socio-psychological motivations with interpersonal consequences, based on their language use. That is, first of all, they regularly mentioned code choices, and second, they did not link switching to folk explanations taking account only of the speaker (rather than the interaction), such as 'he switches because he can't think of the right word' or 'he is just used to speaking different languages'.

Code switching is defined as the use of two or more linguistic varieties in the same conversation, without prominent phonological assimilation of one variety to the other. Most studies have dealt with switching between two or more distinctive languages, but the same motivations account for switching between dialects (Blom and Gumperz 1972) or styles of the same language (Gumperz 1978; Scotton 1985); Switching may be either intra- or extrasentential and often (but not necessarily) involves stretches of more than one word. East African data, at least, shows that the free morpheme constraint on switching proposed by Sankoff and Poplack (1981) does not apply.[3] In Scotton (1983b) numerous switches between an L1 bound morpheme and an L2 morpheme which is not integrated into L1 are shown. For example:

(Swahili) Ni nani alispoil kamba yetu?
'Who spoiled our rope?'

a-	-li-	-i-	-spoil
subject	past tense	object	verb stem

Such hybrid forms occur especially where an international language is used daily as a second language *and* is expanding into settings in which an indigenous language had been the dominant or exclusive unmarked choice. Among educated bilinguals in various African capitals, for example, or in other parts of the Third World, something approaching a melange of two varieties (an international language which either has official status locally or is the unmarked medium of international contacts and an indigenous mother tongue) is common, especially for informal interactions. (The discussion below on overall code switching as an unmarked choice relates to such usage.)

Agreeing on labels for these innovating varieties is a problem, with the use of 'code mixing' alongside 'code switching' as somewhat unfortunate. This is so for two reasons. First, some writers use 'mixing' for what is referred to here as 'switching'; but others use mixing for intrasentential shifts only, reserving 'switching' for intersentential switches. The overlap of reference results in confusion. Second, others use 'mix' for what they see as a development beyond switching, with more integration of the two varieties than under switching (Kachru 1978: 108). The problem is that the term 'mix' implies unprincipled chaos.

The fusion may be such that the two components form something distinct from either donor system. Gibbons speaks of the combination of English and Cantonese used by some in Hong Kong in these terms, as 'an autonomous system' (1979: 116). (Within the model developed here, such a fused variety could develop from an overall pattern of switching as an unmarked choice, especially if it remains in place with frequent use over a period of time. However, this is not a necessary development, nor does it follow that the use of the innovating variety need convey the same social meaning as overall switching does. This will be discussed below.)

In some (or in many?) cases, such amalgamating varieties may be ephemeral, associated with age grading in a way analagous to teenage slang. For example, such a variety called 'Sheng' is current today in Nairobi among the young. While it combines elements of Swahili and English (its name coming from the 's' and 'h' from Swahili and 'eng' from English), the results diverges from both. Sheng does seem to follow many of the syntactic rules of Swahili (but not all); but it has a new lexicon, including some Swahili morphemes (especially the inflectional ones), many English ones (but typically with new meanings), and also some entirely novel morphemes.[4]

Distinguishing code switching from borrowing presents another problem.[5] Trying to resolve this problem on a structural basis, considering degree of assimilation, yields no useful results. First, assimilation is a gradient, not a categorical, concept, and can provide us only with a continuum as a metric for evaluation. Second, while an expected hypothesis is that borrowed morphemes are more assimilated phonologically into L1 than switched morphemes, what about the many clearly established borrowings which show little assimilation? (For example, *town* [taun] 'city center' shows next to no assimilation as a common loan into diverse Kenyan African languages spoken in Nairobi.) Third, what about the relative weight of phonological assimilations vs. morphological assimilation? One may or may not be accompanied by the other. Thus, an educated Tanzanian who knows both English and Swahili may say *u-si-ni-misundastand* (second person singular subject prefix-NEGATIVE prefix-first person singular object prefix-MISUNDERSTAND) 'Don't misunderstand me'. As a verb stem *misundastand* shows little phonological assimilation (since Swahili does not permit closed syllables or consonant clusters such as *-st-*, but it shows deep morphological assimilation (i.e., it accepts Swahili verbal inflections). The fact the same person also might say *ni-ta-cheki mambo hayo* 'I will check on those matters', with *cheki* showing both types of integration does not make it easy to claim that categorical structural criteria identifying borrowings exist.

As I hope will become clear below, however, the problem of distinguishing borrowing and switching is solved if it is approached in terms of social content, not structure. Just as, for example, all phonological or synthactic features in a social dialect are not distinctive and therefore are not crucial defining features of the dialect (they are not all socially diagnostic of social group membership), all incorporations of L2 into L1 are not diagnostic of interpersonal negotiations. Those which carry social significance (as a negotiation) constitute code switching while those which do not are borrowings. (The only complication is that a borrowing can appear as a code switch when it is part of style switching. But this development is entirely consistent with the model: any style (and its components) becomes socially meaningful when it is used in a marked way. For example, a speaker may switch in an informal discussion to a style interlarded with learned loan words. This is a marked choice, possibly to negotiate a position of erudition).

Code switching as an unmarked choice

As noted above, the markedness model most crucially consists of a negotiation principle and a set of maxims which participants in conversation use to calculate conversational implicatures about the balance of rights and obligations which the speaker proposes for the present speech event. The unmarked choice maxim is the keystone of these maxims, directing speakers to 'make the unmarked code choice when you wish to establish or affirm the unmarked rights and obligations set associated with a particular conventionalized exchange.' Making the unmarked choice, then, gives rise to the implicature that the speaker is negotiating a normative position, the status quo (Scotton 1983: 120).

(A) Sequential unmarked choices

What Blom and Gumperz (1972: 424) refer to as situational switching is seen within this model as a movement from one unmarked choice to another. Such sequences occur in a chain of conventionalized exchanges when participants wish to engage in normative behaviour and acknowledge that the change from one type of exchange to another has altered the expected rights and obligations balance, and therefore the relevancy of the indexical quality of one code vs. another. The example above of the security guard and visitor who first interact in Swahili and then, when their shared ethnic membership is known, in Luyia, shows sequential unmarked choices. New information (about ethnic identity) brought about a re-definition of the exchange. Another example makes even clearer how external factors are involved in changing the unmarked choice. Two East Africans from the same ethnic group will chat about personal affairs in their shared mother tongue if they are making the unmarked choice for such an exchange. But if they are joined by a friend from another ethnic group, the exchange is no longer the same. They will switch to a neutral lingua franca now if they are making the unmarked choice.

Because what stimulates the change in code is external to the participants themselves (situational features or their relative saliency are what change), calling this type of code choice situational switching clearly has its motivations. But within the model developed here, situations do not determine choices. Rather, speaker motivations do. Speakers make decisions within a framework of predictable consequences, with situations figuring only indirectly in that they alert speakers (they 'situate' them) to consequences since markedness of choices is determined by situational features. Characterizing such choices as sequential unmarked choices highlights speakers as actors and the element of predictability. While part of what happens is that the situation changes, what counts more is the change in the appropriateness of the present choice to encode the unmarked relationship between speakers, and then their decision (conscious or not) to recognize this new relationship.

(B) Overall switching as the unmarked choice

When participants are bilingual peers, the unmarked choice may be switching with no changes at all in the situation. That is, the pattern of using two varieties for the same conventionalized exchange is itself unmarked. For example, many educated persons from the same Kenyan or Zimbabwean ethnic group alternate between their own first language and English in many conversations with peers.

The motivation for such switching is the same as that for choosing a single linguistic variety which is an unmarked choice: any variety is indexical of the speaker's position in the rights and obligations balance. When the speaker wishes more than one social identity to be salient in the current exchange, and each identity is encoded in the particular speech community by a different linguistic variety, then those two or more codes constitute the unmarked choice. In most parts of Africa, for example, speech communities are multilingual, with each language having particular associations. Ethnic identity is signaled by use of mother tongue. In addition, ability to speak the official language fluently is associated with membership in a multiethnic elite. Other associations are also possible. For example, speaking an indigenous lingua franca well, such as Swahili in East Africa, signals participation in a travel syndrome, usually involving experience in urban multi-ethnic areas. Knowing the language of another ethnic group is also indicative of a special social identy.

The unmarked choice for many speakers having two such identities, when talking with persons similar to themselves, is a pattern of switching between the two varieties indexical of the rights and obligations sets which the speakers wish to be in force for the speech event. The two varieties are both indexical of positively valued identities, but from different arenas, such as ethnic group membership and being part of an educated and/or urban elite.

Each switch need have no special significance; rather it is the overall pattern of using two varieties which carries social meaning (the negotiation of two different rights and obligations balances as simultaneously salient). Note that this feature distinguishes overall switching as an unmarked choice from all other forms of code switching since, for them, each switch signals a new negotiation.

The following example (Scotton 1982a) shows switching as an unmarked choice.

(1) *Setting:* Veranda of a restaurant in Western Kenya. All participants are native speakers of Lwidakho, a Luyia variety. A staffing officer in the

ministry of education, a local school teacher and his wife, who is also a school teacher, greet a secondary school headmaster who has just driven up.

Staffing Office (English): It's nice that we've met. I haven't seen you for long.
Headmaster (English): Yes, it's really long – and this is because I'm far from this way.
Staffing Officer (Lwidakho): Yikhala yaha khulole nuva nuvula haraka. ('Sit down if you're not in a hurry.' Note: *haraka* is Swahili loan for 'hurry'.)
Headmaster (English; Lwidakho): I'm not very much in a hurry. Nuva noveye na khasoda khambe. (Lwidakho: 'If you have to offer some soda, let me have it.')
Male Teacher (English): Tell us about X place. How are the people there treating you?
Headmaster (English; Lwidakho): X is fine, the people are OK, but as you know, they are very tribalistic. Nuwatsa kwanalani navo ni miima jiavo. (Lwidakho: 'But now I am used to their behavior.')
Female Teacher (Lwidakho): Kwahulila vakukuyagaku, gali ndi? (Lwidakho: 'We heard they attacked you and beat you up. How was this?')
Headmaster (Lwidakho; English): Gali madinyu. (Lwidakho: 'It was very serious.') I've seen a place where men can beat up a headmaster. But now they can't tell me personally. Kalunu ku tsiharambe tsya khohola lwayumbaha. (Lwidakho: 'Due to harambee spirit, we've put up a modern dining hall to cater for all students at once) . . . Ndevahe, Peter – Kekokeka Kaimosi yiki? (Lwidakho: 'May ask, Peter – what's happening at Kaimosi?')

A fragment of a conversation between two University of Nairobi students shows a conventionalized exchange for which switching between Swahili and English is an unmarked choice for bilingual peers. This is the case even though the participants share the same first language (Luo) since the setting is a university dining room, with students from other ethnic groups also participating.

(2) Onyango (Luo; Swahili; English): Omera, umesoma katika papers kwamba government imekuwa frozen.
(Luo: 'I say.' Swahili: 'Have you read in the papers that the government is frozen?' Meaning: there is a freeze on employment.)
Owino (Swahili): Kitambo sana. (Sw: 'Long ago.')
Onyango (Swahili; English): Na huoni kuna need ya kujaza zile forms za TSC badala ya kungojea zile za PSC? (Sw: 'And don't you think there's a need to fill in the forms of the Teacher Service Commission rather than wait for those of the Public Service Commission?')

Owino (English; Swahili): Yea, you have a point there. Singejali kuwa part-time cheater. (Sw: 'I wouldn't mind being a part-time teacher.' Note: cheater = 'teacher' in student word play.)

Onyango (Swahili; English): Hutaki kuwa full-time cheater. (Sw: 'You don't want to be a full-time teacher.')

Owino (English): No way.

Other writers in this volume (McConvell on switching among Gurindji Aborigines in Australia and Poplack on Spanish-English switching among Puerto Ricans in New York) recognize a type of switching matching these examples and the above characterization of overall switching as an unmarked choice. They do not, however, fit such switching into a model of code choice as a principled type, as is proposed here. When McConvell mentions this type of switching, though, it is in making a theoretical point which is – within my model – an important motivation for overall switching as an unmarked choice. His point is that the possibility of defining an interaction as belonging to more than one exchange type simultaneously (a 'nesting' of arenas in his terms) should be accommodated in any model. And Poplack's comment about some of the switching in New York, that, 'it could be said to function as a mode of interaction similar to monolingual language use,' is reminiscent of my claim that this type of switching is analogous to using a single code which is the unmarked choice for an exchange, the only difference being that using two codes in a switching pattern happens to be what is unmarked. Once more, her comments that this type of switching shows transitions between varieties and apparent unawareness of participants of the particular alternations between languages would apply to the type of prosody and lack of self-consciousness which would be expected when speakers are simply making the unmarked choice. Further, her description of this type of switching among Puerto Ricans in New York fits the examples from Kenya just cited. She notes that 'in the course of a single utterance the language of the discourse oscillated from English to Spanish and back to English; and during each stretch in one language there are switches of smaller constituents to the other.'

As for the function of such switches, Poplack's observation that 'individual switches cannot be attributed to stylistic or discourse functions' seems to support an important distinction this paper makes above – that overall switching as an unmarked choice differs from other types of switching in that each switching is not socially meaningful on its own. (Rather, only the overall pattern has a discourse function.)

As noted above, overall switching as an unmarked choice seems to be the first step to what has been called the development of a semi-autonomous 'Mix'. Overall switching, for example, seems to include more alternations at the bound morpheme level ('deep switching') than other types of switching, although this claim needs to be supported empirically. But typical examples are the following, taken from natural conversations of bilingual East and Central African university students:[6]

One student to another at the University of Nairobi: Alikuwa amesit papa hapu tu . . .
(A-li-ku-wa a-me-sit =
= he/she-PAST-BE-VERBAL SUFFIX he/she-PERFECT-sit)
(Swahili/English: 'He/she had been sitting just right here . . .')
Note that SIT is used with Swahili inflectional morphemes, not English -*ing*, to convey the progressive meaning 'sitting'.

One student to another at the University of Zimbabwe:
Huana kuda ku-mbo-react-a zvokuda ku-mu-kis-a here kana kuti?
(Ku-mbo-react-a = INFINITIVE PREFIX-NEGATIVE INTENSIFIER 'some-times'-react-VERBAL SUFFIX; ku-mu-kis-a = INFINITIVE PREFIX-THIRD PERSON SINGULAR OBJECT PREFIX-kiss-VERBAL SUFFIX)
(Karanga dialect of Shona/English: 'Didn't you react by wanting to kiss her or to–')

Does overall switching as an unmarked choice occur in all bilingual communities? The answer seems to be 'no'. Elsewhere (Scotton 1986), I suggest that overall switching as an unmarked choice would be hypothesized as unlikely in a narrow diglossic community where there is strict allocation of the two varieties involved. But not only is the degree of normative compartmentaliza-tion of the varieties important, what must be considered is the evaluation of the varieties (as vehicles of the identities they encode), as is discussed more fully below.

Let us first consider some data. Poplack (this volume) notes that this type of switching (she refers to it at times as 'skilled' switching but elsewhere as 'true' switching) occurs only infrequently in an Ottawa-Hull study of French-English switching. She says this is the case 'despite the fact that the participant constellation, mode of interaction and bilingual situation appear to be similar to those in the Puerto Rican study.' (Most of the switching she reports among the French Canadians would be classified as making marked choices in terms of this model).

A similar lack of switching as an overall pattern for informal interactions was reported for instructors of English at the University of Panama at least a few years ago (Alnouri, personal communication). Staff room interactions were almost all entirely in Spanish for these native speakers of Spanish who taught English. One possible reason for not switching to English was that such usage would provide invidious comparisons among persons whose livelihood depended on their English competence. But another reason may have been that there was hostility toward the United States at the time over the Panama Canal. Therefore, a persona as an English speaker was not valued for informal interactions with Panamanian peers.

These examples support the hypothesis that overall switching as an unmarked choice between bilingual peers is only frequent when both varieties are indexical of identities which are positively evaluated for the specific exchange type. For example, this means the point is not that English is never associated with positive values by French Canadians, or that they do not see themselves as bilinguals. Rather, this hypothesis would predict that an overall pattern of switching is infrequent because an identity encoded by English is not valued specifically for informal exchanges with French Canadian peers. Obviously, data from other communities, including attitudinal studies, would be necessary to support this hypothesis in any meaningful way. But the overall insight that specific type of switching possible will depend on evaluations of the varieties involved (and that evaluations are not of one fabric, but are exchange specific) seems valid.[7]

Code Switching as a Marked Choice

Switching away from the unmarked choice in a conventionalized exchange signals that the speaker is trying to negotiate a different rights and obligations balance as salient in place of the unmarked one, given the situational features. Such switching constitutes a marked choice, a flouting of the unmarked choice maxim.

Because a marked choice is a violation, it is always disruptive, although it can be so in a positive or negative sense. That is, a marked choice can be positive by narrowing social distance if it is indexical of a relationship of solidarity, given the normative matrix of associations between varieties and social meanings in the community. Or, it can be negative in that it increases social distance because it encodes anger or the desire to make a power differential salient (when it would not be salient ordinarily). As noted above, marked choices are interpreted by matching them with the exchanges in which they would be unmarked choices. Thus, in the following speech event a passenger begins speaking to the bus conductor in the passenger's own native language, not in the unmarked choice for this event, Swahili. Everyone present laughs (including the passenger, who seemed to intend his use of his language as a joke). How is the choice of his own language to be interpreted? By reference to those exchanges in which it would be the unmarked choice. And those are largely exchanges in which solidarity is salient. Thus, as a marked choice, using his native language is a negotiation for solidarity with the bus conductor, if only facetiously. While the conductor rejects the bid for solidarity as such, he does give the passenger a discount, indicating the bid to alter the unmarked rights and obligations balance has worked.

Setting: A bus in Nairobi, with Swahili as the unmarked choice for the conventionalized exchange of passenger to conductor. A Luyia man who has just got on the bus speaks to conductor:

Passenger (Lwidakho) (Speaking in a loud and joking voice): Mwana weru, vugula khasimoni khonyene. ('Dear brother, take only fifty cents.') (Laughter from conductor and other passengers)
Passenger (Lwidakho): Shuli mwana wera mbaa? ('Aren't you my brother?')
Conductor (Swahili): Apana. Mimi si ndugu wako, kama ungekuwa ndugu wangu ningekujua kwa jina. Lakini sasa sikujui wala sikufahamu. ('No, I am not your brother. If you were my brother, I would know you by name. But, now I don't know you or understand you.')
Passenger (Swahili): Nisaidie, tu, bwana. Maisha ya Nairobi imenishinda kwa sababu bei ya kila kitu imeongezwa. Mimi ninaketi Kariobang'i, pahali

ninapolipa pesa nyingi sana kwa nauli ya basi. ('Just help me, mister. The life of Nairobi has defeated me because the price of everything has gone up. I live at Kariobang'i, a place to which I pay much money for the bus fare.')

Conductor: Nimechukua peni nane pekee yake. ('I have taken 80 cents alone.')

Passenger: (English; Swahili): Thank you very much. Nimeshukuru sana kwa huruma ya huyu ndugu wango. ('I am very thankful for the pity of this one, my brother.')

Scotton and Ury (1977: 16-7) cite another example showing a marked choice in a conversation on a bus in Nairobi. But in this case, the passenger's marked choice is to encode authority and educational status, not solidarity. The conductor counters by matching the passenger's marked choice, showing that he too can compete in any power game (involving here ability to speak English): '

Setting: A conductor on a Nairobi bus has just asked a passenger where he is going in order to determine the fare (in Swahili):

Passenger (Swahili): Nataka kwenda posta. ('I want to go to the post office.')

Conductor (Swahili): Kutoka hapa mpaka posta nauli ni senti hamsini. ('From here to the post office, the fare is 50 cents.')

(Passenger gives conductor a shilling from which there should be 50 cents in change.)

Conductor (Swahili) Ngojea change yako. ('Wait for your change.')

(Passenger says nothing until a few minutes have passed and the bus nears the post office where the passenger will get off.)

Passenger (Swahili): Nataka change yangu. ('I want my change.')

Conductor (Swahili): Change utapata, Bwana. ('You'll get your change, mister.')

Passenger (English): I am nearing my destination.

Conductor (English): Do you think I could run away with your change?

Another example shows how a marked choice is used to narrow social distance. Even though the speech event in this case is discontinuous, its parts constitute a single scenario and therefore show switching in a broad sense.

Setting: A young, well-educated Luyia woman is driving her car into a Nairobi athletic club where she is a member. She has stopped her car and wants the gatekeeper to open the club gate. A middle-aged man, the gatekeeper also turns out to be a Luyia — although that is not obvious until later. An ethnically neutral lingua franca, Swahili, is the unmarked choice for this speech event no matter whether speakers share ethnicity or not. This is probably so because, in the face of the substantial status differential between the gatekeeper (as an unskilled, little educated worker) and the upper middle class club members, ethnicity has little or no salience as a factor in affecting the rights and obligations balance.

Gatekeeper (To young woman stopped in the middle of the gate)
(Swahili): Ingia kwa mlango mmoja tu. ('Enter by using only one gate.')
Young woman (Looks behind her and sees another car pulled up so that she
    cannot move easily) (Swahili): Fungua miwili. Siwezi kwenda revas!
    Kuna magari mengine nyuma.
    ('Open both. I can't reverse! There are other cars behind me.')
(Seeing the situation, the gatekeeper very grudgingly opens both gates.)
Young woman (Driving by the gatekeeper, she says to him) (Swahili): Mbona
    wewe mbaya sana leo? ('Why are you so difficult today?')
(She says to her companions in the car — in English, 'The man is a Luyia.' She
determines this by his pronunciation.)
(Several hours later, she drives through the gate as she leaves.)
Young woman (to gatekeeper) (Maragoli, a Luyia variety): Undindiyange
    vutwa. ('You were being unkind to me.')
Gatekeeper (Swahili; Maragoli): Pole, simbere nikhumany ta. ('Sorry. I didn't
    know it was you.')

The young woman's use of Luyia for the final part of this interaction was a conscious effort to establish co-ethnic identity, she reported.[8] After all, she expected to have to deal with the gatekeeper again and did not want the next encounter to be as irritating as this one had started out to be. By switching from the unmarked choice of Swahili, encoding the neutral relationship of club member: club employee, to a Luyia variety, she is asserting common ethnicity and negotiating a different relationship. The gatekeeper's reply, 'I didn't know it was you,' was interpreted by the young woman as meaning 'I didn't know you were of my ethnic group' (since he definitely did not know her personally). Both his switch from Swahili to Luyia and the content of this utterance encode a movement away from the unmarked relationship for this exchange.

There are many variants of switching as a marked choice, with many of them relatively brief in duration — only a word or two. Yet, the same motivation characterizes such momentary switches as longer ones: a bid to dis-identify with the unmarked rights and obligations balance for the exchange. It is as if the switch is made to remind other participants that the speaker is a multi-faceted personality, as if the speaker were saying 'not only am I X, but I am also Y'. This ploy, in and of itself, is a powerful strategy because the speaker 'enlarges' himself/herself through marked choices in a mainly unmarked discourse, asserting a *range* of identities (Scotton 1985: 113). In addition, of course, the specific associations of the variety making up the marked choice are also part of the attempted negotiation.

A very common type of momentary marked switching is change in code for emphasis.[9] Such switching often involves repetition (in the marked code) of exactly the same referential meaning conveyed in the unmarked code. The fact there is this repetition makes it very clear that the new information is the change in code and therefore its social associations. The following examples, both involving a refusal to give money, show this. In both, the marked choice is a negotiation to increase the social distance between the speaker and his supplicant, since the switch is to a variety symbolizing authority and also unmarked for formal interactions. Such a choice reinforces the speaker's denial.

Setting: A farmer in rural Western Kenya is asking money of a salaried worker who is in his home area on leave. The conversation takes place in a bar where all speak the same mother tongue, Lwidakho, the unmarked choice for this exchange (Scotton 1983: 128)

Farmer (finishing an oblique request for money) (Lwidakho): . . . inzala ya
     mapesa, kambuli. ('Hunger for money. I don't have any.')
Worker (who had been speaking only Lwidakho before the request)
     (English): You have got a land.
     (Swahili): Una shamba. ('You have a farm/land.')
     (Lwidakho): Uli mulimi. ('You have land.')

Setting: A Zimbabwean university student is refusing to give a fellow student money. He has already refused once in their shared mother tongue, the Ndau dialect of Shona; but the petitioner persists. The student switches to English.

Student (English; Ndau): I said, 'Andidi'. I don't want!

'Permissible' marked choices

Marked choices under certain circumstances in conventionalized exchanges are allowable. These choices are marked because they do not encode the unmarked rights and obligations expected for the overall exchange. But at the same time, they are almost unmarked 'in context' because they signal what becomes a conventionalized suspension of the current rights and obligations balance. Two types seem universal:

(A) Those which encode deference. Such choices are made when the speaker wishes special consideration from the addressee, or when the speaker wants to perform a 'face-threatening act' (Brown and Levinson 1978) but also wants to maintain a good relationship with the addressee. Scotton (1983: 123) refers to such choices as following a 'Deference Maxim' which, in a revised form, is 'Show deference in your code choice to those from whom you desire something or to mitigate a face threatening act.'

A major way of expressing deference is to accommodate to the addressee by switching to the variety used in his/her turn, or to a variety otherwise associated with the addressee (e.g., his/her mother tongue). Many of the subtle shifts in phonological features which Giles and his associates refer to under their accommodation hypothesis would be included here (e.g. Giles and Powesland 1975; Thackerar, Giles, and Cheshire 1982). Another way of showing deference is to switch to a variety (or sub-variety) whose unmarked use is to express respect. For example, the use of an elaborate directive form, which is in a marked style for the expected rights and obligations balance, when performing a face-threatening act illustrates this (e.g., Professor to student: 'If it is not out of your way, I would appreciate it if you would please check on whether the library received my reserve list'.)

The use of a term of respect, which is part of a style, dialect or language whose use is not called for by the unmarked rights and obligations balance, also is an instance of following the Deference Maxim. Scotton and Zhu (1984) report that many customers in Beijing service encounters will call unskilled personal *shi. fu*, a term whose meaning is now changing, but generally meaning either 'elder craftsman' or at the very least 'skilled worker'. Scotton and Zhu refer to such switching as 'calculated respect' since the choice elevates the addressee so that the speaker can gain some advantage.

(B) Those which take account of lack of ability to speak the unmarked choice. A conversation starting out in the unmarked choice may shift into a marked choice because of limits on speaking abilities. Scotton (1983: 125) accounts for such choices as following the virtuosity maxim: 'Make an otherwise marked choice whenever the linguistic ability of either speaker or addressee makes the unmarked choice for the unmarked rights and obligations set in a conventionalized exchange infelicitous.'

Many times the switching away from the unmarked choice because of lack of fluency is overtly acknowledged by the speaker, who says, 'I'm sorry, but I can't speak X very well' meaning – in the terms of this model – 'I know the unmarked relationship calls for the use of X.' (Note that it seems to be a marked choice for the other participant – the one who *is* fluent in the unmarked choice – to initiate a switch under the Virtuosity Maxim. That is, the speaker following the Virtuosity Maxim must self-select. For another speaker to take the initiative often elicits a negative affective response).

The following conversation (Parkin 1974: 194-5) illustrates using a marked choice to show deference, as well as a switch to the unmarked choice because of lack of virtuosity. A Kikuyu market seller in Nairobi greets a Luo customer in his own language, clearly a move designed to flatter the Luo by acknowledging his personal distinctiveness. The customer accepts this accommodation, but it soon becomes apparent that the seller cannot speak much Luo. The customer switches to the unmarked choice of Swahili, jocularly accusing the seller of attempting flattery. Thus, the deference negotiation fails, showing that, as the model claims, code choices are made with normative expectations of consequences, but at the same time are negotiations whose success depends on the dynamics of the individual speech event.

Setting: A Kikuyu woman stallholder greets a Luo male customer in a Nairobi market. (Dashes indicate switching.)

Seller (Luo): Omera, nadi! ('How are you, brother?')

Customer (Luo): Maber. ('Fine.')

Seller (Kikuyu; Swahili): Ati-nini? ('What-what?')

Customer (Swahili): Ya nini kusema lugha ambao huelewi, mama? ('Why (try) to speak a language you don't know, madam?)

Seller (English): I know Kijaluo very well! (English with Swahilized form, Kijaluo).

Customer (Swahili; English; Swahili): Wapi! — You do not know it at all — Wacha haya, nipe mayai mbili. ('Go on! You do not know it at all — Let's leave the matter; give me two eggs.')

Seller (Swahili; Luo; Swahili): Unataka mayai — ariyo, omera — haya ni — tongolo — tatu. ('You want two eggs, brother. OK, that's thirty cents.' Note: 'two', 'brother', and 'thirty' are Luo.)

In his analysis of such conversational exchanges, Parkin uses games as an analogy, emphasizing the to-and-fro movement of turn taking and the influence of turns on each other. The dynamic nature of conversation and the possibility for a variety of choices are also important aspects of the markedness model presented here. This model, however, depicts more a 'grammar of consequence' than a 'grammar of choice'. While the speech event itself may be likened to a competition, with speakers making choices to accumulate points, the scoring is only incidentally dependent on the choice in a previous turn or someone else's choice, according to my model. Rather, the specific choices which are made and the outcome depends more on the indexicality of choices, and, accordingly, their expected consequences. This is what makes it a grammar of consequences.

A marked choice or a sequence of unmarked choices?

One problem for the overall model is to distinguish a marked choice following or embedded in an unmarked choice from a sequence of two unmarked choices. They can be distinguished in two ways. First, as noted above, there is always some change in factors external to the on-going speech event when there is a shift from one unmarked choice to another; the topic changes, or new participants are introduced, or new information about the identity of participants which is salient in the exchange becomes available, etc. Second, a sequence of unmarked choices is expected, given the change in factors. In contrast, a marked choice is unexpected. Furthermore, it evokes an affective response, as noted above.

The claim that the distinction between unmarked and marked choices has psychological reality can be empirically tested, although I know of no existing studies. Such expectations and affect are amenable to measurement. Significant differences between marked and unmarked choices would be predicted, although they would be gradient, not categorical.

Ervin-Tripp's discussion of expected vs. unexpected directive forms is relevant here (1976: 61-2). She notes, 'In normal circumstances, when an expected form occurs, *listeners need make no affective interpretation at all*' (italics in original). She goes on to contrast this reaction with that of an unexpected directive:

'If social features are clear, but the form is unexpected by his own coding rule, the hearer assumes that the speaker is imputing different social features than he thinks he has, and reacts to the imputation as deference, sarcasm, arrogance, coldness, undifferentiated annoyance, or a joke. *These inferences appear to be relatively systematic, to the point of being like marking rules*' (italics added).

Switching to exclude? Permissible marked choices or not?

In many multilingual societies, switching to a language not known by all participants is a common means of exclusion, often conscious. At the least, it withholds information from those not knowing the language of switching. It may also contain negative comments about those excluded. Such switching is predicted to be most frequent when there is a sharp power differential between those participants who switch to the new code and those who are excluded, for example, parents vs. children. The switching itself conveys that the speakers share an identity others do not have and narrows the social distance between them while increasing that between speakers and those left out. Because of the relatively greater power of the speakers, others may not like this marked choice, but they must permit it.

When the power differential is less great, such switching may not be condoned, but considered rude. Among other things, the speakers are overtly accused of 'backbiting" and of course they are figuratively speaking behind the non-participants' backs. Given the unmarked rights and obligations balance, such switching is clearly a marked choice. But is it? The markedness of exclusive switching in many parts of Africa, for example, seems very unresolved. Exclusive switching there normally is to an ethnic language. Those who accept such switching may do so because ethnic identity and giving priority in social relations to affinity with ethnic brethren are facts of life in many parts of Africa. Switching which is indexical of these facts simply seems unmarked to many. But not all agree. And, not surprisingly, it seems to be members of the larger, more powerful groups who do more exclusive switching.

This state of affairs indicates that there is not necessarily a categorical consensus including all speech community members on the relative markedness of varieties available. In this case, for example, an interethnic conversation may still be considered a conventionalized exchange by all concerned, but they may not agree on the markedness of a non-neutral ethnic language. (It remains a conventionalized exchange because participants do recognize unmarked choices; that is, they do recognize 'scripts' for the exchange. It is just that they do not recognize the same scripts. If the views about markedness become very fragmented, such exchanges may become unconventionalized. This seems to be what happened in Montreal in the late 1970's when the relative unmarkedness of French vs. English became a political issue, especially for exchanges in public institutions (Heller 1982: 116-7).[10]

A typical example of switching to exclude in a multiethnic conversation in Nairobi follows.

Setting: Four young Kenyan men who have completed secondary school and who work in the same government ministry in Nairobi are chatting. Two are native speakers of Kikuyu, one of Kisii, and one of a Kalenjin language. Swahili and/or Swahili/English are unmarked choices.

Kikuyu I (Swahili): Sasa mumesema nini juu ya hiyo plan yetu? Naona kama siku kama siku zinaendelea kwisha. ('Now, what do you all say about the plan of ours? I think time is getting short.')

Kikuyu II (Swahili; English): Mlisema tu collect money, lakini hakuna mtu hata mmoja ambaye amenipatia pesa. ('You said collect money, but there isn't even one person who has got money for me.')

Kalenjin (Swahili): Makosa ni yako kama mweka hazina. Tulisema uwe ukitembelea watu mara kwa mara lakini hufanyi hivyo. Watu wengi hawawezi kufanya kitu bila kuwa harassed. ('The fault is yours as treasurer. We said you should visit people (us) from time to time but you don't do that. Many people can't do a thing unless they are harassed.')

Kikuyu I (Swahili; English): Mjue ni vibaya for the treasurer akimaliza wakati wake akiona watu ambao hawawezi kupeana pesa. ('You should know it's bad for the treasurer to waste his time if he sees people who can't give money.')

Kisii (Swahili): Mweka hazina hana makosa hata kidogo. Mtu anatakiwa lipe pesa bila kuulizwa. ('The treasurer hasn't made any mistakes. Each person is required to pay without being asked.')

Kikuyu II (Kikuyu): Andu amwe nimendaga kwaria maundu maria matari na ma namo. ('Some people like talking about what they're not sure of.')

Kikuyu I (Kikuyu): Wira wa muigi wa kigina ni kuiga mbeca. No tigucaria mbeca. ('The work of the treasurer is only to keep money. Not to hunt for money.')

Kisii (Swahili; English): Ubaya wenu ya Kikuyu ni kuassume kila mtu anaelewa Kikuyu. ('The bad thing about Kikuyus is to assume that everyone understands Kikuyu.')

Kalenjin (Swahili; English): Si mtumie lugha ambayo kila mtu hapa atasikia? We are supposed to solve this issue. ('Shouldn't you use a language which every person here understands? We are supposed to solve this issue.')

Kikuyu II (Swahili; English): Tunaomba msameha. Sio kupenda kwetu. Ni kawaida kwa most people kupendelea lugha yao. ('We are sorry. It isn't that we favor our side. It's normal for most people to prefer their own language.')

Code switching as a strategy of multiple identities

In uncertain situations (non-conventionalized exchanges) when an unmarked choice is not apparent, speakers nominate an exploratory choice as the basis for the exchange. The nominated variety is recognized as indexical of a certain rights and obligations balance existing in the conventionalized exchange for which it is unmarked. By analogy, it is proposed that the 'new' exchange be treated as an instance of the 'old'.[11]

Many times, however, at the outset of a conversation a speaker is not sure that any one balance would be preferable to another, even as a candidate, for the exchange. In such cases, a speaker may open an exchange with one choice, but be prepared to switch to another choice, depending on the addressee's own code choice in his/her response. If the speaker changes in his/her second turn to the addressee's choice (first turn), this is a form of showing deference, or accommodation. By using two codes in two different turns, however, the speaker also has been able to encode two identities – and the breadth of experience associated with them. For this reason, participants may find it socially useful to treat certain speech events as non-conventionalized exchanges, if it is at all possible. (Scotton and Zhu 1983 discuss some other social advantages of maintaining various ambiguities in linguistic systems.)

Initial contacts with strangers in other than service encounters typically are treated as non-conventionalized exchanges. In the following example, a young man switches from Swahili to English, apparently in an effort to please the young woman with whom he wants to dance.

Setting: A dance at a Nairobi hotel. A young man (his native language is Kikuyu) asks a young woman to dance.

He (Swahili): Nisaidie na dance, tafadhali. ('Please give me a dance.')
She (Swahili): Nimechoka. Pengine nyimbo ifuatayo. ('I'm tired. Maybe a following song.')
He (Swahili): Hii ndio nyimbo ninayopenda. ('This is the song which I like.')
She (Swahili): Nimechoka! (I'm tired!')
He (Swahili): Tafadhali – ('Please.')
She (interrupting) (English): Ah, stop bugging me.
He (English): I'm sorry. I didn't mean to bug you, but I can't help it if I like this song.
She (English): OK, then, in that case, we can dance.

Conclusion

An explanation for code switching has been proposed which emphasizes linguistic choices as negotiations of personal rights and obligations relative to those of other participants in a talk exchange. This explanation follows from a markedness model of code choice which claims that speakers make choices and others interpret them by considering their probable consequences. This process involves a consensus concerning the relative markedness of any choice for a specific exchange and a view of all choices as indexical of a negotiation of rights and obligations between participants. Because all community members have this theory of markedness, they are able to use conversational implicatures to arrive at the intended consequences of any code switching. (As has been noted, this explanation is not merely speculative but is based on studies of the social interpretation of switching by subjects in their own communities (Scotton and Ury 1977; Scotton 1982a). However, as has been mentioned also, not all claims of the markedness model have been empirically tested, although that they can be tested seems clear).

The principle guiding some earlier explanations of code switching in East Africa was the need to detail situational factors. For example, while Whiteley (1974) explicitly recognizes the failures of certain situational factors to account for switching in rural Kenya, his solution is only a more thorough study of the situation. Thus, he writes, 'It does not seem possible to correlate the choice of any particular language with a shift along the scale of formality', but then offers as a solution that 'much more needs to be known about the total social situation than can be gleaned from the language diaries (1974: 331)'.

The point of view taken here is quite different, of course. Situational factors *are* paramount in determining the unmarked choice in a conventionalized exchange: the unmarked rights and obligations set is derived from the salient configuration of social features for the exchange, and the unmarked linguistic choice as indexical of that set. But because not all exchanges are conventionalized and because the relevant features and their hierarchy will differ from exchange to exchange, it is impossible to provide any set of features as universally crucial independent variables. The features themselves even may be dependent variables in the sense that their saliency is context sensitive. In addition, feature salience is dynamically related to a specific exchange in that it may co-vary with content and linguistic choices in progressive turns by participants (e.g. the example above involving the security guard and visitor or Genesee and Bourhis 1982).

Some other more general explanations do acknowledge personal motivations (as does Parkin 1974 for East Africa, mentioned above), although not exactly along the lines of the markedness model. For example, Blom and Gumperz (1972) recognize that non-situationally motivated switching occurs, referring to it generally as metaphorical switching. Their primary emphasis, however, remains on the concepts of setting, social situation, and social event to explain choice (1972: 433). In Gumperz's later work, however, switching is recognized much more as a strategy which the speaker employs at will to generate conversational inferences. He writes, 'Code switching signals contextual information equivalent to what in monolingual settings is conveyed through prosody or other syntactic or lexical processes. It generates presuppositions in terms of which the content of what is said is decoded.' And specifically in relation to what he terms metaphorical usage, he writes, 'This partial violation of co-occurrence expectations then gives rise to the inference that some aspects of the connotations, which elsewhere apply to the activity as a whole, are here to be treated as affecting only the illocutionary force and quality of the speech act in question (Gumperz 1982: 98).' While some aspects of the treatment here are reminiscent of such statements, more of an attempt is made in the markedness model to provide a comprehensive and principled treatment, explicitly assigning roles to a normative framework in implicating consequences and to individual, interactive choices as tools of specific negotiations.

Much more psychologically centered is the accommodation hypothesis and related hypotheses of Giles and his associates (mentioned above) which seek to explain switching and specifically subjective reactions to the process. The accommodation model handles very well switching motivated by a desire to narrow the social distance between the addressee or not, such as those choices encoding deference. However, it seems limited because it seeks to explain all choices in terms of either accommodation or non-accommodation to the addressee. It is argued here that choices have a broader range of motivations. Most important, many are much more speaker-centered (such as choices encoding authority or education). Further, a framework of markedness seems essential in order to deal with the consequences of choices.

In conclusion, this paper has argued that the guiding research question for studies of switching should not be so much, what social factors or interactional features determine code choice? But rather, what is the relation between linguistic choices and their social consequences, and how do speakers know this? From this, more specific questions follow: is there an unmarked choice for a specific exchange? Given that the unmarked choice will have dominant frequency, for what effect do speakers employ switching away from this choice? If there is not an unmarked choice, how do speakers make sense out of choices made?

The several hypotheses and the overall markedness model suggested here respond to these questions. First, it is claimed that choice is not so much a reflection of situation as a negotiation of position, given the situation. People make the choices they do because of personal motivations. Second, it is proposed that these motivations can be characterized and all switching explained parsimoniously in the framework of unmarked, marked, and exploratory choices outlined here. Finally and in general, it has been argued that expected consequence structures code choices. Speakers are restrained only by the possibility and attractiveness of alternative outcomes. This involves, of course, their own linguistic abilities and, more important, their framework of expectations.

Notes

1. Much of the thinking going into this paper grew out of field work in rural Western Kenya and in Nairobi in the summer of 1977 under a grant from the Social Sience Research Council — American Council for Learned Societies, and in Nairobi again and in Harare, Zimbabwe, in 1983 under a

Fulbright Senior Fellow Research Grant. Many of the examples cited come from this research. Support is gratefully acknowledged. I also thank Cory Kratz, Kumbirai Mkanganwi, and Judith Njage for comments on an earlier version.

2. In Scotton and Ury (1977), 70 subjects were asked open-ended questions about four audio-recorded conversations. In Scotton (1982a), 35 subjects were played audio recordings of six conversations and then asked to select one of five possible answers from a fixed list. In both cases, it was stressed there were no 'right' or 'wrong' answers.

   Three of the four test conversations in the 1977 study illustrated switching as a marked choice. The majority of the subjects provided responses about 'what happened in the conversation' entirely consistent with the claims here about the social negotiation encoded by a marked choice; further, their interpretations were very similar. The fourth conversation showed switching in a non-conventionalized exchange. Perhaps not surprisingly, subjects did not cluster very well in their interpretations; however 69 % did mention the different social associations of the three languages involved as a reason for switching (Scotton and Ury 1977: 14—16).

   The six test conversations used in Scotton (1982) were examples of overall switching as an unmarked choice and switching as a marked choice, including one showing deferential switching. In general, over 90 % chose the same interpretation and this was the one consistent with the claims of this model (Scotton 1982: 442—3). More details are available from the author, including statistical test results.

3. This finding is based on more than 100 hours of recordings of natural conversations made in Nairobi and about 20 hours of recordings in Harare in 1983.

4. 'Sheng' is discussed in an article in the *Daily Nation* of March 14, 1984. One example cited is *Buda amenijamisha* 'Father has annoyed me' (as a reason for not going home). The origins of *buda* for 'father' are unclear. The verb stem *-jam* comes from the English but means 'feel stuck or annoyed'. It has Swahili inflections, including the causative suffix. Similar examples were found in my 1983 data corpus from recordings of pre-teens in certain areas of the city.

5. Overall switching as an unmarked choice is most difficult to separate from borrowing. For example, a Luo cooking teacher in Nairobi, addressing in Swahili a class of other teachers, peppered her presentation with such utterances as this:

   Wengine wanachemusha (sic), wengine wana*steam*, na mambo mengi mengi. Wengine wanakaanga kama mtu ambaye anakaanga nyama.

('Some boil [bananas], some steam, and a lot of other things. Some fry like a person frying meat.')

The use of *steam* is probably motivated by the fact that 'to steam' in Swahili requires a longer expression, *kupika kwa nguvu ya mvuke*. Thus, *steam* seems best described as a loan, since it regularly replaces a longer Swahili expression. The same is true of Shona expressions of number which have been almost totally replaced by English forms in urban Shona (more or less assimilated phonologically). To express number in Shona requires long phrases. I thank Kumbirai Mkanganwi for this observation.

But what about words such as *fry*? In the passage above, the teacher uses the Swahili verb -kaanga 'fry'. Yet, within five minutes she uses English *fry*:

Yaondoke kidogo. Kama vile unatake ku*fry*. Ni tamu isipokua (si) ni a bit dry. Sisi, hio ndio njia tuna preserve . . .
('It [water] evaporates a bit. Just as if you want to fry. It is tasty except that it is a bit dry. This is the way we preserve . . .')

Is such a usage as *fry* switching or borrowing? Clearly, *fry* is not a re-placement loan. Is this a *nonce* borrowing? Or is this passage simply an example of overall switching as an unmarked choice? Because the lesson in question contains many other English words and phrases, this does seem to be a case of switching (given the audience).

6. A Swahili poem by Kineene wa Mutiso (1983) contains a good deal of 'morphemic switching'. The poem is about a conversation between a secretary and someone who has come to her office. Here is one quatrain:

Brother sije ka *sorry*, *Bosie* utam*see*
Kwanza tupiga *story*, ama hauna *say*?
Hata ukiwa me*marry*, kwa nini tusi*enjoy*?
Sema ma*home* ku*how*, na kote kwenye ma*joint*.
('Brother, lest you worry, you'll see the boss
First let's talk, or do you have nothing to say?
Even if you are married, why can't we enjoy?
How are things at home and in all the nightspots?')

7. Nartey (1982) suggests, too, that the sociocultural environment may impose constraints on the type of switching possible. He, however, refers

specifically to whether switching is possible after a bound constituent (providing data showing such switching does occur in the conversations of young, educated Ghanaians).

8. Personal observation and interview on the spot.

9. Another type of momentary switching to a marked choice is to avoid taboo words. For example, a Shona lecturer in Zimbabwe speaking about Shona marriage customs used Shona throughout his lecture to an audience of Shona-speaking university students until he had to mention sexual relations. He switched to English for the two words, *sexual intercourse*, and then went on in Shona. (I thank Caleb Gwasira for this example). Even within a single language, the use of euphemisms for semi-taboo subjects or objects is a form of marked switching (from one style to a specialized style), with the shift serving to distance the speaker from the taboo item.

10. Heller's comment (1982: 118) emphasizes how, through the use of exploratory choices, a consensus is reached:

    'This negotiation [of language] itself serves to redefine the situations in the light of ongoing social and political change. *In the absence of norms, we work at creating new ones* (italics added). The conventionalization of the negotiating strategies appears to be a way of normalizing relationships, of encoding soical information necessary to know how to speak to someone . . .'

11. A related strategy, which encodes neutrality more than exploration, is the extended use of two varieties in an uncertain situation so that some entire conversations may be in one variety and some in another. Such a pattern is very similar to overall switching as an unmarked choice because it simultaneously presents two identities while also neutralizing them. Scotton (1976) explains the high incidence of reported use of two languages (rather than either one alone) in urban work situations as such a strategy of neutrality. For example, in Kampala, Uganda, many educated persons reported speaking both English (the official language) and Swahili (a widely used lingua franca) with fellow workers of different ethnic groups. Speaking English signals a person is educated and has the necessary expertise for a job, but English is also the language of formality in Uganda, and even pretentiousness. Speaking Swahili there signals an ethically neutral African identity and egalitarianism (since it is known by persons from diverse socio-economic backgrounds); but Swahili also has associations primarily as the lingua franca of the uneducated in Uganda. Which language to use with fellow workers? Results show that a middle choice is preferred: switching or alternating between the two.

References

Abdulaziz-Mkilifi, M. H.
  1972   Triglossia and Swahili-English bilingualism in Tanzania. *Language in Society* 1: 197–213.
Abdulaziz, M. H.
  1982   Patterns of language acquisition and use in Kenya: rural-urban differences. *International Journal of the Sociology of Language* 34: 95–120.
Blom, Jan-Petter and John Gumperz
  1972   Social meaning in linguistic structures: code-switching in Norway. *Directions in Sociolinguistics*, ed. by John Gumperz, and Dell Hymes, pp. 407–434. New York: Holt, Rinehart, and Winston.
Brown, Penelope and Stephen Levinson
  1978   Universals in language usage: politeness phenomena. *Questions and Politeness*, ed. by Esther Goody, pp. 56–310. New York: Cambridge University Press.
Ervin-Tripp, Susan
  1976   Is Sybil there? The structure of some American English directives. *Language in Society* 5: 25–66.
Genesee, Fred and Richard Bourhis
  1982   The social psychological significance of code switching in cross-cultural communication. *Journal of Language and Social Psychology.* 1: 1–28.
Gibbons, John
  1979   Code-mixing and koineising in the speech of students at the University of Hong Kong. *Anthropological Linguistics* 21: 113–123.
Giles, Howard and Peter Powesland
  1975   *Speech Style and Social Evaluation.* New York: Academic Press.
Grice, H. P.
  1975   Logic and conversation. *Syntax and Semantics: Speech Acts*, ed. by Peter Cole and Jerry Morgan, pp. 41–58. New York: Academic Press.
Gumperz, John
  1982   Conversational code switching. *Discourse Strategies*, by J. Gumperz. pp. 59–99. New York: Cambridge University Press.
  1978   Dialect and conversational inference in urban communication. *Language in Society* 7: 393–409. (revised as Ethnic style as political rhetoric in *Discourse Strategies* by J. Gumperz, pp. 187–203. New York: Cambridge University Press.)

Heller, Monica S.
1982 Negotiations of language choice in Montreal. *Language and Social Identity*, ed. by J. Gumperz, pp. 108–118. New York: Cambridge University Press.

Hymes, Dell
1972 On communicative competence. *Sociolinguistics*, ed. by John Pride and Janet Holmes, pp. 269–293. Harmondsworth: Penguin.

Kachru, Braj
1978 Towards structuring code-mixing: an Indian perspective. *International Journal of the Sociology of Language* 16: 27–46.

Kineene, Mutiso wa
1983 Vioja afisini. *Mwanko*. Nairobi: Swahili club of the University of Nairobi.

McConvell, Patrick
this volume Mix-Im-Up: aboriginal codeswitching, old and new.

Nartey, Jonas N. A.
1982 Code-switching, interference or faddism? Language use among educated Ghanaians. *Anthropological Linguistics* 24: 183–192.

Nation
1984 Sheng, new urban language baffles parents. Wednesday Nation magazine, March 14, 1984.

Parkin, David
1974 Language switching in Nairobi. *Language in Kenya*, ed. by W. H. Whiteley, pp. 189–216. Nairobi: Oxford University Press.

Poplack, Shana
this volume Theory and evidence in the study of codeswitching.

Sankoff, David and Shana Poplack
1981 A formal grammar for code-switching. *Papers in Linguistics* 14: 3–46.

Scotton, Carol Myers
1986 Diglossia and code switching. *The Fergusonian Impact*, ed. by Joshua A. Fishman *et al.* Berlin: Mouton.
1985 What the heck, sir: style shifting and lexical colouring as features of powerful language. *Sequence and Pattern in Communicative Behaviour*, ed. by Richard L. Street and Joseph N. Capella, pp. 103–119. London: Edward Arnold.
1983 The negotiation of identities in conversation: a theory of markedness and code choice. *International Journal of the Sociology of Language* 44: 115–136.
1982a The possibility of switching: motivation for maintaining multilingualism. *Anthropological Linguistics* 24: 432–444.

1982b An urban-rural comparison of language use among the Luyia in Kenya. *International Journal of the Sociology of Language* 34: 121–31.

1976   Strategies of neutrality: language choice in uncertain situations. *Language* 52: 919.41.

Scotton, Carol Myers and William Ury

1977   Bilingual strategies: the social function of code switching. *International Journal of the Sociology of Language* 13: 5–20.

Scotton, Carol Myers and Zhu Wanjin

1983   *Tongzhi* in China: language change and its conversational consequences. *Language in Society* 12: 477–494.

1984   The multiple meanings of *shi. fu*, a language change in progress. *Anthropological Linguistics* 26: 325–344.

Thakerar, Jitendra N., Howard Giles, and Jenny Cheshire

1982   Psychological and linguistic parameters of speech accommodation theory. *Advances in the Social Psychology of Language*, ed. by Colin Fraser and Klaus R. Scherer, pp. 205–255. New York: Cambridge University Press.

Thibaut, John and Harold Kelley

1959   *The Social Psychology of Groups.* New York: Wiley.

Whiteley, Wilfred, H.

1974   Some patterns of language use in the rural areas of Kenya. *Language in Kenya*, ed. by W. H. Whiteley, pp. 319–350. Nairobi: Oxford University Press.

A conversation analytic approach to code-switching and transfer

J. C. P. Auer
Universität Konstanz

Background of this study

This paper summarizes some main findings of an analysis of code-switching and transfer (in the following, the term *language alternation* will be used to cover both) carried out in Constance, W. Germany, among the children of Italian migrant workers with a Southern Italian background.[1] The investigation was part of a larger study on the native language of Italian migrant children (*Muttersprache italienischer Gastarbeiterkinder im Kontakt mit Deutsch*)[2] and is based on an extensive corpus of spontaneous and non-spontaneous speech used by these children interacting with each other, the field-workers, or their parents. Nineteen children between the ages of six and sixteen formed the core group of this study. These children were observed to use (various varieties of) Italian and German alternatingly, in a number of situations. 400 instances of such alternations were submitted to conversation analysis; another 1400 instances were used for quantitative-differential analysis.

In my contribution, I want to sketch the conversation analytic model that was developed out of the materials and that can account for the main types of interpretations language alternation receives in the community under investigation. In addition, I will briefly touch upon differential issues. Before going into details, however, some general remarks on the global linguistic and ethnographic situation of the Italian migrants in W. Germany may be necessary.

The linguistic situation of the urban Italian 'communities' in Germany differs from what is known about other contexts of language contact after migration; it also differs from the linguistic situation of other ethnic groups in the FRG, such as the Turkish or the Yugoslavian communities.

The difference is due to the political status of the Italian migrants who, as members of the European Community, have the right to move relatively freely between Italy and Germany. Whereas the influx of adult workers from non-EC countries has been stopped, and those returning to their countries of origin are no longer allowed to come back, the Italian 'communities' are continuously reshaped by the arrival of new members, as well as by the multiple migration of those who came and go again. This comparatively high mobility, which, particularly in a southern German town like Constance, is still enhanced by geographical closeness to Italy, is one of the reasons for the weak or even absent positive self-definition of the Italians as one ethnic group or community. Although the first Italian migrants − first men, later wives and families − arrived in Constance 30 years ago, the Italian population still lacks any political and almost any cultural infrastructure. Activities on the community level, such as attempts to create social foci (*centri italiani per i lavoratori*), have been treated with utmost suspicion; at the same time, the Italians' inability to create such foci is perceived by them as one of the few stable and widely accepted stereotypes that are part of the Italian population's negative self-image. In fact, if we can speak of a community at all, it is a largely negatively defined one.

The comparatively high degree of mobility led us to abandon the terms 'immigrants' and 'emigrants' in favour of the more neutral term 'migrants'. It applies not only to the first generation adults, but also to the second generation. Many Italian couples send their children back to Italy for a while to live with their relatives, and/or to go to an Italian school, before allowing them to stay in Germany again.

For the present study, this high degree of mobility was relevant in the following way. The children that form the core group of our investigation were either born in Germany or had come to this country early in childhood; although some of them went back to Italy for shorter periods, their dominant socialization took place in the host country. Nonetheless, the social environment of these children is not homogeneous, for the Italian 'community' in Constance includes children of varying biographical backgrounds. If they wish to, they can establish peer relationships with children and youngsters who have only come to Germany recently and are clearly dominant speakers of Italian (dialect). On the other hand, they, too, may choose their friends among those who have been socialized predominantly in Germany (and, for the most part, are dominant speakers of German (dialect)). Finally, they may, of course, avoid all ties to the Italian ethnic group to which they were born, and exclusively affiliate with Germans.

Accordingly, the children's and youngsters' linguistic repertoire is quite complex. The dominant language of pre-kindergarten socialization in the family is, in many cases, the parents' local, southern Italian dialect (in our materials, mostly dialects of the Basilicata, Calabria, Sicily). In kindergarten and primary school, the German dialect is acquired as the most important variety for inter-ethnic peer networks. Between 5 and 8, all the children we investigated had become German-dominant; their German was a more or less dialectal (Alemannic) variety. Regional or standard Italian comes latest in the acquisition process. It is used in the Italian *doposcuola* (a couple of hours per week), and heard in the Swiss Italian mass media. Most families are not in a position to act as a language mediator for the Italian standard, for even regional Italian only plays a peripheral role in family interaction.

After childhood, many young Italians develop a more positive, and more self-confident attitude towards Italy and Italian. But although this change of attitude favours the acquisition of a more standard variety of this language, the problem of learning a language that, in the migrants' everyday world, hardly has any speakers, remains. Being, as it is, a diffusely perceived target, standard Italian is hard to acquire. Instead of showing progress towards that target, the speech of many young Italians continues to be characterized by a very high degree of fluctuation and variation.

But questions of language acquistion are only part of the issue. The rich repertoire of the second generation Italians also opens up the possibility of functionally employing variation in their repertoire. We have investigated such functions via the analysis of complex variational signs such as code-switching, code-shifting, code-fluctuation (including *italiano stentato*) (cf., for instance, Auer and Di Luzio 1983 a, b).

Variation in the repertoire has to be dealt with in a way that is sensitive to the general social and linguistic situation of the 'community'. As this 'community' is heterogeneous, it is not very likely to have developed rigid regulations or norms of language use and language alternation. Within certain limits imposed by co-participants' linguistic competences, language choice is indeed open to negotiation quite regularly, often throughout an interactive episode. Patterns of language choice begin to emerge in small scale network structures, but there are no larger scale "domains" in Fishman's sense. This calls for an analytic tool that is able to catch the subtlety of the on-going linguistic and social processes; we think that this tool is available in the framework of a linguistically enriched conversation analysis.

Another consequence of this social and linguistic instability is that the patterns of language alternation found in the data can be expected to be related to the type of network in which they are being produced. It is reasonable to predict that language alternation of a different type will occur in networks whose members have diverging language preferences (due to their biographical background) than in those where such a divergence is absent, be it because all members share the same history of migration, be it because certain members of the network are dominant in the sense of imposing their preferences on the others. This calls for a differential account of language alternation on the basis of network types.

In our investigation, we focused on children and youngsters with a predominantly 'German' socialization because we think that it is this group of second generation 'guest workers' who will decide the linguistic future of the migrant 'communities'. In order to make predictions about the future development of the Italian part of the speakers' repertoire, it was necessary to find out something about the role this Italian repertoire plays in the everyday life of the children when compared to the German part of the repertoire. Are the varieties of Italian at all necessary in Germany? If so, in what situations are they employed? One can look for an answer to these questions by closely observing linguistic behaviour, and, in fact, this was one line of procedure. A more rigorous answer to the question is possible, however, when small scale linguistic behaviour is analyzed on the basis of transcriptions of audio and visual recordings. The analyst of such recordings is in a better position than the participant observer to pay close attention to the small details involved in the organization of linguistic activities. The basic question facing the micro-analyst in the case of language alternation is this: If children regularly switch from variety A to variety B in order to organize linguistic activities X, Y, etc., and from B to A in order to organize linguistic activities V, W, etc., then what status is being attributed to these varieties by and because of the ways in which they are being employed in conversation? Regularities of language choice and language alternation, if treated in this way, reveal the status of the varieties contained in the linguistic repertoire of the speakers.

In addition, I had a more theoretical interest in the analysis of language alternation that relates to the notion of bilingualism itself. Linguistics owes an extensive and inconclusive literature to the futile discussion of how competent someone has to be in order to be considered 'bilingual'. Dozens of attempts have been made at a definition. The impasse reached can only be overcome, if bilingualism is no longer regarded as something inside the speaker's head, but as a displayed feature in participants' everyday behaviour. You cannot be bilingual in your head, you have to use two or more languages 'on stage', in interaction, where you show others that you are able to do so. I propose then to examine bilingualism primarily as a set of complex linguistic activities, and only in a secondary, derived sense as a cognitive ability. From such a perspective, bilingualism is a predicate ascribed to and by participants on the basis of their visible, inspectable behaviour. As a result, there is no one set definition of bilingualism. Being bilingual is turned into an achieved status, and how it is achieved, in different ways and by different speakers, is precisely what we need to investigate. We need a model of bilingual conversation which provides a coherent and functionally motivated picture of bilingualism as a set of linguistic activities.

A model of bilingual conversation

Two basic category pairs provide the 'underlying' procedural apparatus for arriving at local interpretations of language alternation embedded in their individual contexts. These are the category pairs *transfer* vs. *code-switching* and *participant-* vs. *discourse-related* language alternation. From a hearer's point of view, the speaker has to indicate solutions to the following problems corresponding to the two category pairs:

I. Is the language alternation in question connected to a particular conversational *structure* (for instance, a word, a sentence, or a larger unit) (transfer), or to a particular *point* in conversation (code-switching)?

II. Is the language alternation in question providing cues for the *organization of the ongoing interaction* (i.e., is discourse-related), or about *attributes of the speaker* (i.e., is it participant-related)?

In answering these questions, and in providing indications that make them answerable, bilingual participants operate a basic category grid which provides a fundamental four-way differentiation of the signalling device under investigation. It is important to keep in mind that 'discourse-related code-switching' 'participant-related code-switching', 'discourse-related transfer' and 'participant-related transfer' are not generic categories grouping language alternation types, that is, they are not superordinates to subordinated alternation types such as addressee selection, citations, and so on. Instead, the latter should be seen as situated interpretations arrived at in context, whereas the former are generally available procedures designed to carry out these local interpretations. It is these more general procedures and not the types of language alternation which are used as interpretive resources by participants in the first place.

Let us begin by taking a look at the dichotomy *discourse-* vs. *participant-related switching*. In the organization of bilingual conversation, participants face two types of tasks. First, there are problems specifically addressed to language choice. A given conversational episode may be called bilingual as soon as participants orient to the question of which language to speak. Second, participants have to solve a number of problems independently of whether they use one or more languages; these are problems related to the organization of conversation in general, e.g. to turn-taking, topical cohesion, 'key' (in Hymes' sense), the constitution of specific linguistic activities. The alternating use of two languages may be a means to cope with these problems. For illustration, let us turn to some data extracts:[4]

Extract (1) (VIERER G 37–39)

((Clemente is telling a story in order to prove how little respect German children have for their parents. He reports an interaction between a German boy and his mother.))

```
37 : 14   m:    kom=è kome a fattë?
     15   Cl:   na - na - un - un kompan'o del - kë kë va nella
     16         klassë ko me a dettO ke io lO devO a - prendere
                nO: per g'oka:rë - io sono andantë dopë në -
     17         noi le volemë=mondare una - - Seifenkiste - -
38 : 01   m:    mi devi spiegare kos=è sta Seifekiste hẹ hẹ
     02   ((Agostino, Camillo and Alfredo laugh))
     03   Cl:   i weiß itte
     04   Al:         sag einfach na karrotsEllë ko le rO:të
     05   Cl:   aja: ja genau - - na dopë a venuta la la su
     06   Ag:               u:nd?
     07   Cl:   ma:dre noi ab/ ehm - - e=nato a spannë i - - pannë
                no: nda dopë lei dOmanda ma : : ti: tu n eh de
     08         de=fattë i komptë - nda : : - nël suo fil'ë - -
     09         ditt
     10                              (1.0)
     11         nientë
     12                              (1.0)
     13         dopa heh? - (ja it ìe a) sẹntsi=i: - kompti - -
     14         mae - h (tu : :) hẹ hẹ hẹ hẹ 'h ḍopẹ=ḳomẹ=ạ=
                              oo  oo
     15   Ag?:                       ḥ
     16   Cl:   =ḍẹttẹ; 'h=
```

```
        17  Al.:  =sags in deutsch halt wenn=s et it
→     18  Cl:                                        Mensch du mit deiner
                                                            ((high pitch, imitates
        19          miese Laune fahr doch ab   h   h   h h h
                            shouting))
        20                                      ((Ca., Al. & Ag. laughing))
        21  m:                                          kome, kome?
        22          Mensch du mit? ki è - il bambino a detto
        23          alla mamma
        24  Cl:    e : : la dittë a la ma a — ditt=a : — tu=eh ke ke
        25  Al:        laut!
        26  Cl:    lei kwella: — ku — këlla Laune —
39 : 01  Al:    Cle — sags auf deutsch er wird scho verstehe=aber
        02  Ca:             (. . . . . . . . . . . . . . . . . . . . . . )
        03  Al:    deutlich!
        04  Cl:    nja —
        05  Ag:    Mensch du mit deiner miesen Laune fahr ab
```

TRANSLATION (German parts in CAPITAL LETTERS)

```
37 : 14  m:    how did it what did he do?
        15  Cl:    a-a-a-a friend of the — who who goes in the class
        16          with me said that I have to — take him you know for
                    playing — I went then (we) —
        17          we wanted to set up a — — SOAP BOX — —
38 : 01  m:    you have to explain to me what that is this SOAP BOX
        03  Cl:    I DON'T KNOW
        04  Al:            JUST SAY a pram on wheels
        05  Cl:    OH YES I SEE — — a — then has came the the his
        06  Ag:            SO?
        07  Cl:    mother we ha/uhm — — — she came to HANG UP the — —
                    clothes you see in the then she asks but you you n uh ha
        08          have (to do) your homework — in — in her son — —
        09          he said
        11          nothing
        13          then eh? — (. . . . . . .) without=the — homework — —
        14          (but) — h (you : :) he he he he 'h then=what=did=she=
        16          =say; 'h=
        17  Al:    =SAY IT IN GERMAN IF YOU CANNOT (SAY) IT
→     18  Cl:                                    HEY YOU AND YOUR
                                                        LOUSY IDEAS
```

```
   19        PUSH OFF h h h h h
   21  m:                  what, what?
   22        YOU AND? who was – the boy said it to
   23        his mother
   24  Cl:   yes he said it to his mo he – said to – you=eh who who
   25  Al:           SPEAK UP!
   26  Cl:   she this : – with – this IDEAS –
39 : 01  Al:   CLE – SAY IT IN GERMAN HE WILL UNDERSTAND=BUT
   03        CLEARLY!
   04  Cl:   WELL –
   05  Ag:   YOU AND YOUR LOUSY IDEAS PUSH OFF
```

The interaction is between four youngsters (Clemente, 13, Camillo, 13, Alfredo, 14 and Agostino, 15) and an Italian student and fieldworker (m.). The four form an insulated network cluster which is characterized by a high frequency of switching and transfer of all types. Clemente, the youngest, is also the most German-dominant of the four. In our extract, he tries to tell a story to m. Many aspects of his way of talking suggest that he is having enormous difficulties formulating what he wants to express in Italian (see the hesitations, vowel lengthening, repetitions and reformulations, incomprehensible passages). The efforts he makes to speak (Standard) Italian for m. (a variety he hardly knows), and not to make use of German (which he speaks fluently), lead him into hybrid forms, transfer from German (cf. the *spannë* in 38 : 07) and Italian dialect (cf. the *nda* instead of *nel*, 38 : 08), hypercorrections (cf. *a venuta* in 38 : 05 as the maximally distinct form from dialectal schwa-reduction *venutë*), and a generally wide range of variation.[5] Clemente's difficulties reach a climax when he attempts to translate what the German boy in his narrative said to his mother – the punch line of the story. He finally switches to German to make himself understood (line 38 : 18 f). In reconstructing the local interpretation of this instance of code-switching, the various hesitation phenomena and, on a grammatical level, the *italiano stentato* produced by the boy give us the decisive cues. They reveal that it is his competence in Italian which doesn't allow him to continue, and that switching into German rescues the narrative (if at all) because of his superior competence in this language. Switching thus displays an imbalanced bilingual competence. A second possible interpretation relating Clemente's switching to the direct speech he is about to report, can be shown to be of no more than secondary relevance for participants, for another participant explicates how he interpreted Clemente's hesitations: Alfredo, in lines 38 : 18 and 9 : 01 appeals to Clemente to use German (in line 17, his *sags in deutsch halt* is to be continued with a 'if you can't . . . say it in Italian'). We can therefore be quite sure that our interpretation of the speaker's switching into German as being related to his lacking competence in Italian is also shared by the co-participants in this episode.

The second type of participant-related switching doesn't display a participant's competence, but his or her *preference* for one language over the other. Of course, the two are not always independent. For instance, participants often use self-ascriptions of incompetence as accounts for their preferences.[6] Extract (2) is an instance of preference-related code-switching. Participants are Irma (11) and m., the field-worker. Irma lives in a German-dominated network, including only one Italian boy (her brother). She has a clear preference for German, whereas m. (as do almost all adult Italians) prefers Italian. Language alternation is due in this case to m.'s and Irma's insisting on and thereby displaying their respective preferences. While m. consistently uses Italian for all of his contributions, Irma only switches into Italian once (for the Italian variant of her brother's name — *Tonio* instead of *Toni* — which answers m.'s *ki* in line 03). Usually, she speaks German:[7]

Extract (2) (MG 10 I B, 2)

((talk about Irma's name))

	01	Ir.:	Toni ((=her brother)) nennt mich Makkaroni;
	02		– – Makkaronimännchen
			((lamenting))
→	03	m:	ˆki
	04	Ir.:	Tonio!
	05	m:	ki E/ ah:
→	06	Ir.:	de Toni eh (immer) Toni mi(t)=m=
→	07	m:	=E=pperkE? perke: ti kiama
→	08	Ir.:	früher hat=r immer gsagt

```
09        Makkaronimännchen °wieviel Uhr und so,° – –
10        jetz nennt=er mich au Irma: –
```
_____

TRANSLATION
```
        01  Ir.:  TONI CALLS ME MACARONI; – – MACARONI
        02        MANNIKIN
→       03  m:    who
        04  Ir:   TONIO!
        05  m:    who's that/ah:
→       06  Ir:   TONI UH (ALWAYS) TONI WITH=THE=
→       07  m:    =and=why? why does he call you
→       08  Ir:                     HE USED TO SAY MACARONI
        09        MANNIKIN WHAT'S THE TIME AND SO ON, – –
        10        NOW HE CALLS ME IRMA TOO; –
```

Our interpretation that such a patterned usage of the two languages can tell us (and participants) something about Irma's and m.'s preferences (at least, in the given constellation) is based on the more general expectation that for two participants it is 'unmarked' to agree on a common language for interaction rather than using languages at random. This is in fact the case in the sociolinguistic situation we are dealing with, although certainly not an universal feature of bilingual communities.

Extracts (3) and (4) illustrate *discourse-related code-switching* for certain conversational tasks which are relevant in monolingual contexts as well.

(Luziano is 10, Pino is 9.)

Extract (3) (MG 3 I A 70/71)

((m. has taken Luziano and Pino in his car to his house. The car has stopped, the three are about to get out.))
```
    70 : 06  m:    là là si apre, là sotto
       07  Lz.:  ah là.
→   71 : 01        Pino – – willscht rau:s – wart mal
       02        wart mal Pino
```
_____

TRANSLATION:
```
    70 : 06  m:    here here you can open it, down there
       07  Lz.:  oh there.
```

```
71 : 01        PINO – SO YOU WANT TO GET OUT – WAIT,
     02        WAIT PINO
```

Extract (4) (MG I A 50)

```
((In m.'s car, on the way to a city district called Wollmatingen))
     01    Lz.:    il mio dzio ahm – abita=pure a Wollmatingen
     02    m:      ah
     03                                          (0.5)
     04            lo vai a trovare on'i tanto?
     05    Lz.:    °ah° (.) kwalke vo:lta=
     06    m:      =mhm
     07                                          (5.0)
→   08    Lz.:    da kommt Luft raus
     09    m:      si : , – mhm,
```

TRANSLATION:
```
     01    Lz.:    my uncle uhm – also lives in Wollmatingen
     02    m:      ah
     04            do you go and see him now and then?
     05    Lz.:    ah (.) sometimes=
     06    m:      =mhm
     08    Lz.:    HERE THE AIR COMES OUT
     09    m:      yes, – mhm,
```

In example (3), Luziano's switching in line 71 : 01 helps to
bring about a change in the participant constellation. His *ah là*
has acknowledged m.'s instruction on how to get out of the car;
but in the following utterance, the boy takes on the role of
the 'knowing adult' himself vis-à-vis Pino. The activities are set
off by the use of different languages against each other. Together
with non-linguistic cues such as gaze and gesture (which cannot
be analyzed on the basis of the audio-tape), it is language alternation which effects this change in constellation. In (4), the discourse function served by code-switching is topic change. Luziano
has been talking about his uncle in 01–06, but in 08, after a
relatively long silence, he refers to the car. Again, switching
from Italian into German is one of the means used to terminate
one and to initiate the next stretch of talk.

If we compare participant and discourse-related language
alternation we note that the main difference is the object of

the signalling process. Whereas in the case of participant-related alternation, co-participants display or ascribe certain predicates to each other (competence, preference), they signal a change of conversational context in the case of discourse-related switching.[8] This is why language alternation of the second type is what Gumperz calls a contextualization strategy: a strategy by which participants signal what the are doing at a particular moment. We may also use Goffman's term *footing* and say that code-switching can effect a change from one footing to another when related to discourse.[9] Looked upon as a way of contextualizing verbal activities, code-switching can be compared to other contextualization cues such as change of loudness or tempo, change of body position or gaze, etc.

Some important types of discourse-related switching found in our materials are

— change in participant constellation
— change in mode of interaction (for instance, between a formal interview and a casual conversation, or between a move in a game and conversation)
— topic change
— sequential contrast (for instance, between an on-going sequence and a subordinated repair sequence, or side-remark)
— change between informative and evaluative talk, for instance, after stories (including formulations and other summing-up techniques).

In addition to these local interpretations of code-switching occurring between or within single speakers' turns, there are others which overwhelmingly or even exclusively occur within turns, such as

— marking of non-first firsts (e.g. of repeated questions or requests)
— marking of reformulations/elaborations
— setting off prefaces from stories or other 'big packages' (Sacks)
— setting of 'setting' and 'events' in narratives
— distinguishing various types of information in an utterance (for instance, 'given' and 'new', or 'focus of contrast' and the rest of the contribution, to use Chafe's terms).

The last types hold a middle position with regard to the second major distinction, that between *code-switching* and *transfer*. (Note that the two basic dichotomies provide bilingual participants with four prototypical cases of language alternation; between these prototypical cases, there are numerous less prototypical ones, which are attributed conversational meaning on the basis of their distance from the prototypes. Heller (Introduction, in this volume, pp. 11 and 15) is indeed right: category boundaries *are* fuzzy, and any attempt by the analyst to dissolve this fuzziness in favour of the Procrustean bed of clearly delimited categories will lead to a loss of realism in description.)

Looking at language alternation in conversation, especially in sequential terms, one notices two major patterns. According to the first, language alternation from language X to language Y is followed by further talk in language X, either by the same or by other participants. According to the second pattern, language alternation from language X to language Y is followed by further talk in language Y, by same or other participants. Apparently, there is a difference in how language alternation affects the language of interaction (the 'base language'). In the first case, we speak of transfer: no renegotiation of the language of interaction is observed. The stretch of speech formulated in the other language has a built-in and predictable point of return into the first language. In the second case, we speak of code-switching: the new language invites succeeding participants to also use this new language. In fact, not using this language may be interpreted as disregarding the first speaker's language preference and/or competence (in the case of participant-related switching) or the new 'footing' (in the case of discourse-related switching).

Extracts (5) and (6) illustrate transfer from German into Italian. (Participants are the same as in Extract (1). The episode SCHNECKENFRESSER was recorded two years after VIERER. It will be noted that whereas Clemente still has a preference for German, Alfredo is quite willing to speak Italian (dialect) now.)

As in the case of code-switching (see extracts (1) to (4)), we have to distinguish between participant- and discourse-related transfers:

Extract (5) (VIERER B: 37–38)

((narrative about a typing test the speaker took))

```
37 : 07  Al:    skrivi dopo — kwandë la maestra vidë ke sai skrive
                ((lento))                          ((acc.))
    08          — molto ti fa komminc'are a skrive — h koll=o —
                ((lento))
    09          l=oro10g' g' o=diec' I minutI kwante fai;
    10  m:      °aha,°
    11  Al:             dOppë — da tuttI kwelle pac' ine ke pë skrive
    12          sveltI c'E skrittë,
    13          tutti Anschläge kwandë/volte — 'hhh
    14  m:                                    °mhm,°
    15  Al:    sin zum Beispeil: due mille=o — c'inke c'ento: —
    16  Ag:    due mille c'inkwe c'ento
                (pp e molto presto))
    17  m:     par ole
    18  Al:         Ansc hläge
    19  m:              Anschläge kwã=m (. . .)
                                       ((pp))
38 : 01  Al:    arOppë — guarda le: — Fehler — allOrë i=errori
                ((lento))
    02          e tutto sbal' c'i vonno lovare ventic'inkwe
                                             ((hesitating))
                Anschläge — c'ai/ —
    03  m:      °o kapito°
```

TRANSLATION:

```
37 : 07  Al:    you write then — when the teacher sees that you can write
    08          — a lot she makes you start to write — h
                with=the=w —
    09          the watch=when (?) you do ten minutes;
    10  m:      aha,
    11  Al:        then — of all the pages that you were able to
    12          write fast which you (?) have written,
    13          all the TOUCHES how many/times — 'hhh
    14  m:                                    mhm,
    15  Al:    THERE ARE FOR INSTANCE
                two thousand=or — five hundred
    16  Ag:    two thousand five hundred ((corrects Al.'s pronunciation))
```

17 m: words
18 Al: TOUCHES
19 m: TOUCHES (. . . . . .)
38 : 01 Al: and then − she has a look at the − MISTAKES − I mean
                the mistakes − and (for) every mistake they are going to
                subtract twenty-five TOUCHES − which is/ −
03 m: I got it

Extract (6) (SCHNECKENFRESSER 91 : 25)

((Cl. and Al. are complaining about two older people living in their house))

02 m: perke non lavorano però eh stanno tutto=il
03   g'orno a kasa
04 Al: ke E vẹkkië e g'a pendzionann nun g'annë fil'ë,=
05 m: =he : :
06 Cl.:   na aber nicht der Mann; − der Mann schafft no;
07 Al: u mO u mO
08   u Mạnn E : : c' s' te: kiu s' − kiu schlimm angOrë;
09   (1.0)
10 Al.:   na vO : t (.)
11 m: °°mhm°°

((follows Italian narrative))

_ _

TRANSLATION:
02 m: because they don't work eh they stay at home all day
03   long
04 Al: because (s)he is old and retired already they don't have children;=
05 m: =he : :
06 Cl: NO BUT NOT THE HUSBAND; −
                THE HUSBAND STILL GOES TO WORK;
07 Al: the HUSBAND the HUSBAND
08   the HUSBAND is sometimes even wor − worse;
10   once (.)

((follows narrative))
((Note: mo is dialectal for <u>Mann</u>))

In (5), Alfredo is about to explain a rather complex matter, i.e.
how the final results were calculated in a typing test. He runs into
difficulties in the case of *Fehler/errori* and *Anschläge* ('touches')

which are marked as such by vowel lengthening, hesitation, short silence and above all the self-repair in line 01 (*allorë i=errori*) and the initiated but uncompleted self-repair in line 02 (*c'ai* :/from *cioè i*. . .). The transfer from German is displayed as related to the speaker's (momentary) lack of competence in Italian: it is the German word which comes to his mind first. In (6), we find one of the more important types of discourse-related transfer which I call anaphoric. Alfredo refers to the person introduced in Camillo's previous German turn and uses *Mann* as a topical link between the two utterances. *U Mann* here means 'this man you are talking about'.[10] Certainly, this type of back-referencing could also have been accomplished by the Italian equivalent (*l=uomo*); however, anaphoric typing is based solely on semantic similarity in this latter case, whereas it is based on semantic and formal identity in the first.

Although most of the instances of transfer we find in our materials are on the lexical level (here, nouns are by far the most frequent), our definition of transfer does not restrict the term to this level. We only require that transfer not relate to a certain *point* in conversation (as code-switching does) but to a certain (well-defined) unit which has a predictable end that will also terminate the use of the other language. Accordingly, transfer on higher structural levels must be included as well, for instance language alternation to set off citations, or even songs, sayings, poems, rhymes and other 'kleine Gattungen'. In all these cases, transfer is discourse-related.

Two additional remarks concerning the distinction between transfer and code-switching: (1) first, our expectation is that after code-switching, it is the newly introduced language that will be taken up by the co-participant. This is only a conversational preference, not an absolute 'rule' or 'norm'. On the one hand, there are cases of code-switching in which recipients refuse to accept the new footing together with the new language; and cases in which recipients accept the new footing, but not the new language (a phenomenon which would have to be interpreted on the level of language preference ascription); on the other hand, there are cases of transfer which 'prepare' or 'trigger' switching into the other language. What is important is the distinction between switching *points* and transferred units; (2) Secondly, my notion of transfer does not correspond to and is not to be confused with the one usually met in the literature on language contact and second language acquisition. The latter is supposed to cover the phenomena subsumed under 'interference' before that concept went out of fashion. Let us call them transfer$_L$, where the subscript L stands for 'linguist'; for transfer$_L$ is defined and described from the linguist's point of view. He or she can take into account 'diachronic' and other facts that do not necessarily concern participants. Transfer$_L$ is in continuous danger of being a linguistic artifact, due to a monolingual point of view, that is, of taking the monolingual systems of the two languages in contact as the point of reference (German as spoken by Germans in, e.g. Hanover, and Italian as spoken e.g. in Milano). The (bilingual) speaker may not make a distinction between two independent and strictly separated systems. Often the varieties in the repertoires of bilingual speech communities show independent developments setting them off against the coexisting monolingual norms ('convergence'). Transfer$_P$ (P for participant) is defined from the member's perspective. Accordingly, if we want to claim that an item such as *Mann* is a transfer$_P$, we have to show that the speaker *makes use of* the other-language status of *Mann*. It is not enough that *Mann* can be found in a German dictionary, and not in an Italian one. The 'proof procedures' for transfer$_P$ and transfer$_L$ are therefore quite different. Usually, transfer$_L$ is the weaker alternative with which we have to content ourselves if we cannot demonstrate that the production of an 'other'-language item has a function (be it of the discourse- or of the participant-related type). Transfer$_P$ requires demonstrating how the participant displays a 'reason' for language alternation, in the way this alternation is produced, which is visible to his or her co-participants (as in our extracts 5 and 6).

Transfer$_L$ is observed in the following utterances, also from our materials, but from a different speaker: Daniele is part of a network that is dominated by newly arrived Italian boys. Interaction in this network is characterized by the almost complete lack of code-switching. Language alternation occurs in the format of (mostly discourse-relate) transfer$_P$, but most transfers are not marked as such by the speaker:

Daniele: mia (*sic*) padre fa: l=spazi:no: e: − mia madre fa: la Putzfrau (50 : 08/9)
TRANSLATION: my father is a road sweeper and − my mother is a CLEANING WOMAN

Daniele: o: vergon'atevi davanti $\left\{ \begin{matrix} il \\ al \end{matrix} \right\}$ Mikrophón − 71 : 07)

TRANSLATION: or do you feel embarrassed in front of the MICROPHONE

Daniele: volete delle Kartoffel (73 : 11)
TRANSLATION: do you want CHIPS ((lit.: potatoes))

Daniele: mme l'i mettë tutti sopra al Sparbuch kwelli ke mi gwardan'o=ilà; (97 : 12)
TRANSLATION: (s)he puts them all on my SAVING ACCOUNT (the money) which I make there;

Here, we cannot speak of transfer$_p$ in the sense of (individually) functional language alternation, but only of transfer$_L$ in the sense of *code-fluctuation*[11] which is possibly interpretable in global terms. The distinction between language alternation and code-fluctuation is based on the way textual variation between two items presents itself to conversationalists.

Who switches how?

The following remarks on individual differences among the Italian children investigated must be prefaced with a *caveat* as this part of the study is not finished yet. Above all, differential statements need to be embedded in a wider linguistic and ethnographic description of the speakers than can be given here.[12]

The first question we have to ask is: If Italian migrant children alternate between languages, what is the *direction* of code-switching and transfer? There is an enormous amount of evidence which supports the following hypothesis:

Hypothesis 1:
In the overwhelming number of cases, code-switching is from the Italian into the German part of the linguistic repertoire. Transfer is from German into Italian passages.

This clear dominance of German holds for more or less all types of alternation mentioned above, with the exception of turn-internal switching, which is unspecific with regard to direction. In the case of competence-related alternation, practically all transferred items are from German, and all instances of code-switching are from Italian into German. The conclusion to be drawn from this is that because the preponderance of German is not restricted to pre-ference-related switching, all types of alternation, in addition to whatever else they may do in conversation, display an imbalance between the Italian and the German part of the repertoire. Most of the children have a much stronger tendency to switch codes when the 'base language' is Italian, and almost all children readily transfer lexical items from German into Italian, but rarely vice versa. If we look at the type of 'footing' that coincides with discourse-related switching, the much greater interactional 'value' of German as opposed to Italian is underlined even more. German is the switched-to language coinciding with a transition from formal to informal interaction or from giving information to evaluating it. German is used for ironic or humorous statements, for side-remarks, for the punchline of a story or a joke, etc.

The instances of language alternation that do not conform to this picture are often of a particular type. They are not from German into Regional Italian, but from German (or Regional Italian) into the local southern Italian dialect or its approximation. Without going into details[13] it can be said that for those children who (still) have the choice between more than one variety of Italian, the local dialect may have the same function in relation to German (or Regional Italian) as German does in relation to Regional Italian.

This is to say that a transition from more to less formal speech, from topical talk to side-remarks, or the setting off of humorous or funny statements, may either correspond to a switching from 'Regional' Italian to dialectal Italian, or to one from 'Regional' Italian to German (dialect); it will not coincide with a transition in the opposite direction, however. The third case (switching between Italian dialect and German (dialect)) is rare and less predictable: it may take either direction. Thus, in a maximally exploited repertoire, we can get the following switches:

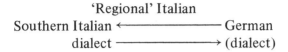

A second hypothesis concerns the overall frequency of language alternation. Here, the following picture emerges:

Hypothesis 2:
Frequency of language alternation is most often similar for members of the same interactional network.

It seems that members of the same network adapt to each other and develop a common style of linguistic behaviour which may or may not be characterized by code-switching and transfer. This is true independent of the quality of the particular network.

Types of network contacts are relevant for a more detailed characterization of the individual speaker's linguistic behaviour:

Hypothesis 3:
If a child's primary network contacts are children of a similar biographical background, language alternation will mostly assume the format of discourse-related switching, otherwise, there may be discourse-related transfer, but most often, language alternation is restricted to the participant-related types.

This means that children who do not have any contacts with other Italian children, or who are part of networks which incorporate children with different histories of migration (recently arrived Italian dominant speakers), show the lowest percentage of discourse-related switching. Those who have their primary network contacts with children who have lived through a similar socialization process show a higher percentage of these switches. Thus, only the existence and the homogeneity of networks seems to provide the necessary conditions for the development of language alternation as a contextualization strategy. If a child who has been brought up and/or was born in Germany has close friends or siblings who have only come here recently, discourse-related switching will be rare.

A final hypothesis concerns the internal differentiation of the largest group of alternations, i.e. discourse-related switching:

Hypothesis 4:
The employment of code-switching as a contextualization strategy varies with age.

Among the earlier employments of discourse-related switching (most frequent between the ages of 10 to 13), switching to initiate a change of participant constellation is most likely because of its intimate relationship to preference-related switching. For quite often, changing the language when addressing a new partner is only the functional aspect of adapting to his or her language preference which diverges from that of the preceding addressee. More sophisticated uses of code-switching, for example, changing the topic, or the mode of interaction, or establishing sequential contrasts, etc., as well as the various types of turn-internal switching only become frequent at around age 13 or 14.

Conclusion

Language alternation can be approached from a number of perspectives. Three stand out in the literature: the grammatical, the macro-sociolinguistic and the conversation analytic approach. From the grammatical perspective, a number of restrictions on code-switching within the sentence have been formulated (cf. Poplack 1982; Gumperz 1982; and others). These restrictions are important for a general theory of grammatical processing in bilinguals, for they allow one to draw certain conclusions about the psycholinguistic reality of the bilingual's two grammars. However, they are only relevant in a minority of cases of language

alternation in our materials. The Italian children we have investigated usually change languages either for individual lexical items,
or for whole sentences. But even in intrasentential switching,
grammatical restrictions do not tell us anything about the interactional 'value' or 'meaning' of transfer and code-switching as
conversational activities.

Surprisingly perhaps, the same applies to the macro-sociolinguistic perspective (cf., for instance, Breitborde 1983). Again,
general statements are made, concerning the distribution of
code-switching in certain situations, or among participants holding
certain 'roles' and 'statuses' in a given society, but little or nothing
is said about the contribution of language alternation to the
ongoing interaction, that is, about its local functioning. Thus,
although neither the value of the grammatical nor that of the
macro-sociolinguistic perspective can be denied, it seems that
both have to be incorporated into a third, more basic perspective
which is to investigate the contribution of language alternation to
members' sense-making activities. This may fruitfully be done
in the framework of conversation analysis, which, taking into
account grammatical restrictions where necessary, can work up
and relate to larger scale sociolinguistic statements.[14] Some
fundamental distinctions that are relevant for the production and
interpretation of language alternation in conversation have been
presented in this paper.

On the basis of these distinctions, the place of language alternation between the German and the Italian part of the repertoire,
in the speech of Italian migrant children in Germany, can be
summarized as follows:

— The two parts of the repertoire are not kept distinct. There is a
  high degree of variation; in particular, a high degree of lexical
  transfer$_L$ was noted. These lexical transfer are not usually
  adapted to the phonology or grammar of the receiving language:
  indeed, I have argued that it would be mistaken to speak of a
  receiving language here at all. We are simply dealing with intra-
  repertoire variation.
— Code-switching is frequent, but mostly occurs at sentence
  boundaries. Sentence-internal switching is only relevant in some
  few, insulated and dense networks.

— Code-switching is not necessarily related to a metaphoric function (in Gumperz' sense). Often, it 'just' takes part in the organization of discourse. As a contextualization strategy, it is comparable to prosodic parameters such as intonation, loudness or pitch level.
— Most speakers have a preference for German. By code-switching, they display this preference, or their better competence in that language. Code-switching is always an attempt to renegotiate the language of interaction, at least temporarily.
— Both competence-related switching and competence-related transfer demonstrate that in the present situation, typical aspects of language contact mix with aspects of second language acquisition (of 'Regional' Italian).

It is reasonable to conclude from all these indicators that at the macro-level, the sociolinguistic situation of the second generation Italian migrants is still unstable and may develop in two directions: complete linguistic adaptation including loss of Italian and Italian dialects in the repertoire, or stabilization as a bilingual community. This uncertainty certainly corresponds to the social mobility of the Italian 'communities' which, in turn, is to be seen against the background of political (European Community) and geographical (distance) factors. A more definite answer will be possible as soon as we move on to a next step of analysis: the comparison of different Italian communities abroad.

Notes

+   I wish to thank Steven Gillies for correcting my English.
1. A more detailed analysis grounded in the transcripts is given in Auer 1983/1984, 1981 and 1984a.
2. Cf. Di Luzio 1983 for an outline of the project, and Auer and Di Luzio 1983a, b; Bierbach (1983); and d'Angelo 1984 for some results. The M.I.G. project was located in the *Sonderforschungsbereich 99* at the *Fachgruppe Sprachwissenschaft* of the University of Constance from 1980 to 1985.
3. cf. d'Angelo 1984.

4. The usual transcription conventions of conversation analysis are employed. However, note that

/	:	phonetic break-off
(.)	:	phonetic pause
—	:	pause not exceeding 0.2 sec.
ḥ ḥ ḥ	:	laughing.

For the transcription of the Italian passages, quasi-phonetic symbols are used:

E, O, I	:	open variables of $\underline{e}, \underline{o}, \underline{i}$
c', g'	:	alveo-palatal affricates
s', z'	:	alveo-palatal fricatives
l', n'	:	palatal laterals and nasals
ë	:	schwa.

English translations give a simplified version.

5. Cf. Auer and Di Luzio 1983a, b for an analysis of this type of variation (*italiano stentato*).
6. For details, cf. Auer 1981.
7. Irma insists on German in initiative sequential positions (lines 01/02), in responsive sequential position (line 09) and in a contribution which disregards the co-participant's prior turn altogether (lines 8 ff). In a more extensive discussion of the data, it could be demonstrated that these three positions are not equivalent with regard to preference displays. Responsive utterances in the other language are stronger indicators of diverging preferences than initiative ones (where I mean by 'responsive' and 'initiative' the respective slots in sequential formats such as question/answer, etc.). Disregarding the preceding other-language contribution can be a way to avoid a responsive position in which switching would have underlined one's preference, for the sake of an initiative contribution (cf. Auer 1983 for details).
8. We are talking about primary levels of interpretation here. On a secondary, 'global' level, matters of competence and preference also relate to the organization of discourse, for finding a common language of interaction obviously is a prerequisite for interaction. Vice versa, discourse related switching can allow ascriptions of competence and of preference to individual speakers.
9. Cf. Gumperz 1982; Goffman 1979.
10. Apart from anaphoric transfer, lexical transfer is not very often employed for discourse-related purposes in our data. In rare cases, transfer is usually part of a contrast pair built up between a same-language and an other-language item. For an example, cf. Del Coso-Calame et al., MS.
11. Cf. Auer and Di Luzio, 1983a, b.
12. Cf. d'Angelo 1984 for ethnographic details.

13. Cf. Di Luzio 1984.
14. Jordan and Fuller (1975), Heller (1982), Valdés and Pino (1981), and McClure (1977) belong to the few authors who have attempted to approach code-switching in conversation analytic terms, although the investigations are restricted to certain types of language alternation. More comprehensive accounts are given by Gumperz (1982), in his famous distinction between situational and metaphorical code-switching, and by Zentella (1981). I have dealt with Gumperz' model elsewhere in detail (Auer 1984a). Zentella's distinction between factors "on the spot," pertaining to the "observables of interaction" (1981: 147), and factors "in the head" which are not directly observable leads into somewhat artificial classifications, when, for example, "topic", "psychological setting" and addressee's language preference are grouped together as "on the spot" factors, whereas a momentary loss for words, or a change of the speaker's role are said to be factors "in the head".

References

Auer, J. C. P.
    1981   Bilingualism as a members' concept: language choice and language alternation in their relation to lay assessments of competence. *Papiere des SFB 99*, Constance, No. 54.
    1983/   Zweisprachige Konversationen. *Papiere des SFG 99*, Constance,
    1985   No. 79. English translation: *Bilingual conversation*. Amsterdam, 1984 (Pragmatics and Beyond).
    1984a   Conversational code-switching. In: Auer and Di Luzio (eds.).
Auer, J. C. P. and Di Luzio, A.
    1983a   Structure and meaning of linguistic variation in Italian migrant children in Germany. In: R. Bäuerle, Ch. Schwarze & A. v. Stechow (eds.), *Meaning, Use and Interpretation of Language*. Berlin, pp. 1–21.
    1983b   Three types of variation and their interpretation. In: L. Dabène, M. Flasaquier & J. Lyons (eds.), *Status of Migrants' Mother Tongues*. ESF, Strasbourg, pp. 67–100.
Auer, J. C. P. and Di Luzio, A. (eds.)
    1984   *Interpretive Sociolinguistics: Migrants – Children – Migrant Children*. Tübingen.
Bierbach, C.
    1983   'Nun erzähl' mal mas!' Textstruktur und referentielle Organisation in elizitierten Erzählungen italienischer Kinder. In: E. Gülich & Th. Kotschi (eds.), *Grammatik, Konversation, Interaktion*. Tübingen, Niemeyer.

d'Angelo, D.
1984 Interaktionsnetzwerke und soziokultureller Hintergrund italie-nischer Migranten und Migrantenkinder in Konstanz. *Papiere des SFB 99*, Constance.

Del Coso-Dalame, F., De Pietro, F. & Oesch-Serra, C.
MS La compétence de communication bilingue. (Université Neuchâtel).

Di Luzio, A.
1983 Problemi linguistici dei figli dei lavoratori migranti. In: G. Braga (ed.), *Problemi linguistici e unità europea*. Milano: Angeli, pp. 112–119.
1984 On the meaning of language alternation for the sociocultural identity of Italian migrant children. In: Auer and Di Luzio (eds.).

Goffman, E.
1979 Footing. *Semiotica* 25: 1–29.

Gumperz, J.
1982 *Discourse Strategies*. Cambridge: Cambridge University Press.

Heller, M.
1982 Language strategies and ethnic conflict in the workplace. Manu-script, Ontario Institute for Studies in Education.

Jordan, B. & Fuller, N.
1975 On the non-fatal nature of trouble: sense-making and trouble-managing in *lingua franca* talk. *Semiotica* 13: 11–31.

McClure, E.
1977 Aspects of code-switching in the discourse of bilingual Mexican-American children. In: Saville-Troike, M. (ed.), *Linguistics and Anthropology*. Washington, pp. 93–115.

Valdés, G. and Pino, C.
1981 Muy a tus ordenes: compliment responses among Mexican-American bilinguals. *Language in Society*. 10: 53–72.

Zentella, A. C.
1981 *Hablamos los dos. We speak both. Growing up bilingual in El Barrio*. Unpulished Ph.D. dissertation, University of Pennsylvania.

Contrasting patterns of code-switching in two communities

Shana Poplack
University of Ottawa

Recent interests in the constraints on bilingual behavior, and in particular, code-switching, show trends which seem to have come full circle.[1] By early accounts (e.g. Labov 1971), the behavior embodied in code-switching was the exception to the systematic and rule-governed nature of language variation. Researchers such as Gumperz and his students subsequently showed convincingly that code-switching was at least subject to pragmatic and/or inter-actional conditioning, was highly sensitive to the characteristics of the participants, and could be used for a variety of conversational functions (e.g. Gumperz and Hernandez-Chavez 1971; Blom and Gumperz 1972; Gumperz 1976/82). The issue of purely linguistic, or syntactic, constraints on code-switching was either not addressed or dismissed with the claim that there were none (e.g. Lance 1975). Empirical studies of actual speech behavior by, among others, Gumperz (1976/82), Hasselmo (1970, 1972), Pfaff (1979), and McClure (1981) revealed regularities which soon caused linguists to reject this view and even to adopt the opposite extreme, leading to a proliferation of particularistic and often poorly motivated statements of precisely where in the sentence a bilingual may or may not switch. It was soon seen that such ad hoc constraints, though they might hold in a majority or even all instances, were not generalizable from one language pair to another or even across different studies of the same pair in different contexts. Later, the view that some more general constraints might hold, constraints based on a universal compromise strategy of some sort, and predictable on the basis of the grammatical properties of the two languages involved in the alternation, gained currency. We return to this view below. More recent papers have contested this universalistic approach (e.g. Bentahila and Davies

1983), or have situated constraints at other than the syntagmatic level (e.g. Joshi 1983; Prince and Pintzuk 1983), or have rejected all but some language-specific conditions, reminiscent of the positions of the earlier work cited above.

In reviewing this and other current work, two issues become obvious. One is that researchers often confound different bilingual behaviors, including code-switching, but also borrowing on the community and individual levels, incomplete language acquisition, interference, and even acceptability judgements, and use them all as evidence about code-switching patterns. In this paper we stress that these linguistic manifestations of language contact are fundamentally different, both in their constitution and in their implications for the structures of the languages. Thus it is illogical to use a datum which may in fact be a fully integrated loanword, like *attorney general* in English, as evidence about word order violations in French-English code-switching. The second issue also pertains to the nature of appropriate data: attempts at assessing the true status of these different bilingual phenomena are futile unless they first distinguish community-wide from individual, and perhaps idiosyncratic, behavior. Conditions elucidated on borrowing and code-switching should in the first instance be community-wide, or part of the bilingual *langue*, since individual manifestations can only be understood against the background of the community norms. Too many variables which are crucial determinants of this behavior cannot be inferred without detailed knowledge of:

1. the bilingual ability of the informant in each of the languages,
2. the detailed nature of the two monolingual codes in question as they are actually used in some bilingual community, and as distinct from the "standard" varieties of either, and
3. the existence of particular community-specific or "compromise" solutions to the problem of reconciling two codes with conflicting rules within the same utterance, solutions which may be ungrammatical and/or unacceptable in other communities.

The nature of an utterance involving elements from more than one language may be predictable from a particular combination of these factors. Yet there is no way of inferring this information from any but systematic examination of the languages as used in the speech community. Thus use of informants of unspecified bilingual competences or linguistic backgrounds, or of isolated or exceptional examples, without situating them within patterns of community usage, is simply not relevant evidence for the existence of norms of bilingual behavior. A sufficient understanding of an individual's bilingual behavior seems beyond the reach of any but systematic corpus-based research carried out within her or his community.

We illustrate the role of the speech community in understanding bilingual behavior with a series of studies of two bilingual communities, which are superficially similar from both sociological and linguistic points of view, but use very different strategies for handling incorporations from English. In so doing, we return to the issue of distinguishing different contact phenomena. Early on, Haugen (1956) proposed that bilingual phenomena be located along a continuum of code distinctiveness, with switching representing maximal distinctness, integration (or borrowing) representing maximal levelling of distinctions, and interference referring to an overlapping of two codes, contrary to contemporary norms. While theoretically, these categories are eminently reasonable, in real life, bilingual behavior is not so easily classified. Indeed, as Hasselmo (1970) observed, although the intention of the speaker may be to choose either to switch or to use an integrated loanword, the constructions actually produced are often ambiguous.

Spanish/English contact among Puerto Ricans in New York

A first series of studies was carried out in a stable bilingual Puerto Rican community in East Harlem, New York (e.g. Language Policy Task Force 1980; Poplack 1980, 1981). Analysis of data collected by Pedro Pedraza, a group member, as part of a program of long-term participant observation of language distribution and use in the neighborhood, revealed that code-switching between English and Spanish was such an integral part of the community linguistic repertoire that it could be said to function as a mode of interaction similar to monolingual language use. An example of the sort of code-switching frequently heard in this community may be seen in (1), where in the course of a single utterance the language of the discourse oscillates from English to Spanish and back to English; and during each stretch in one language there are switches of smaller constituents to the other.

(1)   But I used to eat the **bofe**, the brain. And then they stopped selling it because **tenián, este, le encontraron que teniá** worms. I used to make some **bofe! Después yo haciá uno d'esos** concoctions: the garlic **con cebolla, y haciá un mojo, y yo dejaba que se curara eso** for a couple of hours. (04/601)[2]

       'But I used to eat the **bofe**, the brain. And then they uh, stopped selling it because they had, uh, they found out that it had worms. I used to make some **bofe!** Then I would make a sauce, and I'd let that sit for a couple of hours.'

We examined a large number of these switches to find out how they functioned in discourse (Poplack 1980). One of the characteristics of this kind of "skilled" or fluent code-switching (as opposed to switching for lack of lexical or syntactic availability, and as opposed to the "flagged" switches we discuss below) is a smooth transition between L_1 and L_2 elements, unmarked by false starts, hesitations or lengthy pauses. And in fact, these data showed smooth transitions between the switched item and adjacent sentence elements in 97% of the cases. Other characteristics include an apparent "unawareness" of the particular alternations between languages (despite a general awareness of using both codes in the discourse), insofar as the switched item is not accompanied by metalinguistic commentary, does not constitute a repetition of an adjacent segment, is made up of larger constituents than just a single noun inserted into an otherwise L_2 sentence, and is used for purposes other than that of conveying untranslatable or ethnically bound items. Again, only about 5% of the Spanish/English switches were used in one of these ways (ibid.).

Now, there are two purely linguistic problems that have to be solved in the course of alternating between two languages without the benefit of pausing, retracting, repeating, or otherwise indicating that you are about to pass from one language to the other. One is the resolution of eventual conflict between the word orders of

the two languages involved in the alternation. In the c
Spanish and English adjective placement, for example, wh
basic Spanish order is NA and the basic English order is AN, ᵤ
switch to English after N means forfeiting the opportunity to
produce A in Spanish while never having had the chance to say it
in English. The second problem is local morphophonological conflict between the two languages, as when an English verb used in a
Spanish context must be inflected for tense and mood.

Detailed analysis of the Spanish/English code-switching data
revealed that there were only two general syntactic constraints on
where intrasentential switching could occur (Poplack 1980, 1981;
Sankoff and Poplack 1981): the free morpheme constraint, which
prohibits mixing morphologies within the confines of the word,
and the equivalence constraint, which requires that the surface
word order of the two languages be homologous in the vicinity of
the switch point.

As a result of the operation of these constraints, sentences containing switches turned out to be locally grammatical by standards
of both Spanish and English simultaneously, suggesting highly
developed linguistic skill in both. Indeed, there were only 11
violations of the equivalence constraint, or well under 1 % of the
1,835 switches studied, though the switches had been produced by
both balanced bilinguals and non-fluent speakers (Poplack 1980).

In considering how these latter were able to code-switch frequently and still maintain grammaticality in both languages,
we found that the Puerto Rican community in East Harlem
could be characterized by three switch types: tag, sentential and
intrasentential, each requiring increasingly greater control of
both languages to produce. These were distributed across the
community according to bilingual ability, with the most highly
bilingual speakers switching mainly within the bounds of the
sentence.

Code-switching vs. borrowing

Now the majority of the material involved in the code-switching
studies cited above consisted of switches of sentences or con-

stituents of sentences which were unambiguously Spanish or English. But the smaller the switched constituent, and particularly at the level of the lone lexical item, the more difficult it is to resolve the question of whether we are dealing with a code-switch or a loanword. Since a code-switch, by Haugen's definition, is maximally distinct froom the surrounding discourse, while a loanword should be identical to recipient-language material on the basis of synchronic considerations alone, differentiating the two might seem to be an easy matter. However, superficially the two may be indistinguishable in appearance. Phonological integration, an oft-cited diagnostic, may not provide a clue if the speaker pronounces all his English words, whether borrowed or not, according to Spanish patterns (i.e. with a Spanish "accent"). Morphology may also be irrelevant if the form requires no affixation, as in the case of a singular noun. Similarly, because of "interlinguistic coincidence" between English and Spanish, syntactic stretches in the two languages are often homologous. The co-occurrence of forms from two languages may also be due to interference or incomplete second language acquisition.

In seeking a way to identify full-fledged loanwords, a number of indices measuring various aspects of the linguistic and social integration of borrowed words were developed (Poplack and Sankoff 1984). These were abstracted from the types of criteria used implicitly or explicitly by scholars of bilingualism (e.g. Bloomfield 1933; Fries and Pike 1949; Weinreich 1953; Mackey 1970; Hasselmo 1970, etc.) to characterize loanwords, and included measures of frequency of use, native language synonym displacement, morphophonemic and/or syntactic integration, and acceptability to native speakers.

The frequency of use and phonological integration indices were found to measure phenomena which are closely related and proceed concurrently, a result which provides solid confirmation of the claims in the literature that borrowed words which are frequently used are made to conform with recipient language linguistic patterns.[3] English-origin material integrated into Puerto Rican Spanish, i.e. established loanwords,[4] could thus be defined as those concepts for which the identical, phonologically adapted designation was used by many or all speakers.

In summary, in the bilingual behaviour of the Puerto Rican community in East Harlem there exists a mode of discourse characterized by frequent switching in a smooth and "unflagged" way between stretches of grammatical English and stretches of grammatical Spanish, the stretches consisting of words, phrases, sentences or larger discourse units. In addition, there are English lexical contributions to Spanish, manifested in terms of loan-words, which follow a well-defined linguistic and social trajectory.

Moreover, there is an operationalizable dichotomy between loanwords and switches. In the ideal case, a word or sequence of words which remains phonologically, morphologically and syntactically unadapted to Spanish could be considered English, i.e. a code-switch from Spanish, while one which is integrated with Spanish patterns could be considered Spanish. Though these criteria could not always be applied, for the reasons detailed above, we also had recourse to the empirical findings that 1) virtually all of the eligible Spanish-English code-switches respected the equivalence constraint, and 2) English-origin words which are used frequently are integrated into Spanish phonological and morphological patterns. Thus, given any single English-origin word in Puerto Rican Spanish discourse, if the same word was used by many speakers and hence uttered with Spanish phonology and morphology, and if in non-equivalent Spanish-English structures (e.g. adjective placement), it followed Spanish rules, then we could consider it a loanword and not a code-switch.

French/English contact in Ottawa-Hull

A second series of studies forms part of an ongoing research project investigating the French spoken in Ottawa-Hull — the national capital region of Canada — and the effects on it of close and sustained contact with English (Poplack 1983a). The Ottawa-Hull urban complex is divided by a river which is both a geographic and linguistic border: on the Quebec side (Hull), French is the majority and sole official language, while on the Ontario side

(Ottawa) it has minority status. One goal of this project is to characterize and compare the French spoken in the area in both its status as official language and in its minority guise. Five neighborhoods were selected on both sides of the border, each with a different proportion of English mother-tongue claimants, in order to test the hypothesis that influence from another language is a function of the recipient language's status in both the immediate and wider environment.

Each was sampled according to strict random sampling procedures, resulting in a fully representative sample of 120 francophones native to Ottawa or Hull respectively, stratified according to age and sex. Lengthy, informal interviews were carried out with informants by local francophone interviewers.

As in the Puerto Rican case, negative stereotypes of the French of the region and notably of that spoken on the Ontario side are widespread, particularly as regards the effects on it of coexistence with English. Our ongoing investigation of speakers' own attitudes toward the language(s) they speak reveals a complex system of linguistic values, not too dissimilar from those obtaining in the Puerto Rican (and other minority) communities (Poplack and Miller 1985). First the French language itself, though endowed with affective import, is widely seen as having less instrumental value than English, with the inverse assessments made of English. On the other hand, speakers commented freely on the "unfairness" of having to learn English when anglophones rarely make the effort to learn French. The use of English in largely French contexts which we will examine below can therefore not be simply ascribed to prestige factors or "impression management". Second, linguistic insecurity vis-à-vis European French (*le français de France*) is generally admitted, although Canadian varieties (with the notable exception of informants' own dialects) are imbued with some covert prestige. Not surprisingly then, the majority of informants on both sides of the border feel that they personally do not speak "good French", characterizing it most frequently as anglicized and *joual* 'slang'. Descriptions of "anglicized French" include the metaphor of mixing, which we interpret to refer to the widespread use of borrowing in the area as well as to code-switching, and another evoking "true" or intrasentential code-switching. Interestingly enough, the latter was limited to Ottawa residents, who, as we shall see, in fact engage in this type of switching somewhat more than the Hull speakers. Indeed, Ottawa speakers showed far greater familiarity with code-switching in general, in terms of overtly recognizing its existence, admitting to engaging in it personally, showing neutral rather than negative affect towards it, and even correctly identifying their own reasons for doing it: they claim that the English way of saying it is often shorter, more succinct, and more apt or expressive.

The French speakers' attitudes contrast sharply with those of the Puerto Ricans in the previous study. Though the Puerto Ricans were also fully cognizant of the prevalence of code-switching in their community and saw nothing wrong with it, their reason for switching was in essence because they "were bilingual" and this mode of discourse was appropriate to their dual identity (Attinasi 1979; also Zentella 1982). As a rule, they did not consider that one language was better for specific interactional or conversational purposes, or that certain concepts could be more felicitously expressed in one language than the other. We shall see below how this difference in attitudes is consistent with dramatically different code-switching behaviors in the two communities.

Code-switching in Ottawa-Hull

Turning now to the actual speech patterns of the Ottawa-Hull informants, exhaustive examination of their incorporations from English in approximately 290 hours of tape-recorded French conversation,[5] revealed some 1766 sequences which could be unambiguously identified as code-switches. Note that though it was largely possible to distinguish code-switching from borrowing in the Puerto Rican Spanish-English data, this is by no means always the case. In Ottawa-Hull (as in many other bilingual communities), French discourses may contain liberal amounts of English incorporations whose status as loanword or code-switch is at first blush unclear, as they may be consistent with both French and English morphology or syntax, as in the examples in bold type in (2):

(2) a. Il y avait une **band** là qui jouait de la musique **steady**, pis il y avait
        des **games** de **ball**, pis ... ils vendaient de l'**ice cream**, pis il y avait
        une grosse **beach**, le monde se baignait. (M.L./888)
        'There was a band there that played music all the time and there
        were ball games, and ... they sold ice cream, and there was a big
        beach where people would go swimming.'
     b. Il y avait toutes sortes de chambres là, tu sais là, un **dining room**,
        living room, un **den**, un **family room**, un **rec room**, mais ... mille neuf
        cent quatre-vingt dix-neuf par mois. (L.M./174)
        'There were all kinds of rooms there, you know, a dining room,
        living room, a den, a family room, a rec room, but ... $ 1999 a
        month.'

In the Ottawa-Hull region a large number of other bilingual
phenomena also intervene to further complicate identification, to
which we return below. One thing seems clear, however. When we
exclude the problem category of uninflected single words (or
compounds functioning as single words), other sequences can be
identified as to their language membership on morphological and
syntactic grounds. Thus the English-origin material in bold type
below is being handled like French and not like English, receiving
French affixation in (3) and French word order in (4).

Ɓ - example .

(3)   Sont **spoilés** rotten. (JR/1528) 'They're spoiled rotten.'
(4)   A côté il y en a un autre gros **building high-rise**. 'Next door there's
      another big high-rise building.'

Determination of the status of such forms is treated elsewhere
(Poplack and Sankoff 1984; Sankoff and Poplack 1984; Sankoff,
Poplack and Vanniarajan 1985); the discussion which follows is
limited to the treatment of unambiguously English sequences in
otherwise French discourse, i.e. to code-switches, as opposed to
borrowing, as in the bold-face portions in (5).[6]

(5) a. On va avoir une dépression là que **we'll be rationed if we don't all
        die**. (JB/756)
        'We're going to have such a depression that ...'
     b. Les français apprennent l'allemand parce que **they have to deal with
        them** économiquement là. (PX/1084)
        'The French learn German because they have to deal with them
        economically.'

ex - Co

Table 1 depicts the distribution of code-switches across the five neighborhoods sampled in Ottawa and in Hull.

Table 1. Functions of code-switching in five Ottawa-Hull neighborhoods

	OTTAWA (ONTARIO)			HULL (QUEBEC)	
	VANIER	BASSE-VILLE	WEST-END	VIEUX-HULL	MONT-BLEU
# OF SPEAKERS:	23[a]	23[a]	22[a]	24	24
FUNCTION OF CODE-SWITCH: EXPRESSION/ "MOT JUSTE"	19	18	22	20	13
META-LINGUISTIC COMMENTARY	9	18	9	24	36
ENGLISH BRACKETING	10	17**[b]	8	15	12
REPETITION, TRANSLATION, EXPLANATION	8	8	7	10	7
REPORTED SPEECH	10**	13***	14*	16*	18*
PROPER NAME	4	3	4	5	7
CHANGED INTERLOCUTOR	18*	4	17	2	7
FALSE START	5	7*	4	0.7	0.7
AT TURN BOUNDARY	2	0.7	0.7	0	0
SENTENTIAL	13**	6	12*	2	4
INTRA-SENTENTIAL	3	5	2	6	1
TOTALS[c]	552	423	514	148	136

a) Four sample members whose use of English greatly exceeded that of the other informants and whose status as French L_1 speakers is not clear, were excluded from this study.
b) Asterisks indicate that the effect is essentially due to that number of individuals.
c) Percentages may not add up to 100 due to rounding.

We note first that in the Ottawa communities, people tend to switch three to four times as frequently as in Hull, bearing out the prediction of our hypothesis regarding the influence of English in the environment. It is striking however, that in all of the neighborhoods, on both sides of the border, at least half of all the switches (and considerably more in Quebec) fall into the same four major types: a) when the switch provides the apt expression or what I will call the *mot juste*, as exemplified in (6), b) the switch occurs while discussing language or engaging in metalinguistic commentary, as in (7), c) where the switch calls attention to or brackets the English intervention by the use of expressions such as those in (8), and finally, d) in the context of explaining, specifying or translating as in (9).[7]

(6)   a. C'est un- **a hard-boiled killer.** (CD/1955) 'He's a hard-boiled killer.'
     b. Il dit, "je veux pas avoir des **dishpan hands.**" (IM/14445) 'He says, "I don't want to have dishpan hands".'
     c. Ça aurait été probablement le pays communiste idéal là. **Quote unquote** là. (PX/882) 'It probably would have been the ideal communist country'.

(7)   a. Je m'adresse en français, pis s'il dit "**I'm sorry**", ben là je recommence en anglais. (MMR/3254) 'I begin in French and if he says, "I'm sorry", well then I start over in English'.
     b. Mais il dit, "c'est dur pour nous-autres: *le, la les,* vois-tu? Eux-autres, c'est rien que **the**". (RM/2538) 'But he says, "it's hard for us: *le, la les,* They only have *the*." '

(8)   a. Mais je te gage par exemple que . . . excuse mon anglais, mais les **odds** sont là. (CD/716) 'But I bet you that . . . excuse my English, but the odds are there.'
     b. J'ai accepté le Seigneur là, ben . . . j'étais comme sur un . . . **cloud nine, cloud nine** qu'ils appellent. (MC/2476) 'I accepted the Lord then, well . . . I was like on a . . . cloud nine, cloud nine, as they say'.

(9)   a. Je suis un peu trop anglicisé, anglifié, **anglicized**. (GF/1361) 'I'm a little too anglicized, anglified, anglicized.'
     b. J'ai été aussi pour **acupuncture**. Connais-tu ça de l'**acupuncture**? 'I also went for acupuncture. Do you know what acupuncture is?'
     c. J'ai acheté une roulotte, un **mobile home** là, une maison mobile. (GF/83) 'I bought a trailer, a mobile home, mobile home.'

Use of English fulfills other functions as well, however on a more individual basis. Thus English may be used to report speech as in (10), but this is mainly limited to one or two speakers in each neighborhood. Similarly, a few speakers opt to designate proper names having both English and French designations in English, as in (11). Informants of course switched to English when addressing interlocutors other than the interviewer, although the opportunity only rarely arose, even in the Ottawa neighborhoods, despite the fact that there is more chance there to use and hear English. Even here, the effects are inflated by the presence, during a small number of interviews, of individuals the informants generally address in English. Finally, switching to another language may of course be used to fill lexical gaps. This is how we interpret the behavior we have classed under the category of false starts, self-corrections and disfluencies (12).

(10) Pis il nous a appelé des grenouilles, hein? Bon, des **frogs**. Ben, j'ai dit, j'ai dit "Jess", j'ai dit, **"maybe we're a frog, but we're not dumb."** Pis il dit, **"what do you mean?"** J'ai dit, **"we learn to swim."** Ben, j'ai dit, **"you never seen a frog who don't swim**, hein?" Ben, il dit, **"no"**. Ben j'ai dit, **"you're too stupid."** J'ai dit, **"you don't swim."** Il dit, **"sure"** il dit, **"I can swim."** Il dit, **"sure."** Well, **I says** – j'ai dit, **"show it to me'.** (RM/2462)

'And he called us frogs, you know? Well, frogs (Engl.). Well, I said, "Jess", I said, "maybe we're a frog, but we're not dumb." And he says, "what do you mean?" I said, "we learn to swim". Well, I said, "you never seen a frog who don't swim, eh?" Well, he says "no." Well, I said, "you're too stupid." I said, "you don't swim." He says, "sure", he says, "I can swim." He says "sure." Well, I says – I said, "show it to me".

(11) a. Il avait le choix soit d'aller dans l'armée, dans **Navy** ou dans l'**Air Force**. (AB/2179) 'He had the choice either to go into the Army, the Navy or the Air Force'.

b. Montreal   [mʌntʀijal – mõʁeal] [8]
   Ontario   [anteʀiou – õtaʀjo]
   IGA   [aiʃiej – iʒea]

(12) a. Le- le- le- spontanéité de- de- de- **the spunk** de le faire. (RC/84) 'The- the- the- spontaneity of- of- of- of- the spunk to do it.'

b. C'est- c'est pas distor – tu sais, **it's not distorted**. (GF/2222) 'It's- it's not distor – you know . . . '

Even this use is quite rare, and almost non-existent in the Quebec neighborhoods. However, switching to English for any one of the latter functions is only sporadic in comparison to the first four. Indeed, wherever any one of them appears to have a meaningful effect, this is invariably due to one or two individuals with a particular predilection for the type in question, as indicated by the asterisks on the Table.

Comparison of behavior in the Quebec and Ontario neighborhoods reveals subtle differences in the uses to which code-switching is put beyond the frequency differences noted above, as can be appreciated graphically in Figure 1.

Here we see that in the three Ottawa neighborhoods code-switching to English tends to be done to provide what is perceived to be the best way of saying a thing, or the *mot juste*, a finding which is consistent with Ottawa speakers' description of their reasons for switching: to designate items for which the French equivalent has already been displaced (Poplack and Miller 1985). This use generally far outweighs the others. In Quebec, on the

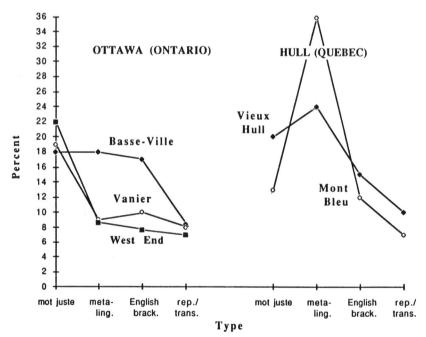

Figure 1. Distribution of favored code-switching types by neighborhood.

other hand, switches to English are largely restricted to meta-linguistic commentary, a device having the effect of showing full awareness on the part of the speaker of using English. In the upper-middle class Mont-Bleu neighborhood of Hull, this strategy accounts for more than 1/3 of all the data, whereas the working-class Vieux Hull shows an intermediate pattern.[9] The Hull speakers' linguistic behaviour is also consistent with their own favorable attitudes towards proper speech, their belief that inter-ventions from English are due to momentary lapses, as well as their attitude that good French must of necessity exclude anglicisms.

Now the use of code-switching to fulfill particular discourse functions, and especially functions such as the ones we have outlined here, is hardly new. This functional or "semantic" approach was introduced by Gumperz over a decade ago (e.g. Gumperz 1976/82; Blom and Gumperz 1972) and has proliferated amongst students of the school of "interactionist sociolinguistics" ever since (e.g. Elías-Olivares 1976; Huerta 1978; Auer 1981; Valdes 1981; di Luzio 1984; Heller 1982; among many others).

The aim here is not to enter into the interpretation of the "meaning" of these individual switches; indeed it is still unclear that each has a stateable meaning beyond the rough labels assigned them. Rather, I want to focus on the global function all of these code-switches fulfill in the discourse: that of flagging, or breaking up the speech flow, and the consequences of this for the investiga-tion of purely linguistic constraints on code-switching. Perhaps the most noteworthy feature of Table 1 is the dramatically reduced frequency in all neighborhoods of spontaneous code-switches at a turn boundary within the same interaction, as in (13), switches of full sentences or independent clauses, as in (14), and especially, intra-sentential switches as in (15).

(13) Interviewer: C'est juste un petit micro, il y a une clip tu peux mettre sur ton gilet là. 'It's just a small mike, there's a clip you can put on your sweater.'
     Informant: **I'm a star!**
(14) Parce que **I was there and** la seule raison c'était parce que je voulais oublier toute. (JB/996) 'Because I was there and the only reason was because I wanted to forget everything.'

(15) a) Tu sais, les condamner à chaise électrique **or** que c'est qu'ils- qu'ils voudraient. (CD/1909) 'You know, condemn them to the electric chair or whatever they want.'

b) Faut que tu **pack your own** au Basics. (KC/336) 'You have to pack your own at Basics.'

c) Le gouvernement de l'Ontario **is an equal opportunity employer**. (CN/832) 'The government of Ontario . . .'

Thus the kind of behavior we had designated as "true" code-switching (i.e. in which individual switches cannot be attributed to stylistic or discourse functions) in the study of the Puerto Rican community, where it was largely confined to skilled bilinguals in appropriate, in-group interactions, is but a minor phenomenon in the Ottawa-Hull French study. Table 1 shows it does not exceed a small percentage in any of the communities studied. This despite the fact that the participant constellation, mode of interaction and bilingual situation appear to be largely similar to those in the Puerto Rican study.

To recapitulate, where the Puerto Ricans code-switched in a way which minimized the salience of the switch points, and where the switches formed part of an overall discourse strategy to use both languages, rather than to achieve any specific local discursive effects, the Ottawa-Hull speakers do the contrary. They draw attention to their code-switches by repetition, hesitation, intonational highlighting, explicit metalinguistic commentary, etc. and use the contrast between the codes to underline the rhetorical appropriateness of their speech. We saw from Figure 1 that this is an overt strategy in the Quebec communities, covert in Ontario. In contrast, the impossibility of systematically interpreting code-switches in terms of any conversational function in the Puerto Rican materials has already been demonstrated (Poplack 1980).

Now the *mot juste* is most frequently a noun phrase or an idiomatic expression. The equivalence constraint on intra-sentential code-switching is thus satisfied trivially or is not pertinent, either because the conditions for placement of this form are homologous in French and English, or because of the devices the speaker uses to deliberately interrupt his or her sentence at a code-switch boundary, as in (16), where a potential grammatical violation is remedied in just this way.

(16) Fait que là ben, je paye un peu moins en- comme on dirait en anglais, **according** à que c'est que je fais. (DM/132) 'So, well, I pay a little less in- as they say in English, according to (Fr. *selon*) what I make.

Thus the data provide few "interesting" tokens which could be used for or against the validity of the equivalence or other purely linguistic constraints on intra-sentential code-switching.

Code-switching differences between communities

To what should the differences in code-switching patterns between the Ottawa-Hull and New York Puerto Rican bilingual communities be ascribed? They cannot be due to linguistic (i.e. typological) differences between the two languages as compared with English, as these are minor and relatively few in number. It is more likely that at least part of the divergence between the two studies is due to differences in data collection techniques: the random sampling methodology used in the Ottawa-Hull study required that the interviewers, though of French Canadian ethnicity and local origin, *not* be group members in the strict sense, as opposed to the participant observation technique employed in the Puerto Rican research. For the same reasons, the large number of speakers interviewed in five separate neighborhoods precluded establishment of the familiarity resulting from years of observing and interacting with the same group of informants on a single city block. Moreover, though interventions in English from the Ottawa-Hull informants were never actively discouraged, they were not overtly encouraged either (by interviewer participation in the code-switching mode). The approach in these interviews was basically French, in keeping with our original goal of studying the French in the region. Since the optimal conditions for code-switching arise when all factors: the setting, participant constellation and situation are considered appropriate, this may account for the preponderance of "special-purpose" code-switching in Ottawa-Hull, as opposed to its virtual absence in the Puerto Rican study. Attractive as this explanation may be, however, it should be pointed out that we have no non-anecdotal evidence, either from the interviews or from systematic ethnographic observation, that there exist situations or domains, untapped by us, where intrasentential code-switching is the norm.

Until such evidence can be found, therefore, we cannot reject out of hand the possibility that these results may represent a true difference in communicative patterns, albeit one which has no simple explanation based on a summary comparison of the characteristics of the two bilingual contexts. The situations of French in Canada and Spanish in the United States share superficial similarities as minority languages, though French has been in contact with English longer than Puerto Rican Spanish has; it has the status of official national language in Canada while Spanish enjoys no such prestige in the United States, and French Canadian ethnics are neither as visible nor as highly stigmatized as are Puerto Ricans in New York. Yet none of these observations seem directly relevant to the code-switching patterns discussed above. Indirectly, however, the different social, historical and political factors have led to differences in attitudes towards use of English in the two situations, which themselves may be partly determinant of the contrasting code-switching patterns. These attitudes may reflect the fact that bilingualism is seen to be emblematic of New York Puerto Rican identity (as compared both with Island Puerto Ricans and non-Puerto Rican anglophones) whereas in the Ottawa-Hull situation, knowledge of English does not appear to be associated with any emergent ethnic grouping. Indeed, bilingualism among francophones (rather than anglophones) has traditionally been the outcome of contact throughout Canada (e.g. Lieberson 1970). Differences in professed affect toward English and toward switching may also play a role.

Moreover, although there is evidence that different methods of data collection may lead to quantitative differences in code-switching behavior even on the part of the same speaker (Poplack 1981), we have no reason to believe that this should result in the nearly categorical qualitative differences observed here: the sum of sentential, intrasentential and spontaneous switches at a turn boundary does not reach 4% of all of the Ottawa-Hull data, while the proportion of flagged or special-purpose switching in Puerto Rican Spanish does not exceed 5%.[10]

If the differences between the two communities are indeed due to true differences in communicative strategies, then this shows a much greater awareness on the part of Ottawa-Hull francophones of their usage of English during French discourse than most casual observers would have expected. But even if the result is an artefact of our methodology, i.e. is due to perceived inappropriateness (because of social distance along the axis of familiarity), we have the striking result that this reaction is neither idiosyncratic nor the property of a small group, but is a community-wide pattern. Its interpretation would then be that in situations where ("true") code-switching is perceived to be inappropriate or has not been negotiated, the response is not necessarily to eschew usage of English altogether, but to use it in ways that show full speaker awareness. Such usage corresponds well with both Ottawa and Hull speaker perceptions mentioned above regarding the role and value of English.

This finding raises other questions concerning the background assumptions of the French speakers in our study. As Gumperz (1982) has pointed out, bilinguals do not ordinarily engage in code-switching before they know whether the listener's background and attitudes will render it feasible or acceptable. Rather they begin interactions with a series of probes aiming to establish shared presuppositions. In addition, the most favorable conditions for code-switching according to him (p. 70) are ones where speakers' ethnic identities and social backgrounds are not matters of common agreement. The situation amongst the Ottawa-Hull speakers is somewhat different. Shared ethnic identity is established before the onset of the interaction.[11] No "probing" as to language knowledge appears in these interviews. Instead, members appear to equate French Canadian ethnicity with knowledge of both English and French, an assessment which is not always correct, as can be seen in the exchange in (17), which recurred not infrequently between interviewer and informant.

(17) Informant: Il y avait de la **wrestling** pis de la boxe pis . . .
     Interviewer: Le **wrestling**, c'était quoi ça?
     Informant: Le **wrestling**, quand les- les **wrestlers** là, comment-ce
                     que . . . ?
     Interviewer: Ah ouais, ouais, okay.

Informant:	De la lutte.

Informant:	There was wrestling, and boxing and . . .
Interviewer:	Wrestling, what was that?
Informant:	Wrestling, when the- the wrestlers, how do you . . . ?
Interviewer:	Oh yeah, yeah, okay.
Informant:	Wrestling (Fr.)

Thus in the Ottawa-Hull region, members' implicit ascription of bilingual competence to each other (cf. Auer 1981) includes the (founded or unfounded) presupposition of competence in English. On the other hand their usage of English is calculated to demonstrate their own full awareness of doing so.

Code-switching vs. other bilingual phenomena

The discussion in the previous sections was based on some 1700 stretches of English-origin material which could be unambiguously identified as code-switches. However, there are thousands more which cannot be so identified in a clearcut way. In an earlier pilot study involving 44 of these same speakers (Poplack 1983 b), we extracted some 2,300 English-origin forms consisting of a single word (or a compound functioning as a single word) from an exhaustive search of their recorded interviews. These were the words operationally excluded from the code-switching data base, as described in the previous section, although some may in fact be code-switches.

Recall that in the Puerto Rican case we were largely able to distinguish borrowing from code-switching even for lone lexical items. How can we ascertain the status of the English-origin words in Ottawa-Hull French discourse?

The straightforward case is that of certain high-frequency forms which are integrated into local French. These forms tend to recur across speakers, to have a single French phonological rendition, and to behave like bonafide loawords in Ottawa-Hull French. It should come as no surprise that most are also attested nation-wide in other varieties of Canadian French (e.g. *chum, gang*).

In other cases, forms may seem equally linguistically integrated into French as in (18), but the frequency criterion is unclear or non-existent.

(18) Je serais pas capable de **coper** avec. (LM/1086) 'I couldn't cope with it.'

Indeed, with studies of the spoken language, even in a data base of this size, most borrowed words are relatively rare, such that those that occur tend to do so only once. Even in the lengthy recorded conversations with our subsample of 44 individuals, we were only able to identify about 500 English-origin words, or about 20%, which were used by at least two different people. This renders the status of words like *coper* indeterminate for the time being.

The situation is further complicated by the fact that "momentary" or nonce borrowings[12] coexist with the integrated loanwords, and the distinction between them is not necessarily recoverable from the structural form of the word. Occasionally the free morpheme constraint, which prohibits mixing phonologies within the (code-switched) word, can be circumvented through the mechanism of momentary borrowing. The examples in (19) show unadapted English morphemes conjoined with French verbal and participial affixes.

(19) quiter   [kwɪ'te]
       enjoyer   [ɛnj̊ɔ'je]
       traveler   [tʀæv'le]
       grower   [gʀo'we]
       polishait   [pʰalə'ʃɛ]
       shockés   [ʃaː'kʰe]
       drowné   [dʀɑw'ne]

This is in contrast with the Puerto Rican usage, which permitted no English root with Spanish affixes unless this root was first integrated into Spanish phonologically and sociologically, but seems to be at variance with the usual French Canadian treatment of integrated loanwords as well.

The Ottawa-Hull francophones also make use of several other strategies which allow them to combine the lexicons, word-formation rules and phonological rules from both languages. Aside from the fully integrated loanwords, synchronically indistinguishable from native French lexical items, we find other words (of greater or lesser frequency) which do not appear constrained to take on the same phonological forms, even when uttered by the same speaker (see also Mougeon et al. 1984). Thus we find coexisting examples such as the ones in (20) (Miller 1984):

(20) meetings   ['miD iŋ] ˷ [mi'tiŋ]
      tough   [tɔv] ˷ [tʰʌf] ˷ [tøf]
      anyways(s) [ɛ́nəwèz] ˷ [ɛ̀nɛwɛ́]
      whoever   [uɛ̀vɔ́ʀ] ˷ [uɛ́vʀ̩]

Alternatively, and more surprisingly, the French affixes are occasionally rendered in an anglicized way, so that the entire word will have English phonology but French morphology.

(21) afforder   [ə'fɔʀDe] for [afɔʀ'de]
      relaxés   [ʀə'lækse] for [ʀəlak'se]

(This situation is further complicated by the fact that English retroflex [ʀ] has penetrated the French phonological system and presently co-varies with apical [r] and velar [ʁ] even in French-origin words.) And in many other cases where the phonological systems differ minimally, only the affixes can be identified as to language (e.g. *mover* 'to move' [mu've]). In addition, a wide range of English items may be borrowed "momentarily" by means of a strategy which is also widespread in other French-speaking communities in Canada. This is a distinctive stress pattern applied to English-origin words in predominantly French discourse, but never to French words, and never in English discourse by the same speakers if they are fluent bilinguals. (Among speakers less fluent in English, it forms part of the stereotypical "French Canadian accent", but the interesting fact here is its use by fluent bilinguals in the restricted context of nonce borrowing.)

Briefly, the main word stress rule shifts the heaviest stress to the rightmost syllable within the word in French, and to the leftmost syllable in English. The two languages also differ as to their rules for assigning syllable stress, or beats. A compromise between English and French stress assignment patterns appears to be taking place in polysyllabic words (and even frozen expressions) of English origin occurring occasionally in French discourse, as in (22):

(22) des **alcoholics**   [ælkəhɑ́lĭk]
      les **neighbors**   [néybə̀ʀ]
      des **arguments**   [ɑ́ʀgjumə̀nt]
      J'aime avoir du **peace and quiet** [pʰiys æn kwɑ́jə̀t]
      'I like having peace and quiet.'

Here we find main word stress assigned according to English rules, shifting stress to the left, while syllable stress is assigned according to French patterns. Final syllables which would normally be unstressed schwas in English thus receive secondary stress.

The resulting word-structures have no counterpart in English or in French, and constitute an example of the innovative solutions which evolve in given speech communities. Their particular function here appears to be to allow nonce borrowing of an English word without "switching" to English (i.e. producing it in English), while still informing the interlocutor that one is attending to the fact of uttering an English word. (These forms may also be accompanied by one or both of rising intonation and the punctuant *là*, which have the further function of bracketing these words.)

Discussion

What are the implications of these results for a general theory of bilingualism? The striking contrasts between the patterns of English influence in just two not very dissimilar communities do not augur well for any simple deterministic view of bilingual behavior. Nor are they promising for attempts to impose global restrictions on the purely linguistic level.

However, the development of any kind of discourse based on more than one code must eventually come to terms with the structural differences between them. For Puerto Ricans, code-switching *per se* is emblematic of their dual identity, and smooth, skilled switching is the domain of highly fluent bilinguals. The use of individual code-switches for particular effects or functions is relatively rare in intra-group communication, consistent with the perceived ability of either language to fulfill any communicative need. The equivalence and free morpheme constraints are simple and natural strategies to achieve this kind of discourse.

The French-English case presented made clear another point: evaluation of the equivalence or any syntactic constraint is a fruitless pursuit in situations where "smooth" code-switching is not a community-wide discourse mode. Here, English use as well as speaker attitudes towards it are consistent with highlighting, flagging or otherwise calling attention to the switch. Indeed, in order for the switch to accomplish its purpose — be it metalinguistic commentary, finding the *mot juste*, providing an explanation and so on — it must be salient, and should not pass unnoticed. One byproduct of this is the interruption of the speech flow at the switch point, effectively circumventing a grammaticality requirement or rendering one unnecessary.

On the other hand, the high rate of use of borrowed material, integrated or not, well-established or momentary, appears to be serving largely referential purposes, so that these should occur without fanfare in the flow of discourse. This explains to some extent the wide range of strategies current in this community to handle English-origin material, in addition to code-switching and fully integrated borrowing. From the brief description of some of these given in the previous section, it should be evident that they do not necessarily show the same regularities or restrictions as the other phenomena, and must be studied in their own right. Moreover, none of the characteristics of the languages involved in the alternation, the contact situations or other aspects of the bilingual context would have permitted us to infer or predict the differences in code-switching patterns outlined here.

In concluding, I have been using the term "code-switching" here to refer to the alternate use of two codes in a fully grammatical way, in the same discourse, and even in the same sentence. Others use "code-mixing", "code-shifting" or other terms for the same purpose, and this poses no problem. What is important is that this phenomenon be clearly distinguished, first conceptually, and then operationally as much as possible, from all the other consequences of bilingualism which involve not alternate use, but the truly *simultaneous* use of elements from both codes. And within this latter category, lexical borrowing on the community level should be kept distinct from "momentary" or nonce borrowing by individuals, on the one hand, and on the other, from incomplete acquisition and language loss. Not least important, all of these phenomena should be distinguished from speech errors which involve elements of both languages, and which may be properly considered "interference". Of course these distinctions are easier to label than to operationalize. In practice, one type of behavior may fade into another. And given a simple utterance containing words from two codes there is not necessarily any *a priori* way of distinguishing a switch from a loanword from one of the other results of language contact discussed here. What appears to be the same phenomenon may have a different status from one bilingual community to another.

This leads to my final point. What data are appropriate to the study and categorization of these phenomena? Clearly, if we are presented with a sentence of unknown pedigree containing elements from two codes, we cannot be sure of anything. We need to know the community patterns, both monolingual and bilingual, the bilingual abilities of the individual, and whether the context is likely to have produced speech in the code-switching mode or not.

Similarly, an acceptability or grammaticality judgement does not reveal whether the item in question is a grammatical code-switch, and established loanword, or a commonly heard speech error among L2 learners. And if the linguist has such difficulty making these analytical distinctions, it is unlikely that the informant should know the answers intuitively.

For an understanding of language contact phenomena, even more than in monolingual studies, corpus-based research on language use in well-documented contexts is indispensable. Subjective reactions, acceptability judgements and intuition all have their place, but they must be tied to knowledge of the community.

Notes

1. We gratefully acknowledge the support of the Social Science and Humanities Research Council of Canada who funded the project of which this

research forms part. Earlier versions of this material were presented at the fourth Scandinavian Symposium on Bilingualism, and the fifth International Conference on Methods in Dialectology, and this paper appears in their Proceedings (*Methods V: Papers from the V International Conference on Methods in Dialectology*, ed. by H. J. Warkentyne (1985), Victoria, B.C.: University of Victoria, pp. 363–386, and *Aspects of Multilingualism*, ed. by E. Wande et al. (1987), Uppsala: Borgströms, pp. 51–77). The term "community" is used in this paper to refer variously to the New York Puerto Rican speech community, Ottawa-Hull francophones and the particular neighborhoods in which they live. This is ordinary language usage; we do not impute to each the ensemble of connotations sometimes associated with the notion of "speech community". Thanks to François Grosjean, Raymond Mougeon, Edouard Béniak and Daniel Valois who read and commented on this paper.

2. The code identifies the speaker and example number.

3. See Mougeon et al. (1984) for an opposing point of view in a situation of language shift.

4. As opposed to nonce borrowing and other types of language mixture discussed below.

5. The systematic combing of such a large data base was made possible by automated manipulation of the computerized Ottawa-Hull French corpus to extract English sequences which had been identified as code-switches during transcription (see Poplack 1983 a).

6. Our basic procedure was to operationally exclude single nouns (or compounds functioning as single nouns) unless there was contextual evidence to indicate they were being treated as code-switches (as in the examples in (8)). Incorporations of single English elements from other grammatical categories were retained as code-switches, with the exception of those which are either well-documented as loanwords (e.g. *so*: Roy 1979; Mougeon et al. 1983), or which in the Ottawa-Hull corpus satisfy the frequency criterion for loanwords.

7. These categories and the others which follow are rough labels for discourse behavior rather than analytical constructs, and include discourse strategies along with linguistic categories. The former will obviously show some overlap, as a single utterance can accomplish more than one function in discourse. Since our concern here is to assess the amount of attention called to or motivation for an English intervention, switches were classed preferentially into categories most clearly reflecting this. Thus bracketing of a switch took precedence over its function to provide the *mot juste*, etc.

8. R = Retroflex r.

9. In fact both the largely monolingual French Vieux Hull and the highly bilingual Basse-Ville of Ottawa show intermediate patterns; in each neighborhood some people behave more like Ottawa speakers and others more like Hull speakers. This is not surprising — code-switching patterns could not possibly be determined solely by neighborhood of residence, being dependent on so many other factors as well. More surprising is the regularity which does obtain here. We focus then on the gross differences between Ottawa and Hull.

10. Indeed, a pilot study of code-switching in Ottawa carried out by a group member using participant observation techniques (Trudel 1985) gave strikingly similar results to the ones reported here.

11. By the response of the potential informant to the interviewer's quest for a "francophone born and raised in the region" and by the interviewer's assessment of the "nativeness" of his French.

12. Grosjean (1982) refers to these as "speech" borrowings.

References

Attinasi, J.
    1979   Language Attitudes in a New York Puerto Rican Community. In Padilla, R. (ed.). *Ethnoperspectives in Bilingual Education Research.* Ypsilanti, MI: Eastern Michigan University.
Auer, J. C. P.
    1981   Bilingualism as a member's concept: language choice and language alternation in their relation to lay assessments of competence. Sonderforschungsbereich 99. Department of Linguistics, University of Konstanz.
    1984   "On the meaning of conversational code-switching". Ms.
Bentahila, A. and E. Davies
    1983   The syntax of Arabic-French code-switching. *Lingua* 59: 301–330.
Blom, J. P. and J. Gumperz
    1972   Social meaning in linguistic structures. In Gumperz, J. and Hymes, D. (eds.). *Directions in Sociolinguistics.* New York: Holt, Rinehart and Winston, pp. 407–434.
Bloomfield L.
    1933   *Language History.* Ed. H. Hoijer. New York: Holt, Rinehart and Winston.
Duran, R. (ed.)
    1981   *Latino Language and Communicative Behavior.* Norwood, New Jersey: Ablex

242   *Shana Poplack*

Elías-Olivares, L.
1976   Ways of Speaking in a Chicano Community: a Sociolinguistic
       Approach. Ph.D. dissertation. The University of Texas at Austin.
Fries, C. and K. Pike
1949   Coexistent phonemic systems. *Language* 25: 29–50
Grosjean, F.
1982   *Life with Two Languages*. Cambridge: Harvard University Press.
Gumperz, J.
1976/ Conversational code-switching. In: J. Gumperz, *Discourse Strate-*
1982   *gies.* Cambridge: Cambridge University Press, pp. 59–99.
Gumperz, J. and E. Hernandez-Chavez
1971   Bilingualism and bidialectalism in classroom interaction. In Cazden,
       C. et al. (eds.). *The Functions of Language in the Classroom.*
       New York: Teachers College Press.

Hasselmo, N.
1970   Code-switching and modes of speaking. In Gilbert, G. (ed.). *Texas
       Studies in Bilingualism.* Berlin: Walter de Gruyter and Co.,
       pp. 179–210.

Haugen, E.
1956   *Bilingualism in the Americas.* Publication of the American Dialect
       society no. 26. University of Alabama Press.

Heller, M.
1982   "Bonjour, hello?": Negotiations of language choice in Montreal.
       In Gumperz, J. (ed.). *Language and Social Identity.* Cambridge:
       Cambridge University Press.

Huerta, Ana.
1978   Code-switching among Spanish-English bilinguals: a sociolinguistic
       perspective. Ph.D. dissertation. The University of Texas at Austin.

Joshi, A.
1983   Processing of sentences with intra-sentential code-switching. To
       appear in Dowty, D. et al. (eds.). *Natural Language Processing:
       Psycholinguistic, Computational and Theoretical Perspectives.*
       Cambridge: Cambridge University Press.

Labov, W.
1971   The notion of "system" in creole languages. In Hymes, D. (ed.).
       Pidginization and Creolization of Languages. Cambridge: Cambridge
       University Press, pp. 447–472.

Lance, D.
1975   Spanish-English code-switching. In Hernandez-Chavez et al. (eds.).
       El lenguaje de los chicanos. Arlington: Center for Applied Linguis-
       tics, pp. 138–154.

Language Policy Task Force
1980 Social dimensions of Language Use in East Harlem. Working paper no. 7. New York: Center for Puerto Rican Studies.
Lieberson, S.
1970 *Language and Ethnic Relations in Canada.* New York: Wiley and Sons.
di Luzio, A.
1984 On the meaning of language choice for the sociocultural identity of bilingual migrant children. Ms.
Mackey, W.
1970 Interference, integration and the synchronic fallacy. In Alatis, J. (ed.). *Georgetown University Roundtable on Languages and Linguistics* 23. Washington, D.C.: Georgetown University Press, pp. 195–223.
McClure, E.
1981 Formal and functional aspects of the code-switched discourse of bilingual children. In Duran R. (ed.), *op. cit.*, pp. 69–94.
Miller, C.
1984 Phonetic criteria for loanword integration in Ottawa-Hull French. University of Ottawa class paper.
Mougeon, R., D. Valois and E. Béniak
1983 For a quantitative study of linguistic borrowing. Paper presented at the Canadian Linguistics Association.
1984 Variation in the phonological treatment of lexical borrowings from English by speakers of a minority language. Paper presented at the XIII conference on New Ways of Analyzing Variation. University of Pennsylvania.
Pfaff, C.
1979 Constraints on language mixing. *Language* 55: 291–318.
Poplack, S.
1980 "Sometimes I'll start a sentence in English *y termino en español*: Toward a typology of code-switching. *Linguistics* 18: 581–618.
1981 Syntactic structure and social function of code-switching. In Duran, R. (ed.), *op. cit.*, pp. 169–184.
1983a The care and handling of a mega-corpus: the Ottawa-Hull French project. To appear in Fasold, R. and Schiffrin, D. (eds.). *Language Variation and Change.* Amsterdam: Benjamins.
1983b The propagation of loanwords within a speech community. Paper presented at the XII Conference on New Ways of Analyzing Variation. Université de Montréal.
Poplack, S. and D. Sankoff
1984 Borrowing: the synchrony of integration. *Linguistics* 22.1: 99–135.

244   *Shana Poplack*

Poplack, S. and C. Miller
    1985   Political and interactional consequences of linguistic insecurity. Paper presented at the XIV Conference on New Ways of Analyzing Variation. Georgetown University.
Prince, E. and S. Pintzuk
    1983   Code-switching and the open/closed class distinction. Ms.
Roy, M.-M.
    1979   Les conjonctions anglaises 'but' et 'so' dans le français de Moncton. M.A. Thesis. Université du Québec à Montréal.
Sankoff, D. and S. Poplack
    1981   A formal grammar for code-switching. *Papers in Linguistics* 14.1: 3–46.
Sankoff, D. and S. Poplack
    1984   Code-switching constraints in functional and typological perspective. Paper presented at the XIII Conference on New Ways of Analyzing Variation. University of Pennsylvania.
Sankoff, D., S. Poplack and S. Vanniarajan
    1985   The case of the nonce loan in Tamil. Paper presented at the XIV Conference on New Ways of Analyzing Variation. Georgetown University.
Trudel, M.
    1985   Une analyse préliminaire de l'alternance de code intra-groupe à Ottawa. University of Ottawa class paper.
Valdes, G.
    1981   "Code-switching as a deliberate verbal strategy: a micro-analysis of direct and indirect requests." in Duran, R. (ed.), *op. cit.*, pp. 95–107.
Weinreich, U.
    1953   *Languages in Contact.* The Hague: Mouton.
Zentella, A.
    1982   Spanish and English in contact in the United States: the Puerto Rican experience. *Word.* 33.1–2; 41–57.

The political economy of code choice

Susan Gal
Rutgers University

1. Comparative codeswitching

In surveying the many detailed case studies of codeswitching published in this volume and elsewhere in recent years, it becomes clear that we are in need of an integrative comparative analysis that will explain not only the striking similarities in codeswitching practices across communities and world regions, but will also allow us to account for the sometimes subtle but always meaningful differences between the practices of different social groups[1]. Indeed, for those observers concerned with the future of linguistic/ethnic groups and their resistance to dominant languages, it is often the differences between communities that have significant political and practical implications.

The study of language in its social context has been a comparativist endeavour from its beginnings, committed to charting cross-cultural contrasts as well as parallels. In early work, Hymes (1964) constructed typologies for ways of speaking in order to discover logically possible and empirically instantiated differences. Weinreich (1953) did the same for the narrower question of language contact. Gumperz (1968) and Fishman (1964) implicitly relied on neo-evolutionary social theory to correlate differing forms of linguistic diversity with differing levels of societal complexity. And in these comparative projects of sociolinguistics, codeswitching has held a central place as the paradigmatic example of systematic, linguistically striking, and socially meaningful linguistic variation.

However, in contrast to the earlier concern with cross-cultural difference, and perhaps under the influence of generative linguistics, most current comparative studies that include codeswitching have seen it as one instance of universal interactional or social-psychological processes (e.g. Bell 1984; Brown and Levinson 1978; Giles and Smith 1979; Gumperz 1982; Scotton 1983). These studies differ in detail, but they agree that the alternations between linguistic varieties – pronouns of address, dialects, linguistic variables, or separate languages – all have the same underlying logic in conversation. One influential version of this argument states that the alternative forms index overarching social oppositions (we/they, power/solidarity), making the choice of one form over the other in a specific context an interpretable act that invites conversational inferences (Gumperz 1982). These inferences are very much like Gricean implicatures, but usually center around the speakers' relationships, (ethnic) identities or conversational intentions. Similarly, other comparisons have aimed to show that in all speech communities the linguistic forms perceived to distinguish social groups of different statuses are the ones used for stylistic effect in conversation (Irvine 1985). These broadly pragmatic studies have been enormously important, revealing interactional principles of impressive generality.

In light of the universalist trend, however, many of the papers in this collection constitute something of a departure. They highlight *contrasts* in codeswitching practices, implicitly or explicitly demanding an explanation for the notable *differences* between communities as well as the similarities. For instance, it has long been known that some bilingual populations allow very intimate mixing of linguistic systems within utterances or even clauses, while in others strict separation or compartmentalization of codes is required. Codeswitching within a single turn of talk is a common, even characteristic activity of some bilingual populations, while it is rare or non-existent elsewhere. Some communities or sub-groups, often in the grip of purist linguistic ideologies, monitor their codeswitching, indirectly alluding to a perceived switch before it occurs or in subsequent talk. Others are unaware of their codeswitches, sometimes even denying that they occur[2]. The language authorized by the state is often used as a symbol of power and prestige within the bilingual group, but this is by no means always the case. Codeswitching is often limited to conversations within a minority group, but there are also reports of its use between groups, even when one of the interlocutors may be monolingual.

To reach an understanding of these differences, we need a comparative analysis that interprets codeswitching practices not only as conversational tools that maintain or change ethnic group boundaries and personal relationships but also as symbolic creations concerned with the construction of 'self' and 'other' within a broader political economic and historical context. This suggests that the study of how codes are deployed in conversation is not only a sociolinguistic problem. Because codeswitching usually involves the use of a state-supported and powerfully legitimated language in opposition to a stigmatized minority language that has considerably less institutional support, it can also provide fresh evidence of what neo-Marxist culture theory (e.g. Williams 1973) identifies as "consciousness": how speakers respond symbolically to relations of domination between groups within the state, and how they understand their historic position and identity within a world capitalist system structured around dependency and unequal development.

To explain variation in codeswitching, an integration of conversational, ethnographic and social historical evidence is required. It is true that, as the papers in this volume amply demonstrate, codeswitching is a conversational strategy used to establish, cross or destroy group boundaries; to create, evoke or change interpersonal relations with their accompanying rights and obligations. But the conversations themselves take place within and between groups whose interactions are shaped not only by Barthian (1969) considerations of ethnic boundaries and competition over resources. As students of ethnicity have argued in response to Barth, ethnic groups have specifiable structural positions of power or subordination in their regional economy and, even groups within socialist states or in apparently peripheral geographic areas are importantly affected by their relation to world capitalist forces. This larger context is crucial in shaping the nature of interactions between and within ethnic groups, the permeability of boundaries, the definitions and evaluations of actions and resources, and the nature of competition across boundaries (e.g. Wolf 1982; Cole

1981). In a parallel way, differing codeswitching patterns can be read not only as forms of interactional management around roles and boundaries, but also as the symbolic practices of different sociopolitical positions (Hill 1985: 735).

In short, both levels of social phenomena, the interactional and the sociopolitical, shape codeswitching practices. But, as Sankoff (1980) has noted, while we can expect to find universals or at least widely occuring types in the structure of face-to-face interaction, the sociopolitical level of analysis cannot be conceived in the same way. The intergroup relations that codeswitching indexes cannot be considered universal types. Rather, they are the result of specific historical forces which produce different social and linguistic results at different times and places. Indeed, I suggest that a broad political economic approach *complements* universalist analyses, allowing the two together to explain differences, similarities, and change over time in codeswitching practices.

In the model for comparative analysis briefly sketched below I argue that the concurrent use of two languages is endowed by speakers with subtly different patterns and meanings which are linked to the ways in which the communities are differently situated within the regional political and economic system. Thus, although strategies of language choice are local conventions maintained by local social networks, the evaluation of codes, and even some aspects of the switching strategies, are nevertheless best understood as symbolic responses to a systemic context much wider and historically deeper than the local community and its current role expectations. Similarly, although historical changes in codeswitching practices have rarely been documented in detail, we know that they do occur (Gal 1979). I suggest such changes can be understood as part of the historic transformation of broader sociopolitical relations.

In keeping with the difference between the interactional and the sociopolitical levels of analysis, it is not the historically and regionally specific interpretations tentatively offered below that will be applicable in other regions and other structural situations, but rather the integrative form of the comparative analysis itself, in which sociolinguistic patterns are placed in a context of economic and political power relations.

2. Cultural and linguistic domination

Sociolinguistic evidence has not often been used by cultural theorists examining the symbolic aspects of power: how relations of domination, having a cultural component, are reproduced and sometimes resisted through local cultural practices. An exception is Bourdieu (1977), who has interpreted variationist sociolinguistic research in these terms. He argues that a standard dialect gains its legitimacy from state sponsored institutions such as education, which inculcate the dialect's authority, imposing it even on speakers of dominated classes who never master it. This produces and reproduces a familiar asymmetry between knowledge and evaluation of languages: a respect for linguistic varieties one does not speak, a deprecation of one's own language. Such asymmetry is a linguistic form of what Bourdieu calls "symbolic domination". He includes bilingual minorities in this analysis.

Woolard (1985) has extended Bourdieu's analysis by arguing that, just as the local response to dominant cultures is sometimes an oppositional culture (e.g. Willis 1977), so the authority of the standard language does not go unchallenged. The unauthorized vernacular forms continue to be used because they enact values of solidarity, opposing the dominant value of status and individual mobility. As with the oppositional cultures discussed by Williams, Willis and others, these vernacular linguistic forms attest to a palpable, if sometimes self-defeating, resistance to domination.

In these generalizations, as in the universalizing models discussed above, social class dialects are equated with minority languages; dominated classes with linguistic minorities. Woolard's sociolinguistic examples demonstrate that the mechanisms underlying the maintenance of a minority language sometimes match those supporting a persistent working class vernacular. Indeed, this tension between dominant and oppositional code, and the role of the dominant language as that *against which* the other is evaluated, are essential to the contextualized analysis of bilingual minorities suggested here. Yet, there are important social and sociolinguistic differences between dominated social classes and linguistic minorities that deserve attention because they significantly affect language use.

Although language minorities — ethnic groups that use language as a boundary marker — can sometimes be conceptualized as underdeveloped "internal colonies" that are structurally equivalent to exploited classes (Hechter 1975), there are numerous counter-examples of highly developed but ethnically and linguistically mobilized groups. A broader perspective suggests that since ethnicity is a form of social organization distinct from class, the relationships of ethnic groups to class divisions and to power is historically contingent (e.g. Cole 1981).

Making this distinction is significant for the analysis of code-switching practices. I have suggested that these practices are shaped by the group's position in the regional political economy. Unlike social classes, ethnic groups can have various relations to the political economic system. In addition, the examples to be discussed below suggest that differences between groups in code-switching patterns are due in part to their historically different class positions and in part to links with co-ethnics in other states, links which do not exist for social classes. Thus, while the code-switching practices of bilingual minorities are rightly viewed as "resistance" to the domination or attempted domination of state-authorized languages, this resistance is not always parallel to that of exploited classes; it can take a number of systematically different forms.

Because variation within a single region is a controlled comparison that presents the strongest test of this systemic approach, my examples in this paper will be drawn largely from Europe, where linguistic groups are among those considering themselves national or ethnic units.[3] The economic and political trajectories of European linguistic groups are a function of their role in the historic European division of labor in which workers, agricultural products and raw materials have moved to regions of the industrial "core" while manufactured products and wages have moved to the more agrarian periphery, fuelling growth in the core and reproducing continued poverty and dependence in the periphery. Over time, the dynamics of this process produce new core regions and new peripheries, but maintain a pattern of complementary and unequal economic development. As this terminology makes clear, I am relying on a view of capitalism's historic expansion advanced in general terms by dependency theorists, elaborated by

Wallerstein (most briefly, 1974), and revised and criticized by many others.

In this view, "core" and "periphery" are not simply geographic designations, but rather positions in a single interdependent system, characterized by differentials between regions in trade, forms of production, levels of growth and forms of labor control. Since the end of the 19th century, when the German provinces started to industrialize and challenged England's economic hegemony, such structural inequality has rendered Western Europe part of the world-wide core, the Mediterranean and Eastern Europe part of the peripheral or semiperipheral regions.[4] Current linguistic minorities can be located in several structural positions in this world system, depending on their particular histories (e.g. how and in what historical period they became minorities) and especially on the timing and legal constraints of their inclusion in the 19th and 20th century expansion of capital (Cole 1983).

3. Codeswitching in systemic perspective: Examples

Far from surveying all of the possibilities, I will sketch a few examples – some of them discussed in sociolinguistic detail elsewhere in this book – of how the past and present structural position of a group can be used to understand its current code-switching practices. The juxtaposition of cases that differ as much in codeswitching as in political economic features is not intended as a set of analytical categories into which other cases fit. Rather they are examples of contrasting social, historical and sociolinguistic processes for which there are partial but illuminating parallels elsewhere in Europe and in other regions.

The most important implication of a systemic perspective for sociolinguistics, as for any comparative endeavour, is the parsimony it offers: a single process, such as the imposition of a state language, can have different effects, over time, in communities situated differently in a single regional economic and political system. Several and sometimes divergent developments thus emerge as parts of a single process. In this systemic view, the effort to find variables – for instance, industrialization, urbanization, economic development, "group vitality" – that will everywhere, in all periods, produce the same effects on minority language use or language evaluation misses the mark. The divergent evaluations of state languages provide an illustration of this systemic logic. State languages are not uniformly accepted by minorities as languages of authority and symbolic power, even if they are consistently supported by schools, police and government agencies. Instead, acceptance depends on the past and current systemic position of the minority group.

For example, Romanian has been the language of Transylvania for over 60 years, but it is largely excluded from the intragroup speech of Germans (McClure and McClure, this volume). The Germans of Transylvania were, until the post-World War II period, an economically dominant and legally privileged merchant and farmer group. Located in a peripheral state (Austria-Hungary, from 1867, Romania after World War I) with ethnic links to the German core, German merchants were among the elite who profited from the unequal trade between core and periphery. In the countryside, they were well-to-do, cash oriented, capitalist farmers who disdained the landless, sharecropping Romanians with whom they shared villages. Currently, in socialist Romania, the Germans have lost both their economic and legal privileges and have joined Romanians in industry and collective agriculture. This post-war integration has been experienced as downward mobility from their former status as independent capitalist merchants and farmers. Their former sense of moral and economic superiority survives to some extent, as does an identification with what they see as a "free" West Germany. These are reinforced by a new legal privilege: by retaining the German language as proof of their ethnicity, Germans can hope to emigrate from Romania to a considerably higher standard of living in West Germany. By allowing a trickle of emigration, Romania wins favorable trade relations with West Germany. For both the ethnic group and the state, the unequal development of western and eastern Europe makes this a desirable arrangement (Verdery 1983, 1985).

Although there has been considerable interaction between Romanians and Germans (Saxons) in post-war Transylvanian villages, separation of Romanian and Saxon/German is the rule, as McClure and McClure's report from the early 1970s shows. Romanian is used largely to monolinguals. Conversational code-switching is very rare. Reports of more recent usage in German villages agree: intermarriage is increasing at a rapid rate, Germans partake in the national economy, but continue using largely German/Saxon among themselves. In the rare cases that Romanian is used among German bilinguals, it is used in speech events not notably high in public status, such as the bawdy songs reported by McClure and McClure, or in jokes and drunken brawls – activities traditionally disdained by Transylvanian Germans (Verdery 1983: 65). Using a spatial metaphor for the status ranking of speech events, we can say that the two languages either stand apart, or Romanian is seeping into German conversations most unprestigiously, from the bottom.

The Hungarians in Austria are tellingly different both in structural position and in linguistic practices (see Gal 1979). Codeswitching occurs regularly, but only in certain sections of the minority population and only with relatively limited conversational functions. In the 1970s, the youngest and oldest generations kept the languages compartmentalized. The eldest used Hungarian with everyone except German monolinguals; the youngest used German with everyone except their grandparents' generation. It was the generation in between, the one that experienced post-war mobility most dramatically, that engaged in codeswitching.

The territory of this small Hungarian group (Burgenland) was annexed to Austria in 1921. They thus became a part of the agriculture population of a core state. As a tiny, impoverished, peasant group with little leadership, they have had no independent influence in politics or economic matters. When, during the post World War II boom, capitalist expansion in the core required labor and drew workers away from agriculture, these Hungarians were among the first to move into jobs in service and heavy industry that proved economically more attractive than their small-scale agriculture. During the increasing prosperity of the 1960s and 1970s, they became well aware that their economic opportunities, as western Europeans, far exceeded possibilities in neighboring socialist Hungary.

Thus, during roughly the same sixty year period that Romanian has been the state language in Transylvania, German has been the language of Burgenland, but with contrary results. For the middle and younger generation of Hungarian speakers, German is the code of prestige and upward mobility, while Hungarian is deprecated as the local peasant language. It is seen as economically useless, in part because it is spoken only in a less developed area. It is true that there is internal opposition to the dominance of German: Hungarian continues to be used because networks of older farmers exert pressures on their younger kin to express local solidarity through that language. But the imposition of German in education and administration has coincided with upward mobility for Hungarians through that language, rendering it the symbol of high status and prestige for most Hungarian speakers. In a pattern exactly the reverse of the German-Transylvanian practice, the Hungarians of Austria insert in their Hungarian conversations the language of state power as a claim to expertise and social authority, or to convey social distance or anger. In terms of the spatial metaphor used above, German is entering intragroup conversations authoritatively, from the top.

To understand more precisely when — in what systemic and historical circumstances — institutional support fails to assure the state language higher status than that of an ethnic minority, further comparisons are essential. Woolard (1985) raises this same issue, and the example of Catalan in Barcelona is illuminating (this volume). Although their histories have diverged significantly since World War II, the experiences of the Catalans of Spain and the Germans of Transylvania show some similarities. Although the Germans are now in decline, while the Catalans have recently gained political strength, historically both were privileged and economically dominant groups within relatively underdeveloped states in the European periphery. Despite the current contrasts in their positions, this partial parallel is suggestive: The institutional dominance of Castilian in Barcelona during many decades did not destroy the prestige and authority of Catalan, based as it was on the continuing economic power of Catalans in everyday life, any more than Romanian has destroyed the prestige of German for the somewhat similarly situated German speakers in Transylvania. Observers of both groups in the 1970s reported that intra-group codeswitching within a single communicative episode was rare, and when it did occur humor was one of its functions.[5]

The contrasting process described for the Hungarian speakers is widespread.[6] It is aptly characterized as "linguistic domination" since it involves the speakers' deprecation of the status of their own language, acceptance of the public authority of the state language, and the restriction of the minority language to solidarity functions. Many other economically weak, primarily agricultural, linguistic groups in Europe's core have gone through a process parallel to that described for the Hungarians of Austria, with similar linguistic results. For instance, despite revivalist and nationalist regional movements, Breton shows an identical pattern of asymmetrical evaluation and decreasing overall use, although detailed information on codeswitching is not available (Dressler and Wodak-Leodolter 1977); the language situation among the languages of southern France presents a strikingly parallel picture (Schieben-Lange 1977), even with respect to codeswitching (Eckert 1980).

In sum, a single factor can have different effects on language use in different parts of a political economic system. A somewhat different example of this is provided by the currently divergent evaluations of the two minority languages, Hungarian in Austria and German in Romania. Both carry connotations of ingroup solidarity. But the post-war political bifurcation of Europe into eastern and western camps, and the much longer-standing differences in economic development and dependence that closely parallel it, have contributed simultaneously to the devaluation and "uselessness" of Hungarian in Austria, while in Transylvania, on the other side of the divide, to the opposite result, a new source of prestige and an instrumental use (emigration) for German.

Finally, the juxtaposition of all of these cases with yet another group, Italians in West Germany, provides evidence of the divergent effects that industrialization exerts, in different systemic contexts, on linguistic evaluations and practices. The Italian speakers in West Germany are neither native farmers nor former elites, but rather labor migrants from the region's impoverished agricultural periphery. Their cheap labor provided the impetus to continued economic growth in the core during the post-war period. For individual workers, migration meant an improved standard of living, but the guestworker system as a whole has reproduced the relative poverty and structural dependence of peripheral regions such as southern Italy on the core economies (Castles and Kosack 1983).

The timing and legal provisions of the migrants' entry into the labor force of the core are important. Migrants filled jobs that socially mobile native workers (including groups such as the Hungarians of Austria) had abandoned. But legal barriers and discrimination encountered in West Germany halted further mobility for the migrants, especially when the world-wide recession of the mid-1970s and the movement of capital to the Third World led to contraction of the German labor market. A rise in unemployment among "native" workers increased hostility against the "guest-workers", who were seen as competition. Despite repeated attempts by the state, both total assimilation and wholesale repatriation of migrants have proved politically impossible. This is especially true in the case of Italians and others from countries that are members of the European Economic Community. Indeed, EEC treaties assure workers the right to move back and forth between countries, ensuring a continuing stream of newcomers, many of them children, into Italian neighborhoods in Germany cities.

The codeswitching practices of the Italians of Konstanz, like their structural position, present notable contrasts with the other cases discussed so far (Auer, this volume). Among the children of Italian migrants codeswitching appears much more common than among Hungarian speakers in Austria, and with many more functions. Indeed, it is less a metaphorical extension of the codes' contrasting connotations, than a device accomplishing virtually any change in footing, any conversational task. Conversations are often characterized by constant negotiation for use of the code that suits the speakers' current "preferences". Since local peer groups frequently include children recently arrived from Italy, as well as those born in Germany and more fluent in German, an interactional effect of the constant codeswitching is to smoothly include in conversation speakers who have considerably different competences in the two languages. Most significantly, as Auer (1984) notes, there are advanced speakers for whom the frequency of codeswitching is so high that it is hard to identify a base language, although the contrast between the codes retains its signalling function, alerting speakers that some conversational inference is necessary.

It is clear that the intimate and frequent mixture of two languages, as in the Italian case, is linked only to some contexts of industrialization. Many of the same structural factors − legally assured opportunities for circle migration, discrimination and lack of social mobility linked to relatively late entry into a contracting economy − are conspicuously present as well in the case of the Puerto Ricans of New York. And the linguistic practices of Puerto Ricans in the New York area, like that of the Italians, but unlike less geographically and more socially mobile migrants, is characterized by extreme frequency of conversational and even intrasentential switching. What is more, as with the Italians in Germany, analysts have argued that interpretation of this does not depend directly on the connotations of the codes involved. Rather, codeswitching is itself a stable syncretic practice that draws in newcomers and is an emblem of the group's ethnic identity (Poplack 1980; this volume).

The discussion so far has focussed on the structural processes affecting patterns of codeswitching within the minority language group. However, as Heller (this volume) has emphasized, codeswitching can also be an inter-group phenomenon, so that symbolic attempts at domination and resistance are enacted in more public societal arenas. A consideration of inter-group codeswitching must include not only patterns of language choice with outsiders (monolinguals or nearly so) but also the widespread constraints on use of the minority language in the *presence* of outsiders as well. Since all such practices constitute a stance toward the claims to public authority and legitimacy of the dominant language, they too can be expected to vary with the minority group's systemic position.

Intergroup patterns range from unabashed switching to the minority language with monolingual outsiders, to a continuum of restrictions in the use of the minority language: no switching if a monolingual is part of the conversation, if a monolingual is part of the audience, or merely one among many potential eavesdroppers (Bell 1984). Ethnic groups whose language practices were interpreted above as results of linguistic domination not only practice the more restrictive patterns but frequently report that they do so out of "politeness" to monolinguals, who might otherwise feel they are being discussed or excluded. Ironically this is often among the arguments used by speakers of the dominant language to justify their attempt to curtail the public use of the minority language. However, not all ethnic groups respond to such pressure by adopting an ethic (or ideology) of politeness. For instance, as one might expect from the earlier assessment of the Germans' systemic position in Transylvania, a major complaint made against them by Romanian neighbors is that they continue to use German among themselves even when Romanians are present (McClure and McClure, this volume; Verdery 1983). Such practices often occasion conflict within the group, between factions with different linguistic ideologies who monitor their own and others' usage.

But surely the most aggressive resistance to the pressure of the dominant language is an intergroup pattern that allows/demands the use of the minority language to outsiders who are monolingual in the domainant language. The florescence of this pattern in Quebec in the 1970s (Heller 1982) suggests that it was a day to day enactment of Francophone political and ideological mobilization and occured in conjunction with the group's increased control of the state's language policy. Thus, the constant negotiation about choice of language in impersonal, public exchanges and among co-workers of different ethnic groups is, at one level, a means of managing interpersonal conflict, and ethnic boundaries, as Heller has argued. It should also be read as a change in consciousness, a means of establishing the authority of the minority language and the power of the linguistic group. In Europe, much additional contrastive evidence from recently mobilized or at least vocal linguistic groups such as the Catalans in Spain, the Hungarians in Yugoslavia, and others, is needed before we can specify the relation between such patterns and larger systemic processes.

4. Conclusion

The relationship between codeswitching practices and the language group's changing political economic position in the world system has been the focus of this paper. However, it is important to repeat that the patterns of language use, whether inter-group or intra-group, are not simply a reflex of that structural position. First, these practices are also constrained by local historical contingencies, so that parallels between groups are necessarily partial. Second, rather than being directly determined by political economic position, the practices are part of the group's actively constructed and often oppositional response to that position. Indeed, for language groups facing a dominant culture that imposes external images of them, linguistic practices and evaluations are among the readily available and revealing sources of information about the implicit self-perceptions and unspoken evaluations of the ethnic "other" that make up consciousness. They are a form of symbolic resistance whose local meanings, though grouped around solidarity, differ notably across cases. Finally, although symbolic in nature, minority practices are often instrumental in creating material effects. While offering active resistance to the dominant culture, they are often contradictory in effect.

Examples of these points emerge from the case studies juxtaposed above. The Italian young people, with their position as migrants from the periphery in an economically stagnant sector of the industrial core, use their bilingual repertoire to create a syncretic form of conversation that continually includes the stream of newcomers, but symbolically rejects both alternatives offered to them by the German state: integration into German society and repatriation to Italy. This genuinely novel form is not only symbolic of a newly forming social entity; it is *instrumental* in creating it. The Hungarian-speaking young people of Austria's Burgenland present another kind of example, highlighting the sometimes contradictory nature of opposition. Resisting institutional and informal pressures to abandon Hungarian altogether, they have continued using the language, in response to counterpressures for solidarity within the community. But as a result of this dual pressure they are reducing Hungarian, by their own actions, to a code of solidarity, leaving German uncontested as the language of public life and of authority, even within their own conversations. Finally, the Germans of Transylvania attempt to maintain the minority language, separate and superior to Romanian, not only as a remnant of historical dominance but also, paradoxically, as the symbol and a major instrument of emigration out of the ethnic solidarity the language enacts.

For sociolinguistics, the explanation of differences in code-switching practices across case studies is as important as understanding the underlying semiotic unity. A comparative perspective is essential for both goals. I have suggested that comparisons framed within a systemic view of political economy offer logical advantages, allowing a unified view of divergent linguistic practices in specific world regions. According to this approach, different regions will require different analyses both of local communicative meanings and political economy, despite apparent similarities in codeswitching. Within the context of a world system, sociolinguistic evidence reveals the workings of social and cultural processes at a number of levels of analysis: not only how personal interactions are managed through the use of linguistic variation, nor simply the dynamics of boundary skirmishes between ethnic groups, but also forms of consciousness developed in unequal power relations, the diverse local responses linguistic groups construct to material and cultural domination.

Notes

1. A fuller version of this argument appears in Gal (1987).

   My thanks to Monica Heller for inviting me to contribute to this volume and for her advice on revising the paper, and to Paul Friedrich, Willett Kempton, Zoltán Kövecses, Michael Moffatt, Katherine Verdery, and Kathryn Woolard for their comments on these ideas. The support of an ACLS Fellowship in 1986–87, while this paper was written, is also gratefully acknowledged.

2. Many of these distinctions were first discussed in detail in the classic papers by Gumperz (1964) and Blom and Gumperz (1972).

3. In contrast to world regions where language boundaries and linguistic boundaries are not perceived to coincide in significant ways (see Hymes 1968), Europe's historical linguistic differences have been highly politicized for two centuries and have been used ideologically in the state-building efforts of elites. At the same time it is important to note that not all ethnic groups are language groups, even in Europe, and that what is usually called an 'ethnic group' in the scholarly discourse of the US is referred to in European scholarship as a nationality or national

minority. I have used these terms interchangeably, along with the more general 'linguistic minority' and 'language group'.

4. Many observers argue that, despite impressive development since World War II, and the entry of the Eastern states into the Soviet orbit, many features of the earlier structural asymmetry between Eastern and Western Europe are currently in force (Luke and Boggs 1982).

5. Notice that the use of the state language for humor contrasts with the more commonly reported pattern of bilinguals judging the home language more appropriate and effective for humor.

6. Hill and Hill (1980) have discussed parallel examples in North America, making the argument in particular for such a relation between Mexicano and Spanish.

References

Auer, J. C. P.
   1984   Bilingual Conversation. Amsterdam: John Benjamins.
Barth, F.
   1969   Ethnic Groups and Boundaries. Boston: Little, Brown.
Bell, P.
   1984   Speech Style as Audience Design. Language in Society 13: 145–204.
Blom, J.-P. and J. Gumperz
   1972   Social Meaning in Linguistic Structures. *In* Directions in Sociolinguistics. J. J. Gumperz and D. Hymes eds. pp. 407–434. New York: Holt.
Bourdieu, P.
   1977   The Economics of Linguistic Exchanges. Social Science Information 16: 645–668.
Brown, P. and S. Levinson
   1978   Universals in Language Usage: Politeness Phenomena *In* Questions and Politeness. E. Goody, ed. pp. 56–289. Cambridge: Cambridge University Press.
Castles, S. and G. Kosack
   1983   Immigrant Workers and Class Structure in Western Europe, 2nd ed. London: Oxford University Press.
Cole, J.
   1981   Ethnicity and the Rise of Nationalism. *In* J. Cole and S. Beck eds. Ethnicity and Nationalism in Southeastern Europe. Pp. 105–134. Anthropological-Sociological Centre, University of Amsterdam.

Cole, J.
    1983   Culture and Economy in Peripheral Europe. Ethnologia Europaea
            XV: 3–26

Dressler, W. and R. Wodak-Leodolter
    1977   Language Preservation and Language Death in Brittany. Inter-
            national J. of the Sociology of Language 12: 33–44.

Eckert, P.
    1980   Diglossia: Separate and Unequal. Linguistics 18: 1056–1064.

Fishman, J.
    1964   Language Maintenance and Language Shift as Fields of Inquiry.
            Linguistics 9: 32–70.

Gal, S.
    1979   Language Shift. New York: Academic Press.
Gal, S.
    1987   Codeswitching and Consciousness in the European Periphery.
            American Ethnologist. 14 (4): 637–653

Giles, H. and P. Smith
    1979   Accommodation Theory: Optimal Levels of Convergence. *In*
            Language and Social Psychology. H. Giles and R. St Clair eds.
            pp. 45–65. Oxford: Blackwell.

Gumperz, J. J.
    1964   Linguistic and Social Interaction in Two Communities. American
            Anthropologist 66: 6: II: 137–154.

Gumperz, J. J.
    1968   The Speech Community. International Encyclopedia of the Social
            Sciences. pp. 361–6. New York: Macmillan.

Gumperz, J. J.
    1982   Discourse Strategies. Cambridge: Cambridge University Press.

Hechter, M.
    1975   Internal Colonialism. Berkeley: University of California Press.
Heller, M.
    1982   Negotiations of Language Choice in Montreal. *In* Language and
            Social Identity. J. J. Gumperz ed. pp. 108–118. Cambridge:
            Cambridge University Press.

Hill, J. and K. Hill
    1980   Mixed Grammar, Purist Grammar, and Language Attitudes in
            Modern Nahuatl. Language in Society 9: 321–348.

Hill, J.
    1985   The Grammar of Consciousness and the Consciousness of Gram-
            mar. American Ethnologist 12: 4: 725–737.

Hymes, D.
  1964 Toward Ethnographies of Communication. American Anthropologist 66: 6: 1–34.
Hymes, D.
  1968 Linguistic Problems in Defining the Concept of 'Tribe'. *In* Essays on the Problem of Tribe. J. Helm ed. pp. 23–48. Seattle: University of Washington Press.
Irvine, J.
  1985 Status and Style in Language. Annual Review of Anthropology 14: 557–581.
Luke, T. W. and C. Boggs
  1982 Soviet Subimperialism and the Crisis of Bureaucratic Centrism. Studies in Comparative Communism. XV: 1–2: 95–124.
Poplack, S.
  1980 Sometimes I'll Start a Sentence in English Y TERMINO EN ESPANOL: Towards a Typology of Codeswitching. Linguistics 18: 581–618.
Sankoff, G.
  1980 The Social Life of Language. Philadelphia: University of Pennsylvania Press.
Schieben-Lange, B.
  1977 The Language Situation in Southern France. Linguistics 191: 101–108.
Scotton, C.
  1983 The Negotiation of Identities in Conversation: A Theory of Markedness and Code Choice. International J. of the Sociology of Language 44: 115–136.
Verdery, K.
  1983 Transylvanian Villagers. Berkeley: University of California Press.
Verdery, K.
  1985 The Unmaking of an Ethnic Collectivity: Transylvania's Germans. American Ethnologist 12: 62–83.
Wallerstein, I.
  1974 The Rise and Future Demise of the World Capitalist System. Comparative Studies in Society and History 16: 387–415.
Weinreich, U.
  1953 Languages in Contact. New York: Columbia University Press.
Williams, R.
  1973 Base and Superstructure in Marxist Cultural Theory. New Left Review 87: 3–16.
Willis, P.
  1977 Learning to Labour. Westmead, England: Saxon House.

264   *Susan Gal*

Wolf, E.
    1982   Europe and the People Without History. Berkeley: University of
            California Press.
Woolard, K.
    1985   Language Variation and Cultural Hegemony: Toward an Integra-
            tion of Sociolinguistic and Social Theory. American Ethnologist
            12: 4: 738–748.

Where do we go from here?

Monica Heller
The Ontario Institute for Studies in Education

The purpose of this volume has been to integrate a variety of inter-
pretivist approaches to the study of codeswitching. By situating
codeswitching in levels of embedded contexts, it is possible to
understand how codeswitching functions as a strategy for defining and negotiating social relations, and so becomes a crucial
element in the maintenance, creation or dissolution of social
boundaries.

The papers in this volume have approached the interpretation of
the local and community-wide significance of codeswitching at a
number of different levels:

— the discourse or conversational frame of different patterns of codeswitching;
— the distribution of different patterns of codeswitching across social situations in a community;
— the distribution of different patterns of codeswitching among members of
  a community.

An overriding theme has been that the nature of the boundary
between speech communities influences or constrains which
members of those communities are likely to have access to the
kinds of linguistic resources and background knowledge which
render codeswitching accessible and meaningful to them as a
communicative and social strategy. Furthermore, the use that
they make of codeswitching, along with other forms of language
contact phenomena, is an index of the communicative and social
goals that codeswitching can serve to attain. The fact that code-
switching is framed or unframed, inter- or intra-sentential, inter-
or intra-turn is directly related to the degree of its conventionality
and to the degree of breakdown of social boundaries.

This indicates a future direction for research on codeswitching which takes as its point of depart a synthesis or integration of the different context-embedded approaches exemplified by the papers in the volume. Such an approach would situate codeswitching within the verbal repertoires of individuals and within the speech economies of communities, and would analyse its function both at the level of conversational task or outcome and at that of social task or outcome. What is needed is an ethnography of communication which has a two-pronged approach: the description of the place of codeswitching in the repertoire of individuals, and the situation both of these individuals and of their use of codeswitching in community social networks.

As most of the papers in this volume have indicated, it is rarely the case that all members of a speech community codeswitch in all the social interactions in which they participate. Rather, codeswitching (including different types or forms of codeswitching) generally characterizes the usage of only those members of a community who find themselves at the boundary between social groups. Saxons in Vingard, Wanyjirra and Gurindji speakers on cattle stations in Western Australia, young upwardly-mobile francophones and older anglophones at the management level of companies in Montreal, all find themselves participating in situations which give them access to the formation of relationships (however tenuous or circumscribed) with members of other groups and to the linguistic varieties controlled by those groups. Their position in the community, at specific historical moments, underlies the development of bilingualism as an element of their verbal repertoire, and of codeswitching as an appropriate verbal and social strategy.

The nature of social and economic activities, the niches (to use Barth's term) occupied by groups within a larger social and economic unit, are related to each other, and are implicated in processes of change. Certain groups, or members of groups, within a community may participate more readily in those processes of change than others, because of their access to the social and economic resources involved. To the extent that changes affect the nature of intergroup relations, those individuals may be directly involved in managing the consequences of change for intergroup relations. Here, codeswitching, or its absence, may contribute to the process of redefinition of inter-personal and inter-group relations. At the same time, the status of groups within the community, and the nature of intra-group relations, may change, with similar consequences for the availability and exploitation of codeswitching as social strategy. The basic principle is that through the accomplishment of discourse or conversational tasks, interlocutors simultaneously define their roles or their role relationships at an interpersonal level.

Interlocutors' very ability to establish conversational cooperation has consequences for the possibility of establishment of social relations, without even considering questions concerning what the nature of those social relations might be (Gumperz 1982; Erickson and Shultz 1982). Codeswitching can be seen as one kind of verbal strategy used to establish conversational cooperation, or to prevent its establishment. To the extent that it is related to the establishment of conversational cooperation, it is part of the definition of frames of reference which constitute the new social reality of ethnic relations and ethnic group status.

By accomplishing conversational tasks through codeswitching, interlocutors accomplish social relationships. By using codeswitching as a discourse device, interlocutors signal a shared understanding of the context which renders the discourse strategies effective and meaningful, and so signal assumed co-membership in a social community. Further, since they are members of social groups, the outcome of negotiations of interpersonal relationships has an impact (at least potentially) on the nature of inter-group relations, as well as on the nature of group-internal processes. Codeswitching therefore must be understood as part of historical processes, whether it contributes to stability or to change. In this regard, much work remains to be done.

Studies of codeswitching have tended to focus on synchronous events: few have traced the development of codeswitching to the present situation (although Gumperz and Wilson (1971) hypothesized that codeswitching may have contributed to processes of creolization on the Indo-Dravidian border). Equally, few have followed the development of codeswitching over time from their first analysis of it (although Heller (1982) used apparent time, that is different patterns used by older and younger employees of the same company, to argue that patterns of codeswitching had changed; Gal (1979) also examined the different patterns of codeswitching characterizing different generations of Hungarians on the Austro-Hungarian border). Even at the micro-level, it has been rare that analysts have examined the medium-term consequences of codeswitching for interpersonal relationships. We know little about how codeswitching contributes to the development of interpersonal relationships over time, and how the nature of those relationships is related to the development, maintenance or change of conventions of interactive behavior.

The approach proposed here is, then, historical, ethnographic and multi-level. As with many microsociolinguistic studies, it identifies local situations within a broader context; that is, it uses the patterns identified through ethnographic description to select a sample of micro-level interactions. Those interactions, or discourses of various forms, are then in turn interpreted both in the context of the event itself as well as in the broader context which informed the initial selection process. This top-down/bottom-up approach permits an analysis which deals not only with the explanation of codeswitching in a given setting but also with the discovery of the contribution codeswitching makes to group-level social processes.

At one level, then, future directions for research on codeswitching include the analysis of the relationship of micro-level to macro-level synchronic and diachronic social processes. We still understand only poorly the kinds of social conditions which facilitate the development and use of codeswitching as communicative and social strategy. The papers in this volume suggest that those social conditions involve individual and group interest in boundary maintenance or boundary breakdown and the existence of multiple frames, and so multiple role relations, which can be collapsed. Still, several areas remain relatively unexplored.

We know little about the extent to which different types of codeswitching are related to different types of boundary maintenance/change processes, or whether the presence or absence of codeswitching is indicative of certain configurations of intergroup relations. We also need to examine further the extent to which the social significance of codeswitching can be transformed into stylistic, or discourse, significance as social conditions change, that is, as codeswitching becomes a convention associated with newly-defined and newly-routinized role relations. Finally, we can explore the generalizability of findings concerning the social conditions under which codeswitching is or is not found; it may be that codeswitching represents one of many ways in which communicative resources can be used to similar ends in similar social situations.

At another level, a context-embedded approach can lead to an analysis of the ways in which codeswitching does develop as a communicative resource, as individuals draw on their linguistic resources to accomplish communicative tasks in specific social interactions. Codeswitching represents an individual's ability to creatively exploit conventional associations between patterns of language use and social activities. By violating conventions, codeswitching forces interlocutors to question their assumptions and expectations, but since the violation is itself patterned, it points to the aspect of the taken-for-granted context which needs to be reinterpreted. Future research needs to examine the relationship between codeswitching and other forms of communicative strategies which serve to re-define frames of reference, implicitly or explicitly, and to examine the ways in which individuals learn to draw on their communicative resources and their other forms of background knowledge to create meaning.

By examining the place of codeswitching in individual verbal repertoires, and its emergence, development or disappearance over time, it should be possible to explore its relationship to other forms of communicative resources and to changing frames of reference. The link between codeswitching and other kinds of communicative resources, principally other forms of language contact phenomena, is crucial, because it provides us with a glimpse of the pool of communicative resources available to speakers and so of the ways in which those resources can be drawn on in the creation of communicative strategies. The development of patterns of codeswitching over time is equally important, as a point of departure for examining ways in which communicative forms are tied to changing social conditions.

There remains a great deal to discover concerning the relationship between patterned communicative strategies and the redefinition of frames of reference, which in turn contribute to the development of new or modified strategies. Codeswitching as a

sense-making activity is an example of ways in which the organization of communicative behavior can be seen to be central to the
construction of frames of reference. The text of codeswitching
derives from and defines its context. We still have much to learn
concerning the means interlocutors use to deploy communicative
resources in the form of codeswitching in order to create text and
intend or infer context. We need to discover where the sense that
codeswitching makes comes from, and what consequences it has
for interlocutors' understanding of the multiple levels of message
embedded in codeswitching discourse. Finally, we must examine
those multiple levels of meaning and the ways in which code-
switching indexes their salience for particular moments in discourse and conversation.

Issues of intercultural relations will continue to be crucial to
our social development: the study of codeswitching can contribute
to an understanding of how individuals approach problems of
intercultural communication, and of personal and group development in culture contact situations. Codeswitching is a strategy
which can signal shared culture or be used to create it. If we are
able to articulate how codeswitching can be used to create shared
frames of reference, we may be able to contribute to the pool of
strategies for equitable intercultural communication currently
sought after by so many. The implicitness of codeswitching is one
of its most salient characteristics, and one which deserves to be
further explored. There is clearly a relationship between such
implicit strategies and face, an important component of intercultural communications where sometimes so little is known
about socially critical aspects of status and role. Ambiguity, to
which codeswitching can contribute, is often essential to the
maintenance or creation of social relations, and to cultivating the
potential for many avenues of development.

The study of codeswitching is also the study of the maintenance, change or breakdown of social barriers, and of the consequences of those processes for individuals' access to important
social and economic resources. Codeswitching can be understood
as an element of both personal and group social mobility. It has its
place among the creative uses of interpersonal communication for
the redefinition of social context, and so for cultural production,
and among strategies used for maintaining current understandings

and so contributing to cultural reproduction. As a strategy, it is connected to conversational outcomes, and these can have consequences for the ability of individuals to form social relationships, to accomplish conversational goals, and to participate in social activities where important resources are controlled. This is particularly important in intergroup interaction, since ethnolinguistic groups differentially control social, economic and political resources, and inter-group encounters are, in effect, gate-keeping encounters. Again, little is known about the consequences that codeswitching can have, either at the individual or at the group level, for access to resources and for intra- and inter-group relations.

Perhaps the major realm of enquiry to be explored concerns the ways in which our use of communicative strategies to make sense of experience contributes to the concrete conditions of our social lives. The relationships we make, or fail to make, have a bearing on the activities we can participate in, the resources we have access to or can call on, the aspirations we can develop for ourselves and for others. Our ability to use communicative resources skilfully to achieve our immediate conversational objectives is essential to our ability to negotiate outcomes in keeping with both our short-range and our long-range plans. Codeswitching, as any other communicative resource, can be a tool, and can be used to create the kinds of meanings speakers want to create. Codeswitching is linked to issues of power and control, on micro-level and macro-level scales.

The study of codeswitching will continue to have a role to play in the study of intercultural relations, of language and culture, indeed in interpretive social science in general. It is not a unique, peculiar form of discourse, and from an analytical point of view it has the merit of relatively clear associations with individual speakers and with forms of social activity, and thus provides an accessible point of entry into complex questions. The papers in this volume, by exploring small scenes in a variety of settings, attempt to shed light on part of those questions, and to contribute to a body of work on the importance of language as social process which promises to remain relevant to both theoretical and practical concerns.

References

Erickson, F. and J. Shultz
    1982   *The Counsellor as Gatekeeper*, N.Y.: Academic Press.
Gal, S.
    1979   *Language Shift.* N.Y.: Academic Press.
Gumperz, J.
    1982   *Discourse Strategies.* Cambridge: Cambridge University Press.
Gumperz, J. and R. Wilson
    1971   "Converence and creolization: a case from the Indo-Aryan/Dravidian
           border," in: D. Hymes (ed.), *Pidginization and Creolization of*
           Languages. Cambridge: Cambridge University Press, pp. 151–168.
Heller, M.
    1982   *Language, ethnicity and politics in Quebec.* Unpublished Ph.D.
           dissertation. Dept. of Linguistics, University of California, Berkeley.

Index